CANADIANS
IN THE BATTLE OF THE
ATLANTIC

Larry Gray

© 2007 by Folklore Publishing
First printed in 2007 10 9 8 7 6 5 4 3 2 1
Printed in Canada

The Publisher: Folklore Publishing
Website: www.folklorepublishing.com

Library and Archives Canada Cataloguing in Publication

Gray, Larry, 1937–
Canadians in the Battle of the Atlantic / Larry Gray.

Includes bibliographical references and index.
ISBN-13: 978-1-894864-66-4
ISBN-10: 1-894864-66-2

      1. World War, 1939–1945—Naval operations, Canadian. 2. World War, 1939–1945—Campaigns—Atlantic Ocean. I. Title.

D779.C3G73 2007   940.54'5971   C2007-904884-6

Project Director: Faye Boer
Project Editor: Tom Monto
Production: Alexander Penrose
Cover Image: Photo Courtesy of Library and Archives Canada, PA-104309
Photo Credits: Every effort has been made to accurately credit the sources of photographs. Any errors or ommissions should be directed to the publisher for changes in future editions. Photographs courtesy of Department of National Defence/Library and Archives Canada (p. 22, PA-112993; p. 35, PA-105255; p. 47, PA-037447; p. 59, PA-139273; p. 66, PA-112359; p. 112, PA-116084; p. 170, PA-134522; p. 187, PA-141300; p. 204, PA-136285; p. 214, PA-134191; p. 263, PA-142540; p. 294, PL-12610; p. 304, PL-12608; p. 315, PL-16700); Musée Naval de Québec (p. 219, FOR001).

We acknowledge the support of the Alberta Foundation for the Arts for our publishing program.

We acknowledge the financial support of the Government of Canada through the Book Publishing Industry Development Program (BPIDP) for our publishing activities.

Alberta Foundation for the Arts   Canadian Heritage   Patrimoine canadien

PC: P5

Contents

Introduction

CANADA'S OCEAN SHORELINE SPANS 43,000 kilometres. Measured to include all bays, inlets and peninsulas, it is 60,000 kilometres. Navigators calculate this expanse of territorial waters at almost 13 million square kilometres. Bounded by the Atlantic, Arctic and Pacific Oceans, with the St. Lawrence River and the Great Lakes striking like a dagger into its very heartland, the country has a considerable nautical history. Her citizens are truly maritime people.

In 1939, Canada was still a young nation. It was woefully unequipped to wage war against Hitler's aggression. Following the declaration of war on September 9, Canada quickly mobilized militia regiments that operated coastal defences. Volunteers flooded recruiting offices, and in December the first units of the 1st Canadian Infantry Division sailed for the United Kingdom. The Royal Canadian Navy (RCN) entered the hostilities with 13 ships: six destroyers, five minesweepers and two small training vessels. Three thousand sailors, 1800 in the permanent force and 1700 reservists, operated the ships. The pride of the Canadian fleet was six 1500-ton-displacement modern destroyers (*Skeena* and *Saguenay*, delivered in 1931; *Fraser* and *St. Laurent*, acquired in 1937; and *Ottawa* and *Restigouche*, which followed in 1938).

These were not aircraft carriers, not battleships, not even cruisers, just lowly destroyers. There was no industrial or technological base to support the Canadian navy. Support services, training and dockyard facilities, logistical and administrative organizations barely existed in Canada.

The German navy set to sea, determined to sever Britain's lifelines and cut the island off from all overseas supplies. The United Kingdom was under siege. Canada committed four of her destroyers to help the Royal Navy (RN) protect the approaches to British ports.

While Parliament debated whether to join mother England on this latest excursion against Germany, the navy sailed. Prime Minister Mackenzie King had ordered the navy to assume a wartime footing on August 28. Two of the destroyers were showing the flag on the West Coast. In Vancouver, *Fraser* and *St. Laurent* shooed visiting dignitaries off their decks and hurriedly left for Halifax on August 31. The day Canada declared war, September 10, they were in the approaches to the Panama Canal. Five days later, they steamed into Halifax and immediately began escorting convoys.

At noon on September 3, 1939, the *Kreigsmarine* sent the following signal to all units: "Open hostilities with England at once." The Royal Navy expected the main threat to come from surface raiders, but wars rarely progress as expected. Seven hours after receiving the signal, the *Unterseeboot U-30* sank the British liner *Athenia,* bound for Montreal with 1103 passengers. One hundred and eighteen people lost their lives. The Battle of the Atlantic had begun and was to last almost six years.

Fighting the U-boat became the Allied navy's greatest task. A huge part of this burden fell to the RCN. Expecting Germany to begin unrestricted submarine warfare against Allied shipping as soon as war started, the Allies began organizing merchantmen into convoys even before war was declared. On August 26, the British Admiralty sent a telegram containing the single word "Funnel" to all intelligence centres. With that transmission, control of all British ships passed from their owners to the Admiralty. Simultaneously, no Canadian-registered ship and no merchant ship in a Canadian port could sail without the express permission of the RCN.

On September 16, *Saguenay* and *St. Laurent* slowly steamed eastward past Georges Island escorting HX-1, the first convoy from Halifax to Britain. Eighteen merchant ships assembled in Bedford Basin and then set out across the North Atlantic. Travelling as a convoy, their progress was restricted by the speed of the slowest ship. Navigating a zigzag course to confuse enemy U-boats further lengthened the passage. Once the convoy was in open sea, somewhere between Newfoundland and Iceland, RN cruisers took over escort duties. They led the flock into the uncertain gloom of a menacing ocean, while the two Canadian destroyers turned back to base. Midafternoon on September 17, the destroyers passed *Fraser* outbound with HXF-1, a "fast" convoy of unarmed ships each making more than 15 knots. (Convoys were identified by their destination or origin and numbered. "HX" means it sailed from Halifax to the UK. The letters "H" and "O" before the number designated whether the ships were bound for "Home" (Britain) or were leaving Britain "Outbound." An "S" was added for slow and an "F" for fast. Thus, HXF was a fast convoy bound for Britain from Halifax.)

On the open ocean, the main threat was from surface raiders, the pocket battleships *Deutschland* and *Graf Spee* and the battlecruisers *Scharnhorst* and *Gneisenau*. At first, the U-boats operated only in closer British waters. In those early days, convoys picked up anti-submarine escorts only in the western approaches to the British Isles.

Until May 1940, Canadian ships were confined to shepherding merchantmen from the east coast to a mid-ocean point in the North Atlantic where powerful RN ships took over. Destroyers' fuel capacity only permitted a direct Atlantic crossing with nothing left for zigzagging in unison with a convoy or carrying out protective sweeps against enemy craft. Then hell became a European reality as the seemingly unstoppable German war machine churned into the Low Countries and France. On May 23, British destroyers off the coast at Boulogne traded shots with German tanks. The next day, *Skeena, Restigouche* and *St. Laurent* sailed out of Halifax bound for Britain, where they would be based as they covered the west end of the convoy route. *Fraser*, leaving her duties in the West Indies, refuelled in Bermuda and headed for the United Kingdom to join her sisters.

The Royal Canadian Navy spent the next six long years as one of the principal combatants in the Battle of the Atlantic. They began wartime duties with a mere 13 vessels and 3000 sailors of all ranks. By the time the Allies won the Battle of the Atlantic, close to the end of the war in Europe, Canada had the third largest navy in the world.

CHAPTER ONE

Not By Enemy Action

IN LATE MAY 1940, HMCS *FRASER* steamed out of the St. Georges harbour in Bermuda. The destroyer carried 10 officers and 171 seamen aboard. Among them were 24-year-old Sub-Lieutenant Bill Landymore, the gunnery officer, and 19-year-old Ordinary Seaman Horace Stark, a wireless telegrapher. Both were Ontario boys. Landymore was born in the town of Brantford and Stark in rural Finch, Stormont County. The Stark family moved to Carleton Place, Ontario, in 1929, where Horace's father taught high school mathematics and history. Under the stern tutelage of his schoolmaster father, Horace completed high school in Carleton Place in June 1939 and joined the Royal Canadian Navy shortly after war broke out.

Stark spent only a minimal time, October 2 to November 27, in Halifax learning the basics of navy life. He was already a qualified telegraphist because his hobby for the past few years had been amateur radio. Stark was licensed and had transmitted worldwide in Morse code under the radio call sign "VE3UH." (The "VE3" identified his station as being in Ontario and "UH" were his personal call letters.) The RCN was mobilizing and needed every skilled tradesman it could get.

Stark was drafted to the River Class destroyer HMCS *Fraser* on November 27, 1939. She was Stark's first ship and Landymore's first Canadian warship. *Fraser,* built in 1931, was a Royal Navy C Class destroyer and had been transferred to the Royal Canadian Navy in 1938.

In late summer 1934, Landymore travelled to Kingston to begin studies at Royal Military College (RMC). Waiting for him were an intense academic regimen, a physically demanding training program and the grueling routine of military duties. Within a week he was on his first parade, standing rigidly at attention in his spotless red tunic, a pillbox hat canted appropriately to the right side of his almost-shaved head and blue trousers with a wide yellow stripe tucked into mid-calf boots that shone from the hours of spit-polishing each student quickly mastered.

Landymore was not from a military family but had been interested in things military while at Brantford Collegiate Institute. At a young age, he had joined a militia regiment, the Dufferin Rifles (which later became the Dufferin and Haldiman Rifles). He progressed to the rank of cadet sergeant. While completing his senior matriculation, he applied and was accepted to RMC. Landymore spent the summer of 1934 in Petawawa, training with the Non-Permanent Active Militia. After his first winter at RMC, he elected to spend his summer in the Royal Canadian Naval Volunteer Reserve (RCNVR).

During his first year in Halifax, seasoned veterans introduced him to navy life, teaching him communications, gunnery and a little seamanship. In the summer of 1936, he went aboard the destroyer HMCS *Saguenay* for training at sea. The ship sailed to Charlottetown, PEI, Pictou, Nova Scotia, and Montréal. Just outside the Charlottetown harbour the officer in charge of RMC cadets decided they needed some small-boat experience. The cadets were lowered over the side in a whaler. Hoisting the sail, they moved smartly away from the destroyer, but just outside the harbour, the breeze dropped absolutely dead. With 30 kilometres to go, down came the sail and out came the oars. The tides were not favourable, and at 9:00 PM that night, they were still pulling. Landymore, a star football quarterback, was very fit, but when they reached Pictou his and the other cadets' backsides, legs and hands were blistered raw. Not that this excused them as next morning, at 6:00 AM, they were roused for fitness training.

In Montréal, the RMC students were unceremoniously dumped off and left standing on the jetty as *Saguenay* took Canadian dignitaries to France as part of the pilgrimage of World War I veterans to witness the unveiling of the Vimy Memorial.

In August 1936, Landymore graduated 20th in his class in academic subjects and well at the top in military matters. He enlisted into the Royal Canadian

Navy as a cadet. The navy cadets set to sea on a training cruise aboard HMS *Frobisher*, a Royal Navy training cruiser. The Royal Navy was held in high esteem throughout the navies of the world. Most nations sent their cadets for training with the Royal Navy. With Landymore's contingent were three Indian cadets, eight Chinese, three New Zealanders and a couple of Australians.

This first cruise went all the way around the United Kingdom with one stop in Bergen, Norway. The cadets were expected to do the work of ordinary seamen. The premise was that it was good for a man who was destined for higher rank to have done the work of a deck hand. Every Saturday morning at 6:00 AM, the cadets were on their hands and knees holystoning the deck. Holystone is a soft and brittle sandstone that was used for scouring and whitening the wooden decks of ships. It probably got its name from the fact that "holystoning the deck" was done on one's knees, as if in prayer. Undoubtedly, the cadets in training uttered many profane prayers.

Their second training cruise was to the West Indies. This was a bad time for the cadets because a mysterious illness ravaged their ranks. By the time the illness was brought under control, one cadet had died and two were permanently paralyzed. The disease was never formally identified, but the consensus is that it was some form of meningitis. Landymore was promoted to midshipman on May 1, 1937, and posted to another cruiser, HMS *Emerald*. *Emerald* was deployed to the East Indies to be based in Trincomalee, Ceylon (now Sri Lanka).

Midshipmen had a wonderful life in the East Indies. There was not a great deal of stress in their activities, and they assumed far more responsibility than if they had been in the Home Fleet, the Mediterranean or the Pacific Fleet. Each morning they participated in a well-organized education program of seamanship, mathematics, navigation and meteorology. After lunch, they were employed as midshipmen of the watch on the quarterdeck and ran their ships.

Ceylon had an RN rest camp in the mountains, near large tea-growing plantations. Spending all one's time in a bake-oven of a ship was considered unhealthy. Therefore, when ships went in to Colombo, Ceylon's capital city, for annual refits and were out of action for eight weeks, each watch of sailors and officers rotated for two weeks in the camp at Dyitialwa. However, the midshipmen were not needed on board during refit, so they had two full months at the camp with nothing to do except have a good time. Their only duties were to train a guard for colours every morning and to teach a platoon how to fire their rifles. They spent the rest of their days playing tennis, field hockey or rugger. They became physically tough as a result.

Late in the summer of 1937, the German cruiser *Emden* berthed at Columbo. The RN hosted the German cadets at the rest camp. The midshipmen entertained them. Every time the German cadets or their officers went into the wardroom (the officers' mess), they used the "Heil Hitler" salute instead of the proper naval salute. The RN people told the Germans that if they were going to persist then they would have to stop while the British sailors sang "God Save the King." All agreed that was not very practical, and both the raised-arm saluting and the singing stopped.

Emerald left for England early in 1938. On the way home, she detoured to the Middle East. As the ship cleared the Suez Canal there was an outbreak of trouble in the British Protectorate of Palestine. Arabs were throwing bombs at Jews leaving synagogues, and Jews were throwing them at Arabs in the marketplaces. *Emerald* went into Haifa, and her crew was sent ashore to cool things down. Midshipman Landymore commanded an armed patrol in the residential Mount Carmel area. There was no shelter for them, but the headmistress of a nearby girls' school allowed the sailors the use of the school for their necessities. Local housewives brought out cookies and lemonade. The ship's crew was there less than two weeks, just until things quieted down. The men returned to the ship and their normal routine as the *Emerald* sailed for England.

On October 12, 1938, Landymore transferred to the Home Fleet and HMS *Glasgow*. *Glasgow* was a new light cruiser, commissioned on September 9, 1937. She had a top speed of 32 knots. Landymore was promoted to the rank of sub-lieutenant on March 1, 1939, and he left the *Glasgow* on May 1, 1939, just before the ship departed to escort the King and Queen on a Royal Cruise to Canada. The young Canadian officers were quite disappointed to be left behind from a ship going to Canada. On paper, Sub-Lieutenant Landymore was posted to HMS *Victory*, the navy name for the Royal Navy Barracks in Portsmouth. In fact, he went to HMS *Excellent,* the shore establishment Gunnery School at Whale Island, Portsmouth. As part of his gunnery training, Landymore went to HMS *Vernon*, the school in Portsmouth that taught countermeasures against mines.

After the completion of their courses, Landymore and Canadian friend Bob Welland (the two had been together since duty on the training ships) presented themselves to Canada House on Trafalgar Square in London. Their purpose was to get an appointment to a Canadian ship. None was available. The officer in charge of Canadian trainees sent them on leave for a week. When they returned a week later, he sent them on leave for another week. This charade continued for five weeks. Leave in London could be a lot of fun—if you had money. The young officers had none and spent their time going to inexpensive museums, keeping their cash to pay for food and accommodation.

Quite despairing of the lack of action from Canada and concerned that the war with Germany would be over before they got aboard a ship, they noticed a door with the gold letters "Personnel" on the glass panel. They were in the Royal Navy Admiralty offices. "Bob," said Landymore, "I don't know about you, but I'm going in there and ask for an appointment to one of their ships." Bold as brass, they puffed themselves up (Landymore was all of 1.75 metres tall and 66 kilograms). The two marched in. An RN Commander met them with the question: "You're sure you want an appointment?" "Yes, sir," they chorused, to which the senior officer asked, "What kind of ship?" "A destroyer," piped up Landymore and Bob said, "Me too." "What were you doing before you came in here?" the RN officer queried. "We've just finished waiting for weeks to get an appointment from Canada, but they don't seem to be able to get us one. We are just cooling our heels without any money in London." "I'll see about it." And he dropped back into his office.

The officer returned in about five minutes. "I've got two ships, the *Windsor* and the *Fame*. I'll flip a coin. Landymore, you call it." Bill did. He won and chose the *Windsor*. In another half hour, both men had their tickets, travel warrants and an advance on their pay. Bill Landymore ended up in Plymouth. HMS *Windsor* was a 100-metre-long destroyer carrying 134 men. She was launched in 1931. Because of its age, the ship had been reduced to reserve status before the war. In the early stages of the war, the Admiralty was forced to employ every available warship. In the early 1920s *Windsor* had been an escort destroyer for the Royal Yacht. She had all sorts of fancy equipment; the stanchions were brass (which had to be polished) and her lanyards and ropes were all interlaced with gold braid. Appropriate for a ship showing the flag of a "Royal Yacht." *Windsor* served on Fleet duties and as convoy escort.

When Landymore joined the ship, he, another sub-lieutenant and the captain were the only regular-force officers on board. All the rest were reservists. Landymore became the gunnery officer. Although the vessel leaked like a sieve, Landymore had a wonderful time. Since none of the other officers knew how to decode a radio message (cypher) and Bill allowed that he had been shown once how to do it, the captain also named him "Cypher Officer." He learned his error when messages began to flood in.

Hitler let loose his army. Following the German invasion of Poland in 1939, Britain declared war, and the British Expeditionary Force (BEF) established itself at the Franco-Belgian border. The BEF consisted of 10 infantry divisions in three corps, a tank brigade and an RAF detachment of about 500 aircraft. In 1940, Germany invaded France and Belgium. The BEF sustained heavy losses during the German *blitzkrieg* advance. Most of the British survivors (roughly 330,000 men) were evacuated from Dunkirk in June, leaving much of their equipment behind.

In September and October 1939, the first months of the war, HMS *Windsor* transported elements of the BEF to France. The rest of the time the ship was employed on convoy duties from England to Europe. She escorted a couple of convoys from Tilbury to Gibraltar. She accompanied the ships only for about a day and a half into the Bay of Biscay, then the merchant ships were on their own.

By March 1940, Canadian naval authorities discovered the young Canadian officers on British vessels. Landymore and Welland returned to Canada as passengers aboard the battleship HMS *Royal Sovereign*. The Admiralty was sending big ships to Canada's east coast to escort the Atlantic convoys. On February 27, 1940, Bill Landymore boarded HMCS *Fraser*, saluted the quarterdeck and strode to the bridge to present himself to Wallace Creery, the commander. Creery made no bones about the fact that he considered Landymore and his friend's actions in England to be those of smart-alecs. The Canadians did not think they had done anything to warrant any punishment. They could hardly sit around and do nothing while the country was at war.

~⌘~

CHAPTER TWO

The Perilous Sea

WORKING IN THE TELEGRAPH ROOM of Bill Landymore's new ship, HMCS *Fraser*, was Ordinary Seaman Horace Stark. He was a teenager from Carleton Place, Ontario. Stark joined *Fraser's* crew on November 28, 1939, and already had finished one transatlantic trip on convoy duty. On December 10, 1939, *Fraser*, with the *Ottawa, Restigouche* and *St. Laurent*, led five large ocean liners out of Halifax's Bedford Basin into the Atlantic heading for England. The ocean liners carried the 1st Canadian Division to the United Kingdom. Because of the liners' speed, the convoy, numbered TC-1, travelled in a straight line, rather than zigzagging.

Stark's proficiency as a telegrapist earned him a promotion to the rank of able telegrapher on January 2, 1940. He spent most of his days in the crowded, smoky radio room, painstakingly copying messages sent in Morse code in four- and five-letter cipher groups.

The Admiralty in Whitehall sent out radio broadcasts across the Atlantic. The Admiralty sent at a rate of 20 to 25 words a minute with no pause between messages, and nothing was ever sent twice. Most watches had two telegraphers on duty just to keep up with the steady stream of incoming messages. The radio operators also maintained a listening watch on the international distress frequencies where merchant ships broadcast calls for help when they came under attack from U-boats or surface raiders.

On May 1, Bill Landymore was promoted to the rank of lieutenant. He was now a qualified watch officer, taking his turn at controlling the destroyer from the bridge. *Fraser* did a few local convoys, not venturing far offshore. Then she was ordered south to Jamaica. She patrolled the approaches to the Panama Canal and monitored the ports of Aruba and Curacao. They watched for ships that had been interned at the start of the war trying to make a run for it to return home.

Fraser was at sea on one of these patrols when the German Wehrmacht overran most of France. On May 24, Canadian warships were ordered to England to take up duties under the direction of the Royal Navy. *Fraser* put in to Bermuda for a hasty refuelling, then headed east.

She arrived in Plymouth on June 3 where she berthed alongside HMCS *Restigouche*. The other Canadian destroyers were evacuating men of the BEF from the beaches at Dunkirk. Approximately 350,000 men were evacuated, but most of their arms and equipment lay abandoned on the shores of France.

Before leaving Plymouth, the Canadian destroyers had their torpedo tubes on the aft end of the ship removed, and each ship was given a three-inch anti-aircraft gun. Rather than participating in the "Miracle of Dunkirk," *Fraser* sailed south to St. Jean-de-Luz on the French border with Spain. Most of the French coast had been sealed off, and this area was the only way for refugees to get out.

Landymore took a party of men ashore to aid in the evacuation. The local men had lost their enthusiasm for war and did not want to leave their families, boats and homes to go to England. Landymore recalled an incident wherein a young American girl drove her brand new Buick down on the jetty where people were embarking. She gestured to one of the warships laying off the harbour and asked if she could get on one of those boats. The young lieutenant said, "There'll be a boat here in about 10 minutes. But you can't leave that car here." "Put it anywhere you like," she retorted. "I'll never drive it again. Do you want it?" And she gave him the key. Landymore asked his sailors, "Any of you want a new Buick?" They laughed and pushed it out of the way.

Meanwhile, in the hectic confines of the radio room, Stark copied a secret message. He ran to the bridge to deliver it to the captain. The message was for the British ambassador, and *Fraser* was ordered to make all speed to deliver it to him at the port of Arachon, 60 kilometres south of Bordeaux, where the ambassador was believed to be. As *Fraser* approached Arachon in rough seas and a heavy rainstorm, a small sardine boat hailed the ship. Tossing and bobbing alongside, the small craft brought the British ambassador,

A convoy of merchant ships assembling in Bedford Basin, Halifax, April 1941

~oOCo~

Sir Rodney Campbell; the South African minister to France, Colin Bain Marais; and the Canadian minister to France to the warship. The Canadian was Lieutenant Colonel Georges P. Vanier, a distinguished army officer of World War I and later Canada's first native-born governor general (1959–67). Vanier was pleased to discover a Canadian ship had rescued him and even more pleased when he recognized Captain Creery as an old friend. *Fraser* later transferred the three envoys to the nearby British cruiser HMS *Galatea*. The two ships (*Restigouche* and *Fraser)*, with several British destroyers and a British cruiser, shepherded a collection of overloaded boats to England from Arachon. The flotilla carried 16,000 soldiers and a multitude of civilians for three days through rough and dangerous waters.

The two Canadian ships entered Arachon to take off their own evacuation shore parties at the end of the evacuation. Just as the last of the Canadians were scrambling up the boarding nets, a German tank and an armoured car pulling a field gun crested the hill overlooking the town and trained their guns on the Canadian ships. The ships wasted no time speeding for the open sea. *Fraser* was carrying 44 British, French and Polish soldiers and many civilian refugees. A light cruiser, HMS *Calcutta* (Vice Admiral A.T.B. Cuteis embarked), arrived on the scene and took over as command ship. The flotilla headed for Bordeaux, then set a course for England. As night fell, the sea was rolling in a moderate swell. A light breeze came up, and visibility lifted to about two kilometres. *Fraser* positioned herself about two kilometres off the starboard bow of *Calcutta*; *Restigouche* took up station the same distance to the port, slightly astern, of the command ship.

About 10:00 PM *Calcutta* ordered her convoy to form "a single line ahead." Because of the probability of attack from the air or from submarines, the flotilla was travelling at the fast speed of 20 knots. For weeks crew on the Canadian destroyers had been in continuous action, and most officers on the ships' bridges were suffering from sleep deprivation. On *Fraser*, Horace Stark was relieved of duty in the radio room and went below to his berth and fell asleep. Sub-Lieutenant Bill Landymore was in the wheelhouse with the quartermaster, a youngster who was oversteering the ship. Landymore was trying to get the young sailor to let the ship settle down and make his steering less pronounced. After the officer spent considerable time with the quartermaster, he left the bridge to get some sleep but decided to go back up to see what was going on.

Landymore had just neared the bridge when he heard the orders "Hard-a-port! Hard-a-starboard! Full astern!" Every bell on the ship began to clang. The screech of rending steel assaulted his ears. At this time, the captain, the first lieutenant (called Number One), two lookouts, a signalman and the yeoman were on the bridge. *Calcutta* slammed into *Fraser* between "B" gun and the bridge and kept going, taking *Fraser*'s bridge with her. The two ships had a combined speed of 34 knots and covered the last 200 metres between them in 11 seconds. The *Calcutta* sliced the *Fraser* into two.

The terrible sound of shredding steel roused Stark, who galloped from the lower deck and crawled through a hole onto the still-floating stern of the ship. He saw *Fraser*'s bow drifting off into the night, bottom up. The stern, where he was, was heeled over to port. Stark crawled through an opening to get to the air. He clung to the wreckage until it began to sink. Forced into the sea, he swam for about 30 minutes before a floating lifebelt came into reach. He grabbed it and, numb with exposure and shock, held on. *Restigouche* picked him out of the water an hour later.

Fraser's bridge was pitch black; all lights had been extinguished. As Landymore's eyes adjusted he saw Captain Creery on his knees trying to climb under the wheelhouse to rescue Able Seaman Todeus, the quartermaster. Todeus was trapped in a small cavity between *Calcutta's* deck and the floor of *Fraser's* bridge, which had buckled. Landymore said "I'll do that, sir" and crawled in as far as he could before coming to a blockage. He couldn't see nor feel enough to know what the obstacle was, so he backed out. Later, rescuers from *Calcutta* went in with lamps and found the unconscious quartermaster pinned against a bulkhead. They extricated the young man, who suffered only a broken ankle. He was lucky. The man who had been standing beside him had been squashed flat.

Without even getting their feet wet, the men on the tangled bridge leaped the two metres down to *Calcutta's* deck. *Fraser's* bridge remained on *Calcutta's* fo'c'sle until acetylene torches burned it off in Devonport Dockyard.

Restigouche and *Calcutta* lowered scramble-nets and boats to rescue survivors. *Restigouche* closed on *Fraser's* bow. Just as she neared it, it capsized and threw the men clinging to its rails into the water amid those already floating there. In spite of the black night and heavy swell, boats from *Restigouche* plucked 14 officers and about 100 men from the frigid water. One bedraggled and frozen sailor rescued was Able Telegrapher Horace Stark.

Restigouche turned her attention to *Fraser's* floating stern wreckage. She manoeuvred into a position with her quarterdeck touching the wreckage. In the heavy swell, the two ships ground against each other for about 10 minutes as 60 crewmen and one stretcher case safely crossed. A scuttling party was put on the destroyer's stern to open the seacocks. The last trace of HMCS *Fraser* slid below the surface a few minutes after midnight on June 25, 1940. She lost 58 seamen. It was not recorded whether or not any of the evacuated soldiers died from injuries. The rescuers provided hot soup, hammocks and beds to the survivors and delivered them to Plymouth.

Horace Stark spent the summer recuperating in England, attending various telecommunications courses. On September 6, 1940, he and most of the remaining crew were re-assigned to HMCS *Margaree*, a Royal Navy destroyer Canada bought to replace *Fraser*. Stark joined her at the Albert Docks in London while she was being refitted.

Landymore's only injury from the collision was a bruise on his right hip. After their return to England, he and his gunnery crew were sent to temporarily man railway anti-aircraft guns. Mounted on flatcars, the guns were taken into the rail marshalling yards at night to counter air attacks. Later in the summer Landymore was sent to Rosyth, Scotland, to replace the navigation officer in *Restigouche*. The *Restigouche* escorted convoys from Rosyth across the north of Scotland to the Western Approaches of the Atlantic. Then he was re-assigned to *Margaree*, still in refit at London's East End docks.

Margaree had no ammunition, so her guns remained silent during air raids. There were one officer and

15 sailors on board at all times. Their prime function was to provide a fire-party during the raids. The lack of power on the ship at night meant the fire-party had to form a bucket brigade to get water from over the side. They also had buckets of sand to deal with incendaries. Each group was on board four nights at a stretch. On the night of September 17, the entire crew "felt" a bomb fly by to land on the dock beside their ship. The feeling was a change in air pressure. Fortunately the explosion happened at low tide, and the destroyer was low in the water and flush with the dock. The crew were below decks in their quarters, so they were not injured when the bomb exploded over their heads. The exposion blew a hole in the dock almost three metres across. The ship suffered only minor damage, a few splinter holes and dents. Because of the bombing, the ship was moved quite frequently.

During one of the watches, on the first of the four nights, Landymore arranged to have a small keg of beer brought on board. All the sailors chipped in so they could each have a glass of beer. Most of the men had received their beer and taken it below to the mess deck. Suddenly a mine came down. Although it exploded about a half kilometre away, it blew Landymore off his feet.

During this time in England, Bill married his wife, Judy, in St. Margaret's Church, Westminster. The wedding went smoothly, although everyone was wary of an unexploded bomb in the courtyard.

꩜

CHAPTER THREE

Short Service in the RCN

ON A SERENE SEPTEMBER DAY IN 1940, the destroyer *Margaree* sailed down the Thames and around to Plymouth. There she loaded her ammunition and various other provisions available only at a navy yard. She was ordered to Londonderry, Ireland, to escort a small convoy, OL-8, to the mid-Atlantic after which the warship would proceed to Canada. On October 20, 1940, the convoy started out with five ships. About 800 kilometres west of Ireland, only two merchant ships were still in convoy and, making 14 knots, dispersed to proceed on their own.

Two days after sailing in rough seas and frequent rain squalls, *Margaree's* first lieutenant ordered reduced speed to maintain visual contact with the mechantmen. At about 1:00 AM, a particularly ferocious storm enveloped the ships for about 25 minutes. Visibility was zero. When the storm lifted, *Port Fairy*, the leading merchantman, found *Margaree* directly ahead to starboard and dangerously close. The merchant ship threw her engines into emergency stop and then full astern. She sounded three warning blasts. As if drawn to the sound, *Margaree* inexpicably turned left, directly across *Port Fairy's* course.

Port Fairy had no options—she cold not avoid the upcoming disaster. Her bow sliced *Margaree* in half at the bridge.

The destroyer's bow drifted clear, rolled over and sank within a minute. Fatalities included the officers standing watch on the bridge and the captain, Commander J.W. Roy, in his sea cabin behind the bridge. None of the officers or men in the forward part of the destroyer survived.

Twenty-year-old Horace Stark went down with the forward part of the ship. He was the first casualty of World War II from the Lanark County town of Carleton Place. His name is inscribed on the town's cenotaph and on the Halifax Memorial in Point Pleasant Park where the great granite Cross of Sacrifice is visible to ships approaching Halifax harbour.

In the wrecked aft section, things were hardly better. A few officers and the crews from the boiler room, engine room, depth charge and the after gun, about 40 men, were alive amid the wreckage. Bill Landymore was in his cabin aft of the wardroom. He knew immediately that they had been in a collision. Not even taking time to pull on his sea-boots, he ran up to the deck in his thick woollen socks. Landymore immediately saw that the bridge had been smashed and was just a piece of wreckage. However, its ladders were still in place. He scaled them to see if there was anyone alive. The bow had been sheared off as straight as if a razor had cut it. Only the bulkhead remained. *Margaree* was lolling in the water. *Port Fairy* manoeuvred alongside, and the three remaining officers (Bill Landymore, Bob Timbrell and Pat Russell) and one killick (enlisted seaman) caught lines and made them fast to the hulk.

Another young officer who survived this sinking was Sub-Lieutenant Robert Timbrell, a native of Victoria. He had just come off watch at midnight and was asleep in his cabin beneath the rear torpedo tubes. Timbrell was the first RCN officer to be decorated in World War II. His Distinguished Service Cross recognized his service commanding a yacht taking soldiers off the beach at Dunkirk. Like Landymore, Timbrell also rose to become an admiral during the post-war period.

The two ships ground together, banging and crashing in the roll of the sea. Men crossed to the *Port Fairy* by pulling themselves up on ropes. One sailor fell off a line and fell into the water. When the two ships smashed together, he was crushed to death.

When all the ratings were off the hulk, the three officers let the lines go. *Port Fairy* drifted away. The three put a Carley float over the side, but Landymore balked at leaving the derelict. He was the officer in charge of all the confidential books and documents. It was his absolute responsibility to get the four lead-weighted chests of confidential documents from the captain's cabin and put them over the side into deep water. Timbrell grabbed Bill and said "Forget it! Let's get the hell out of here!" It was obvious the remains of *Margaree* were going nowhere except to the bottom.

The officers and the killick abandoned the ship for the Carley float. After they fought the sea with paddles for an hour, *Port Fairy* picked them up and took them to her next stop, Bermuda. They eventually made their way back to Canada by hitching a ride on a CNR ship.

It was 1940; the war had barely started—and already two perfectly good destroyers and many Canadian sailors had lost their lives but not because of enemy action. The losses were a bitter blow to the young Canadian navy. If the stricken ships had had radar, it could have provided warning that another ship was close. The only detection devices the sailors had were their eyeballs. Information that may have shed more light on what happened in the two fatal collisions went down with the 142 officers and ratings that were lost in *Margaree*'s sinking. Eighty-six of those lost had survived the earlier sinking of the *Fraser*. The loss of so many volunteer sailors with the two ships was a shock to the civilians at home.

Bill Landymore went on to a distinguished career in the RCN. When he returned to Canada after the sinking of *Margaree*, he was sent to HMCS *Naden* in Esquimault. He taught gunnery, navigation and pilotage to RCN reservists who had been called up for active service but whose skills were rusty. Judy joined him, and the couple had a semblance of normal married life for a few years. In April 1943, orders sent Landymore back to England to take the RN long-gunnery course.

Landymore went back to sea in June 1944, to serve as a gunnery officer on the cruiser HMS *Uganda*. On March 1, 1945, he was promoted to the rank of acting lieutenant commander. *Uganda* was sent to the British Pacific Fleet, but the Canadian government insisted that all serving in the Pacific had to volunteer again for service. A few officers and many of the ship's sailors objected because they had volunteered once already for the duration of hostilities and they were incensed that they were being told they had to volunteer again.

Landymore's post-war career was a series of staff appointments and commands of various Canadian ships. He served two tours of duty in Korean waters as commander of HMCS *Iroquois*. He was mentioned in dispatches in January 1946 and in June 1953, both for his service during the Korean War. Landymore was in command on October 2, 1952, when a Communist shore battery shelled the ship, killing three sailors. He was awarded the Order of the British Empire on February 20, 1954. Landymore commanded HMCS *Bonaventure*, Canada's last aircraft carrier, in 1958.

As a rear admiral, Bill Landymore was the Commander, Maritime Forces when the government instituted the integration of the nation's military forces. Admiral Landymore was vocal in his opposition to the tri-service union and passionately defended the Royal Canadian Navy.

His greatest concern was the navy's professionalism. He feared that Defence Minister Paul Hellyer's unification of the forces would cost the navy its identity. But military officers are not allowed to question political motives. Regrettably, it became apparent that many junior officers did not share Landymore's opinion. He was forced into retirement. Rear Admiral William Moss Landymore hauled down his flag at HMCS *Stadacona,* navy headquarters in Halifax, on July 19, 1966. He and his wife retired to a seaside cottage at Head of Chezzetcook, Halifax County, Nova Scotia.

CHAPTER FOUR

The Ubiquitous Corvette

As soon as the ice started out of the St. Lawrence River in 1940, 14 small steel warships passed towards the sea. They were the first Canadian-built corvettes. The ships were only half-equipped and only partially manned. They were small for warships, 60 metres long and 10 metres wide, but could do 16 knots, and they displaced 860 tonnes and drew five metres of water. In some places during the passage, ice was still thickening, and the warships had to follow an ice-breaker weaving and crashing through the floes.

In 1939, the Canadian government was committed to acquiring a fleet of Tribal Class destroyers. Naval authorities considered these new ships equivalent to light cruisers, with armament capable of matching anything of equivalent class and size the enemy could float. Nevertheless, world events soon thwarted these plans. On September 10, 1939, Canada declared war on Germany, and on September 16, the first convoy left Halifax. Royal Canadian Navy destroyers escorted this convoy. The notion of surface raiders as the principal threat faded on September 3 when U-30 torpedoed the British liner *Athenia*. The Royal Navy interpreted this action as an act of unrestricted submarine warfare

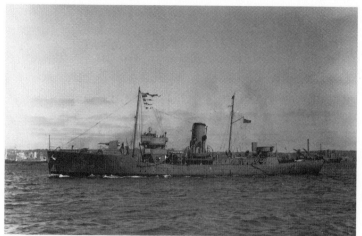

HMCS *Chambly*, April 1941

and shifted its emphasis to the requirement for convoy escorts and anti-submarine protection.

Hundreds of escort ships were required along the convoy routes between North America and Britain, but there were not hundreds of ships to be had. The Canadian shipbuilding industry had little or no expertise in the construction of warships. Technical advice from Britain was sorely needed for that type of project.

However, many Canadian steel-fabricating firms could build the proposed auxiliary ships initially designed as "whale catchers." The tactics used in catching a whale and catching a submarine are quite similar. Both targets surface or dive quickly, and both can swim at fast speeds. Both are highly maneuverable underwater, and both are frequently found in stormy, inhospitable seas. British plans for patrol vessels of the whale-catcher type were readily available, and Canadian yards could build them. Atlantic maritime shipyards were full with commercial orders, so almost all the contracts to build 64 whale catchers went to yards in the Great Lakes, the Upper St. Lawrence and the west coast. Only three whale catchers were built on the East Coast, at the Saint John, New Brunswick Shipbuilding and Drydock Company. Britain and Canada devised a barter scheme whereby Canada ordered Tribal destroyers from British yards in trade for 10 patrol boats built in Canada. The first 10 patrol vessels were promised to the Royal Navy, leaving the remaining 54 on order for the RCN.

These coastal patrol ships acquired the name "corvettes." The Royal Navy called their corvettes "Flower Class" and gave them names of flowers. Canadian corvettes were named after Canadian communities, usually small towns. Representatives of the municipalities and their local service clubs enthusiastically volunteered to be present at the launching and provided various amenities for "their" ship and her crew.

The original design for the corvettes called for a complement of 29 men, all ranks. The complexity of weapons and sensing equipment on board increased and so did the size of the crew. Each ship's crew swelled to 80 within a year and eventually to more than one hundred. Naval officers estimated that they needed almost 7000 officers and men to sail the planned ships. Most of the first corvette captains were former merchant marine officers. Crews came untrained from Canadian streets.

The RCN, at first, was not prepared in any way to train the new sailors. Equipment had to be procured and training establishments built. The transformation of a Saskatchewan farm lad to an efficient naval crewmember treading the deck of a heaving warship boggles the imagination. But that is exactly what the navy did, sometimes pumping out young officers in as little as 90 days.

Eighty percent of the corvettes' crewmembers had never even seen the ocean, let alone sailed on it. Only a handful of senior ratings were skilled in the operation of ship equipment and weapons. The rest learned as they sailed. The ex-merchant marine captains were often the only officers who were qualified as watch keepers or able to perform basic navigation. These old salts were not impressed with navy discipline and were totally unfamiliar with modern warfare at sea. Both the men and their ships were ill prepared for war.

Corvettes were young men's ships. The small ships survived rough weather, but their corkscrew motion through the sea, rising and falling as much as 15 metres, and rolling and yawing through monster waves, was hard on the crews. Sailors had to find their sea legs in a hurry, and many never did adjust. Those poor souls hung over the rail for most of a two-week trip. Even those not seasick experienced continual distress and numbing fatigue. They could not keep the sea out of their ships. Dampness and cold water were the only constants in their lives. As the ship burrowed through each crest, seawater surged over the fo'c'stle and along the heaving deck (wet even on a calm day). It cascaded through any opening into the mess decks and accommodations below. Water was everywhere—in the sailors' clothes, their food and all their belongings.

The corvettes that hustled off to Newfoundland to escort convoys across the unforgiving North Atlantic were intended for only a few days at sea at a time and for patrolling harbour mouths and coastlines. The standard four-inch main gun was of World War I vintage. The British mounted 20-millimetre Oerlikon guns on their bridges, but the Canadians had only .303 Lewis guns and .50 Browning machine guns. Neither was effective against submarines. Even things as rudimentary as the ships' bridge compasses were different. RN warships had gyrocompasses, which were quite stable in high seas and tight manoeuvres. Canadian ships had magnetic compasses, which swung wildly in pounding waves. Nearby electrics and guns firing often made the compasses inaccurate. As late as 1941, Canadian corvettes were simply not ready for war. Proper equipment and trained seamen were not available.

The Admiralty, however, was not overly worried. Only as a last resort would the escorts be called upon to fight. The strength lay in the convoy system itself and the technical advances onshore like the high-frequency direction-finding equipment that pinpointed U-boat concentrations and movements with considerable accuracy. The primary tactic would be avoidance rather than confrontation.

In 1941, Canada's corvettes were armed with basic anti-submarine weapons that posed no special threat to an experienced submariner. A corvette's principal weapons were an outdated sonar system, called ASDIC, and some 60 depth charges. Excellent water conditions and a skilled operator were required to produce useful results from the ASDIC apparatus, named after the Anti-Submarine Detection Investigation Committee of WWI. A weapon classified "secret" during WWII, ASDIC located submerged submarines by using sound waves. The device consisted of an electronic sound transmitter/receiver housed in a metal dome beneath a ship's hull. High-frequency beams—audible "pings"—were sent out. They bounced back when they hit a submarine (or other underwater obstruction). The time that passed before an echo was received showed the range of (distance to) the submarine or underwater object. The pitch of the echo revealed if the object was approaching, moving away or keeping the same distance.

The ASDIC equipment required a highly trained operator to get effective results. The ASDIC operator searched through an arc of roughly 45 degrees in five-degree intervals. The beam went out 2000 metres. If it did not hit anything and echo back, the operator shifted the beam five degrees. The operator moved the beam through the entire arc at five-degree intervals until a contact was obtained. When an echo was received, it was evaluated. By moving the beam a small amount, the operator determined the length of the target and whether or not it was moving.

Each of a corvette's 190-kilogram depth charges, packed with explosives, was about the size of a garbage can. Depth charges were intended to work with the pressure of the water at depth to crush the submarine's hull. The charge's hydrostatic (water pressure–sensitive) detonator could be set for depths up to 100 metres. Half the charges were carrying additional weight to make them sink faster. The stern of the corvette had two launching rails, with two throwers per side. Various patterns were used to make an effective attack. If the submarine was forced to surface, the corvette could shell it with the corvette's unreliable main gun, or, as most captains preferred, simply ram the target. Although U-boats were faster on the surface, the corvette was more maneuverable. Its curving bow could cause considerable damage to the U-boat's pressure hull. The corvette would also suffer, but a U-boat kill was worth it.

Starting in 1941, the RCN faced a new kind of war at sea. Admiral Karl Dönitz, commanding the German submarine fleet, adopted aggressive strategy and tactics. When a convoy was located, radio homing beacons directed the rest of the U-boat "wolf pack" to it. The pack assembled around the convoy then independently attacked. They raced into the massed ships, picked a target, fired their torpedoes and slipped out behind the convoy. In three early battles, marauding wolf packs sunk 43 vesels without the loss of a single U-boat.

In early 1941, British-based escorts took convoys some 2100 kilometres west then picked up inbound convoys headed for English ports. Canadian-based warships ranged to the northeastern edges of the Grand Banks. This still left a "happy hunting ground" for the U-boats in the waters between Iceland and Newfoundland. The British occupied Iceland. Anti-submarine forces operating from there improved the Allies' protection of the merchantman lifeline. Still, there was a gap of several hundred kilometres of cold and rough water. The need to plug this hole resulted in the formation of the Newfoundland Escort Force (NEF) in May 1941. The first corvettes to make their way to St. John's as part of the NEF were the *Agassiz, Alberni, Chambly, Cobalt, Collingwood, Orillia* and *Wetaskiwin*. Their task was to escort and protect merchant convoys as they began to cross the vile North Atlantic. RCNR reservists from the merchant marine commanded five of these ships. Only two, *Chambly* and *Wetaskiwin*, had RCN professional officers as commanders.

The ocean convoy escort system from east coast ports was organized around the NEF, the Western Local Escort Force (WLEF) and the Mid-Ocean Escort Force (MOEF). The WLEF (later called the Western Escort Force) was responsible for escorting convoys from New York and Halifax to ocean routes off St. John's. There the NEF/MOEF took over the eastbound ships. The NEF, WEF and MOEF were Canadian responsibilities, covered mostly by Canadian ships under British control until September 1941, then by Canadian ships under American control until April

1943, when joint British–Canadian control was established. A Canadian, Commodore L.W. Murray, was appointed commander in April 1943 when the command was established. His was the only operational command for a Canadian officer.

Although Newfoundland was not then a part of Canada, Canada had assumed responsibility for its defence. The NEF was the first operational responsibility in "foreign" waters the RCN undertook. To form the NEF, Canada used all its available escort vessels. Destroyers serving in Britain and those in Halifax were allocated to the NEF and moved to St. John's.

So too were the first of 10 corvettes that had been built in Canada for the RN. Escort groups were usually made up of a destroyer and three or four corvettes. By mid-1942, Canada provided about half of all the escort ships ushering convoys across the North Atlantic. However, Canada's corvettes were woefully underequipped for the task. Their design was for coastal work, not mid-ocean slogging.

In the quest for small auxiliary warships that could be built in Canadian shipyards, the navy acquired from the National Research Council plans for "whale catchers." Intended for inshore duty, these corvettes, as the whale catchers came to be called in 1940, were built as the Canadian navy's primary anti-submarine ship. The navy's expansion plans for 1940 included two Tribal class destroyers, 20 corvettes and 12 minesweepers. By war's end, 113 corvettes were ordered for the RCN.

Navy vessels, even small corvettes, are complex fighting machines. Experienced sailors are needed to train novice crews. In the early days of WWII, all the experienced men in the pared-back Canadian navy were already at sea. Even experienced people need time to learn to handle a new ship. Fighting teams need practice, but Canada had no facilities for training. Corvette crews, if they were lucky, had a couple of officers on the bridge who were qualified merchant mariners. However these officers had minimal experience in naval operations. Most often a new crew was sent on its first day at sea with a regular force officer to show them what to do. Below decks, a lucky corvette crew had a few trained permanent-force petty officers and seamen. Newly commissioned corvettes were woefully unprepared to fight a professional enemy at sea. Ships were being built and equipped faster than crews were being trained to properly fight in them—and survive. All the corvettes' crews were sent to sea sadly lacking experience.

CHAPTER FIVE

An Ideal Commanding Officer

"In each ship, there is only one man who, in the hour of emergency or peril at sea, can turn to no other man. There is one who alone is ultimately responsible for the safe navigation, engineering performance, accurate gunfiring and morale of his ship. He is the Commanding Officer. He is the ship…It is a duty which most richly deserves the highest, time-honoured title of the seafaring world…captain."

–Anonymous

ENTER COMMANDER JAMES DOUGLAS "Chummy" Prentice. Prentice was a Canadian who had retired from the Royal Navy in 1938 and returned to live in Canada. He was recalled to service in the RCN, appointed "Senior Officer, Canadian Corvettes" and given the task of whipping the little ships into shape. Striking groups of five corvettes each were based at various East Coast ports. Their role was to hunt and kill U-boats in the harbour approaches.

Prentice was born in 1899 to British parents living in Victoria. At age 13, he declared his intention to join the newborn RCN. Marc Milner wrote in *North Atlantic Run* that Prentice's father believed the RCN to be no more than a receptacle for political patronage. If his son was determined to join a navy, it would have to be the Royal Navy. So, Prentice was admitted to the Royal Naval College in Dartmouth and that same year enrolled as a cadet in the RN. His service was quite ordinary, reaching its peak as first lieutenant commander of the battleship HMS *Rodney*. In 1934, after 22 years' service and passed over for promotion to commander, he realized that his career options were not great. He took early retirement in 1937 (at the age of 38) and returned to British Columbia, finding employment as financial secretary to the Western Canada Ranching Company. He was at his desk in 1939 when war broke out.

He first offered himself to the RN, but, because there were no openings, the RN placed his name on a list of officers available to the RCN. The Canadians offered him a commission at his old RN rank, which he quickly accepted, and he was posted across the continent to Sydney, Nova Scotia on the staff of the Naval Officer in Charge. He was rescued from staff work in July 1940 with a transfer to Halifax to take command of the yet-to-be-commissioned corvette, HMCS *Levis*. In Halifax, Prentice met an old RN staff college friend, Canadian Commodore L.W. Murray. Murray was commanding the Newfoundland Escort Force, and the two men, sharing many interests, became fast friends. Murray had Prentice transferred to his staff as senior officer, Canadian corvettes. The position was little more than titular, but it provided Prentice with a conduit into the affairs of the corvette navy, which he used constantly over the next three years. Murray was posted to the UK as commodore commanding Canadian ships.

Prentice spent the winter of 1940–41 conducting workups of the few new ships that had arrived in Halifax before the St. Lawrence froze up. In March, he was given command of another corvette, HMCS *Chambly*. Prentice was an innovator, and this command gave free rein to his overactive imagination. His prime interest became the operational efficiency of the corvette and how best the ships could be used. Milner points out that, as a rather senior officer (in the rank of commander), his experience, seniority and lack of long-term ambition in this junior service (the RCN) gave him a freedom of expression that none of his peers enjoyed.

Prentice was the ideal commanding officer to the lower ranks. His sense of fairness was legendary, and his eccentricities endeared him to the men on the lower decks. His British accent, love of cigars and his wearing of a monocle became the stuff of myth. Milner relates the oft-told but never authenticated story of a whole division of *Chambly* parading on deck wearing monocles. Without apparently taking notice, the captain completed his inspection and then stood facing his crew. In the ranks, knees began to shake as they expected a royal dressing-down. According to Milner, Prentice threw his head back, flipping the monocle into the air. As the glass fell, he caught it between his eyebrow and the lower eyelid—exactly back in place. He then announced, so the story goes,

View from HMCS *Chambly* of the first group of Canadian-built corvettes, 1941

"When you can do that, you can all wear monocles." Prentice was enthusiastic about his work, and that enthusiasm rubbed off on colleagues and subordinates alike. With a good measure of fairness and a well-developed sense of propriety he pursued efficiency at all levels of shipboard life. Prentice clearly found his niche in the small ships of the RCN.

A warm sun bathed the entrance to St. John's, Newfoundland, on the morning of May 23, 1941. That day Commander Prentice led the first seven corvettes of the NEF through the narrow rock cliffs forming the entrance to the St. John's harbour to establish the new convoy-escort force.

Unfazed by the task ahead, Prentice led his first convoy to sea on June 2. The North Atlantic lay quiet until June 23. *Chambly, Ottawa, Collingwood* and *Orillia*, screening convoy HX-133, discovered and battled *U-203*. The U-boat's commander was 28-year-old *Kapitänleutnant* (eqivalent to an RCN lieutenant commander) Rolf Mützenburg, an experienced surface ship and U-boat commander. Due to a lack of equipment, bad training and poor procedures, communications between the Canadians was chaotic. *U-203* got away, but assisting British warships sunk two other U-boats. The convoy lost six ships that day. Prentice's force returned to St. John's and prepared to try their luck again.

On September 6, 1941, the crew of HMCS *Chambly* let go her lines. Commander Chummy Prentice aimed her bow towards the sea through the split rock forming the harbour mouth of St. John's. Slightly astern and to starboard steamed HMCS *Moose Jaw*, skippered by Freddie Grubb. The two corvettes had been scheduled for a training exercise that day, but Prentice took them to sea to meet Convoy SC-42. This convoy was carrying more than one-half million tonnes of essential supplies from Sydney, Nova Scotia to Britain. However the next day, Prentice's little armada received a radio order from NEF headquarters telling the ships to wait for convoy SC-44, which was expected to pass the Straits of Belle Isle (between Newfoundland and Labrador) on September 11.

This order was unexpected, as intercepted German radio traffic made it quite clear that U-boats were gathering to attack SC-42. On September 8, convoy SC-42, 64 merchantmen spread out over 65 square kilometres of the North Atlantic, was south-southeast of Greenland's Cape Farewell. The convoy altered course due north for one day. Within sight of the mountainous coast, the escort commander ordered a change of heading starboard to settle out on a north-east track and head for Britain. The escort commander hoped the northward course changes had taken them around the submarine patrol line. Escort Group 24, destroyer HMCS *Skeena* (commanded by Lieutenant Commander James C. Hibbert, who was also the commander of the escort group) and three corvettes, *Alberni, Kenogami* and *Orillia*, were escorting the convoy. High winds and seas buffeted the flotilla. The plan was for the convoy to make an average speed of seven knots, but it had to wallow for two days as the ships' engines strained just to keep steerage.

At 11:37 PM, September 9, torpedoes hit SS *Muneric,* loaded with iron ore. Massive holes below her waterline caused her to sink within minutes. Her crew had no chance of escape, and all hands went to the bottom with her. *Kenogami* raced along the track of the torpedo. The sub launched a second salvo of torpedoes, but *Kenogami* was not hit. Sailors on the ship's bridge saw the U-boat floating on the surface but had no searchlights or star shells to illuminate the enemy. The ship's deck gun fired almost blindly at the black shadow and missed. The U-boat easily escaped.

Shortly after midnight clouds covered the sky, extinguishing the moonlight. An easterly gale blew up, and heavy heaving seas buffetted the heavily laden merchantmen.

The convoy tried to turn away from the threatening subs, but by then U-boats were everywhere inside the convoy's perimeter. Seven more merchantmen were sunk before daybreak and another went down at noon. HMCS *Orillia* was designated the "rescue ship" and dropped behind the convoy to pick up survivors. After dong this, she took a severely damaged tanker, SS *Tahchee,* in tow and started north for Iceland. As admirable as this humanitarian gesture sounds, *Orillia's* captain was making a serious error in judgement. The ship's departure left the surviving ships of convoy SC-42 with 25 percent less of their meagre escort.

The Admiralty radioed requesting help for the beleaguered convoy, and Prentice's *Chambly* and Grubb's *Moose Jaw* were only too happy to oblige. As daylight faded, U-boats sank two more of the convoy's merchantmen. *Skeena* fired two star shells to see what was happening. (Destroyers were equipped with searchlights and star shells, but corvettes were not.) *Skeena* saw no surfaced submarines in the rough seas, but Chummy Prentice's rapidly approaching pair of corvettes saw the flares and used them to locate the convoy. By now the convoy stretched over five kilometres, and its front covered almost 12 kilometres.

❧◆❧

A corvette's prime anti-submarine detection device was ASDIC, an early form of sonar. When the highly trained ASDIC operator located a U-boat, the "Action

Stations" bell was sounded and another escorting warship was called in to launch a coordinated attack. The ship that acquired the contact laid off in order to maintain ASDIC contact. The attack was made with depth charges dropped on the calculated position of the enemy contact.

Infamous Captain Frederic J. "Johnnie" Walker, CB, DSO and three Bars, RN, developed and perfected these hunter-killer tactics. His operating instructions to his ships' captains read:

> *Our object is to kill, and all officers must fully develop the spirit of vicious offensive. No matter how many convoys we may shepherd through in safety, we shall have failed unless we slaughter U-boats. All energies must be bent to this end.*

Walker's last command at sea was the sloop HMS *Starling*, where he achieved a reputation as a "scourge of the U-boats." While ashore on leave, on July 9, 1944, Captain Walker died, at the age of 48. According to doctors he died of cerebral thrombosis. In fact, he died of overstrain, overwork and war weariness. His body and mind had been driven beyond all normal limits in the service of his country. Shock at the news stunned Walker's own "gallant *Starling*." At dawn, the ship's ensign was half-masted and lifelines were trailed over the side in an ancient mariner's tribute to a dead hero.

According to Walker's tactics, the attacking corvette should rush at her 15-knot top speed to the calculated position of the enemy. Corvettes had four depth charge throwers that were loaded during the run-in. Each depth charge was set to explode at a specific depth. The idea was for the charges' detonations to create a shock wave that would hit a sub's hull and damage its watertight integrity. The damaged sub would come to the surface where, it was hoped, it would surrender. The shock wave also could damage the attacking ship. Often its ASDIC was knocked out, which was why the first ship summoned another to attack while the first maintained contact. The slow speed of the attacker meant that it was close to the exploding charges. The depth charges caused quite a shock to the ship, especially if they detonated near the surface.

⌘

Back at the beleaguered convoy SC-42, the arriving *Chambly* picked up a strong ASDIC signal and rapidly classed it as a submarine contact. The corvette turned to launch a quick attack and dropped five depth charges. As *Chambly* swung into a second attack, *U-501* surfaced off the port bow of *Moose Jaw*. *Moose Jaw*'s Lieutenant Freddie Grubb ordered his gunners to open fire. However, the main gun misfired, and Freddie turned his corvette to ram the U-boat. Just before the two ships met, the *Moose Jaw* crew fixed the four-inch gun and fired it, putting a round into the U-boat's conning tower. *Korvettenkapitän* (equivalent to an RCN commander) Hugo Förster, the U-boat commander, decided to surrender and ordered the submarine to stop engines. As *Moose Jaw* scraped alongside, its crew found most of the submarine's crewmembers on deck with their hands raised.

Then, in a move that surprised both crews, Förster leaped some three metres from his deck onto the bridge of *Moose Jaw*. Sub-Lieutenant Hal Lawrence was on duty on the bridge. The German captain's greeting to him was, "Do not fire. Do not fire on my men anymore. We have stopped firing. We surrender."

Fearing further boarding attempts, Grubb slipped away from the enemy vessel. However, the U-boat's crew started her engines and steered to cross the bow of the Canadian ship, a perfect position to attack the ship with the sub's deck gun.

Grubb decided again to ram. The German crew ran for their deck gun, but *Moose Jaw's* gunners discouraged them from this plan. Their machine gun bullets peppered the sub's conning tower, and their four-inch gun shot away the main German deck gun.

Meanwhile *Chambly* joined the fray. She lit up the U-boat with her signal projector and the small Aldis lamps that normally were used for signaling. Prentice ordered his crew to launch the whaler and "prepare to board." When Lieutenant Ted Simmons and his boarding party arrived at the sub, its German crew was jumping into the sea.

Mac Johnston, in his book *Corvettes Canada*, records Commander Prentice's description of the action.

Lieutenant Simmons knocked one German overboard who tried to interfere with him and drove two more to the top of the conning tower with orders to show him the way below. They refused, making it clear

that they expected the boat to sink at any moment.
(They had opened the seacocks.)

Lieutenant Simmons started down the hatch, but
got stuck due to his gas mask. He took the gas mask off
and started down a second time in the hope of finding
confidential papers, in spite of the fact that he knew the
boat must have been filling with chlorine fumes. As he
reached the bottom of the ladder, a bulkhead must have
given way for he saw a wall of water coming towards
him. He climbed to the top of the conning tower and
ordered his boarding party to swim to the skiff that was
lying off. The last man had just splashed into the water
when the U-boat sank under his feet.

Those still in the whaler fished most of the Canadians out of the water, but one Canadian did not make
it back. Stoker W.I. "Bill" Brown, 24, of Toronto, was
lost, and his body never recovered. His shipmates
believed his feet, encased in heavy sea-boots, were
caught in the conning tower's chains when the boat
sank. Lieutenant Simmons narrowly missed a similar
fate when the sinking sub sucked him down.

The sunken *U-501* had been a type IXC boat, commissioned in Hamburg on April 30, 1941. Förster was
her first and only captain, and she had been on her
first mission when she sank. The U-boat had one success, the sinking of a merchant ship on September 10,
1941, in the Straits of Denmark. The merchantman
took 11 of her crew down with her. *Chambly* brought
an end to this German vessel's career when it was just
starting.

While Lieutenant Simmons boarded the sub, *Moose Jaw* and *Chambly* busily picked up its survivors. *Chambly* lowered scramble nets over her sides for the Germans to clamber up to the corvette's deck. Thirty-seven sailors were rescued and became prisoners of war. Each was given a survivor's kit containing civilian clothes and was offered hot showers, food and drink. On the corvettes, the Germans ate with their captors, slept in the same area (albeit under guard) and generally got along well with their enemy. When the ship docked in Greenoch, Scotland, the blindfolded Germans were led ashore to a prison camp. To a man, they turned away from their captain.

"For bravery and enterprise in action against enemy submarines," James Prentice received the Distinguished Service Order on March 3, 1942. This DSO was the first awarded to a Canadian naval officer during World War II. His lieutenant, Ted Simmons, was decorated with the Distinguished Service Cross. Prentice and his crew had accomplished the first RCN U-boat kill of the war.

The Navy Department in Ottawa informed Bill Brown's wife and family only that he was missing in action. Commander Prentice did not want them clinging to the possibility that he had survived and was a prisoner of war. When *Chambly* returned to Canada for a refit, Prentice called in torpedo man Syd Moyle, whose home was in Rexdale, a suburb of Toronto, and instructed the 20-year-old sailor to visit the family and tell them the true story of Bill's demise. Moyle was sent on leave to perform the task. The young man wanted never to have to repeat this emotionally charged experience.

Despite *Chambly*'s kill, Convoy SC-42 lost 16 ships, one quarter of its complement, during the three-day battle. U-boats had outnumbered the escort three to one. *Orillia's* departure to tow the tanker had further weakened the protective screen. Other warship commanders had stopped to pick up survivors and left the convoy vulnerable. The one-sided action ended on September 11 when the ships sailed within range of air cover from Iceland. Also, about that time, RN destroyers, corvettes and sloops from the Western Approaches Command joined the escorts and drove away the attacking subs. During the night of September 17–18, the battered convoy straggled into safety at Loch Ewe.

Kreigsmarine officers said they considered Hugo Förster's leap from *U-501* to *Chambly* an act of cowardice. The captain of a ship in any navy is the last, not the first, off a vessel in distress. Other U-boat officers in the prison camp in England intended to try Förster for cowardice, but he was moved to Canada. It is rumoured that after he was repatriated to Germany in a prisoner exchange, German navy officers court-martialled him, and a firing squad executed him.

~∞~

CHAPTER SIX

"All Convoys Are Safe from the Sub You Have Sunk"

IN APRIL 1942, COMMODORE MURRAY had Prentice establish a training group at Conception Bay. Its purpose was to take corvettes on 12-day training exercises. Over the next four months, Prentice trained more than a dozen corvettes and their crews. The "training exercises" usually were sailings in support of convoys over the Grand Banks. Prentice never mended his unconventional ways, and shore-bound admirals complained about his convoy-support techniques. In August, operational commitments forced the abandonment of the training group. However, the need for convoy protection did not lessen. In November, the Western Support Force was established to escort convoys over the Grand Banks, exactly what Prentice had done from April to August.

In 1943, the RCN expected a major German inshore offensive. Protective operations in the Gulf and in the St. Lawrence were stepped up. Forces were also primed and ready on the Nova Scotia coast. Recently promoted Captain (Destroyers) Chummy Prentice changed his ships from convoy escorts into submarine hunters. By March 1943, he had turned convoy escort work upside down. Prentice espoused that the primary role of the escort should be to counterattack. He preached, "All convoys are safe from the sub you have sunk." These offensive operations, along with tactical innovations, enhanced British operations on the eastern side of the Atlantic and increased long-range air support, contributed to decreased shipping losses.

Captain Chummy Prentice left his acting rank of Captain (D) *Halifax* on May 9, 1944, to go back to sea as senior officer on the destroyer HMCS *Ottawa*. While commanding *Ottawa*, on July 6, 1944, he sunk a second submarine. In company with HMCS *Kootenay*, under command of A/Lieutenant W.H. Wilson, *Ottawa* was part of Escort Group 11 (EG-11) patrolling the English Channel. This group was the main anti-submarine group operating in inshore waters. It had been put together to clear sea passage for the Normandy landings a month earlier.

The Germans had developed their new *schnorkelling* U-boats, which Prentice had to battle in the Channel's comparatively shallow water. The Channel was littered with destroyed shipping, among which subs could hide from Allied detection. EG-11 was designated the "Anti-submarine Killer Group" in the Channel, and Prentice challenged the crews under his command to discover a method to deal with enemy boats silently lying in wait on the bottom.

On the morning of July 6, the British frigate HMS *Statice* acquired a firm radar contact on a submarine. Prentice's Canadians were ordered to that location,

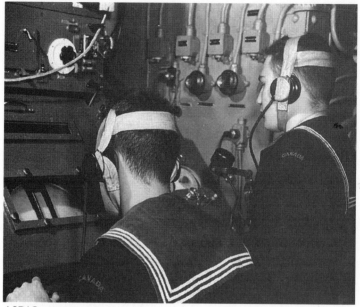

ASDIC operators

~❦~

a point south of Beachy Head, a few kilometres off the Sussex coast. The Channel seabed was an ASDIC operator's nightmare. It was strewn with wrecks, teemed with schools of fish and was beset with strong changeable currents.

The U-boat drifting along the bottom was U-678 under the command of 26-year-old *Oberleutnant zur See* (senior lieutenant, equivalent to the RCN rank of lieutenant) Guido Hyronimus. *U-678* was a type-VIIC boat and belonged to the 7th Unterseebootsflottille, based in St. Nazaire, France. Hyronimus had taken command when the boat was commissioned in Hamburg on

October 25, 1943 and was her only commander. This was Hyronimus' second boat. He had previously commanded *U-670*, again from commissioning in Hamburg on January 26, 1943, until she was lost on August 20, 1943. That day, Hyronimus and his crew were still in training when their boat collided with a target ship *Bolkoburg* and sank. Twenty-one crewmembers died, and 22 survived the accidental sinking. After a short leave in his hometown of Augsburg, Hyronimus took the remnants of his crew with him to the new boat, *U-678*.

U-678 and the other VIIC U-boats were the workhorses of the German submarine fleet. Germans commissioned 568 boats of this class. Each one carried four bow torpedoes and one stern tube. They were also armed with an 88-millimetre (45-calibre) deck gun. On the surface, the submarine could travel at 17.7 knots; submerged, it cruised at 7.6 knots.

Knowing they had been detected, the German crew coasted their boat quietly along the bottom. Their depth varied from 65 to 100 metres. The Canadian destroyers took turns swooping in to drop depth charges aimed at the sub. They were getting confirmation of hits when, at noon, books, clothing, pieces of wood and a cylindrical decoy bobbed to the surface. Shortly thereafter, a slick of diesel oil spread over the ocean's surface. Still not believing the sub was dead, *Ottawa* and *Kootenay,* through that long afternoon, dropped depth charges on their target, which was wallowing at the Channel floor in only 50 metres of water.

Onboard *Ottawa*, Prentice's anti-submarine staff officer was Lieutenant Bob Timbrell. This man had been among the officers last to leave the ill-fated *Margaree* in the RCN's early, dark days. Onboard the *Ottawa*, Timbrell had devised an unorthodox technique to attack the submarine. Prentice was keen to test the merits of any new procedure in search of ways to improve his command's performance. His style of command raised many eyebrows in the Royal Navy, but he was successful. Timbrell had developed a special depth charge. It was armed with an electronic detonator and would be lowered over the side on a wire. On the bottom end of the wire was a grappling hook.

Ottawa dragged the device slowly over the bottom until the hook caught on the U-boat. The wire tightened, and a gunner triggered the charge. *U-678* was ripped wide open in the resulting explosion. Grisly debris provided a positive identification. Fifty-two Kreigsmarine sailors—the total complement of the boat—died.

In mid-August 1944, Prentice's EG-11, composed of HMC Ships *Ottawa, Kootenay* (with Bill Wilson, now an acting lieutenant commander still at the helm) and *Chaudière* (under A/Lieutenant Commander C. Pat Nixon), patrolled the coast of France in the Bay of Biscay. The three destroyers caught two U-boats and methodically destroyed them. A little later, near La Rochelle, they battled *U-621*. This boat's commander was *Oberleutnant zur See* Hermann Stuckmann. Although only 23, he was a veteran submariner. Stuckmann took command of *U-621* on May 15, 1944, and spent the summer fighting Allied landing ships in the English Channel. He sank two of them. Prior to taking over *U-621*, he had served on *U-571* and commanded *U-316* as a school boat in the Baltic Sea. In recognition of his success in combat—four ships and one auxiliary warship sunk; one ship and one warship damaged—Stuckmann was awarded the Knight's Cross on August 11, only a week before he met the Canadian destroyers. Stuckmann and his 55-member crew were all lost when the Canadian destroyers sunk *U-621*.

On August 20, the three Canadian ships coordinated an attack against another solid ASDIC contact west of Brest. The ships took turns laying depth charges and succeeded in sinking *U-984*. *Oberleutnant Zur See* Heinz Sieder, *U-984*'s commander, had celebrated his 24th birthday at sea on June 20 and had been awarded the Knight's Cross on July 8. Under his direction, the crew of *U-984* had damaged one ship and sunk three U.S. merchant vessels and a British destroyer. The U-boat had completed four patrols in 95 days. Sieder and his crew of 44 sailors were all lost.

At war's end, Prentice had four successful engagements against enemy submarines to his credit. He was awarded a Distinguished Service Cross (DSC) and Bar for the last two actions. The commendation for the DSC reads "For courage, resolution and skill while serving in HMCS *Ottawa* in anti U-boat operations." The commendation for the Bar reads "For services in destroying an enemy submarine on 18–19 August

1944." These decorations were both awarded on January 20, 1945.

During the winter of 1944, the Canadian Navy moved its training facilities to Bermuda. The water and the weather there were far better for ASDIC training than winter water near Halifax. In mid-summer 1944, the base HMCS *Somers Iles* (so named after Bermuda's historic name) was established at St. Georges. Captain Prentice had retained his interest in training. At the end of the European war, he was given command of *Somers Iles* and the task of preparing frigates for the war in the Pacific.

Canada made a remarkable contribution to Allied victory in the Battle of the Atlantic. However, this contribution was more through good luck and the persistent doggedness of her sailors than by good management. It is not coincidental the most effective ship commanders were those who had joined the Royal Navy pre-war and learned their trade from experts in large modern warships. During the six years of war, the Royal Canadian Navy grew from 11 warships and 1800 professional sailors to more than 450 ships of many types and nearly 100,000 all ranks. This rapid expansion caused a shortage of properly trained crew that slowed the increase in the true battle effectiveness of Canada's wartime navy.

The war caught all three services, army, air force and navy, unprepared, but only the navy was forced to fight from the start. Canada fielded a large army after it had ample time to get trained and equipped.

Members of the Canadian air force too did not go into battle in Europe until being properly trained in the British Commonwealth Air Training Plan in the safe skies over Canada.

From the start, Canada produced basic warships, but Canada's production of up-to-date electronics and other equipment did not keep pace with the rapidly changing tactical naval environment. The Canadians always seemed to be the last to receive new equipment, such as improved radar, sonar and communications equipment. Having this equipment would have contributed a great deal to successful actions and to effective ocean convoy escorts. The RCN's unbridled growth led to inefficiency and unacceptable losses in Canadian-escorted convoys. One accomplished Royal Navy escort commander, Captain Donald MacIntyre, referred to the RCN's escorts as "travesties of warships" and Canadian convoy battles as "wild and confused." Government ministers and navy senior officers pushed industry to meet target numbers even if it meant producing ill-equipped hulls. Then they rushed the training of the men to sail them.

Canada's inability to support her navy caused grave worries. The Battle of the Atlantic was a struggle the Allies could not lose and survive. But the officers and men of the RCN rose to meet and overcome the impossible challenge en route to success.

CHAPTER SEVEN

The Tribals

TRIBAL CLASS DESTROYERS FIRST APPEARED in the Royal Navy just before World War II. Their design gave them an aggressive appearance. There was no doubt that these destroyers were warships. The forward-raked bow and rearward-raked funnels and masts gave the ship a powerful striking appearance. The Royal Navy gave the ships names of warrior tribes and designated the destroyers "Tribal Class." The 16 Tribals in the RN at the start of World War II were among the elite of the British force. They proved to be excellent fighting ships and served in every sea theatre of the war. Only four of the 16 survived the war.

The Canadians decided that seven Tribals were required as part of the RCN's expansion plans to make the navy a formidable force. Each of these destroyers carried eight 4.7-inch guns and four torpedo tubes. The Tribals' high speed and heavy armament made them the most powerful destroyers then in service. However, until late in the war, Canadian shipyards did not have the technical expertise to construct these complex, high-performance vessels. In 1940, the Canadian government placed an order for four Tribals to be built in Britain.

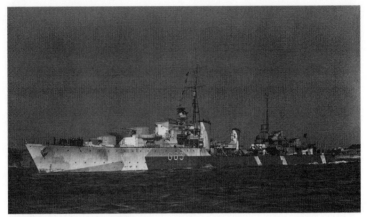

HMCS *Haida*, July 1944

~∞)(∞~

HMCS *Iroquois* and *Athabaskan* were launched in 1941, *Haida* and *Huron* in 1942. The need for formidable convoy escort ships like these four became urgent when the Germans adopted U-boat wolf-pack tactics. The submarines began travelling on the surface (in areas outside the range of Allied aircraft) and attacking at night. Allied countermeasures consisted mainly of forming protective escorts around the convoys. Large targets, like convoys, however, proved difficult, almost impossible to defend. Canadian navy senior officers planned to build a destroyer navy to enhance the ability of the RCN to carry out this convoy-escort role, to work with the main British battle fleet and to conduct torpedo attacks on enemy warships. (To build up Canada's destroyer fleet, the Halifax yard, with British assistance, constructed four Tribals: *Micmac*, *Nootka*, *Cayuga* and the second

Athabaskan. None of these were commissioned before the end of the war, so they did not see action.) Later, Canada naval command shifted to prefer a new type of convoy escort, frigates, of which 60 were ordered starting in 1943.

Construction of *Iroquois* and *Athabaskan* started on September 19, 1940, at the Vickers-Armstrong High Walker Yard in Newcastle-on-Tyne. *Iroquois* was intended to be the first Canadian Tribal Class destroyer. After losing the Battle of Britain, Hitler concentrated on night bombing of British industry and cities. In April 1941, the *Luftwaffe* bombed east coast towns. One of these raids severely damaged the hull plates and stringers of the frame scheduled to be *Iroquois*. Beside her, *Athabaskan* escaped Hitler's anger. Lengthy repairs to *Iroquois'* broken hull, compared to the rapid rate of construction of her sister, meant that *Athabaskan* would be in the water long before *Iroquois*. Senior naval and shipyard officials decide to switch names so that *Iroquois* would be the name of the first launched, according to the original schedule.

The newly renamed *Athabaskan* was left to lick the wounds of her first injuries. *Iroquois* went on to illustrious adventures, but her younger sister-ship, *Athabaskan*, was beset by hard luck.

On November 18, 1941, on a typically English overcast day, Lady Tweedsmuir, widow of Canada's first WWII governor general, braved a cool onshore breeze to burst a bottle of champagne on the ship's bow and declare, "I christen thee *Athabaskan*." The RCN's second

Tribal Class destroyer slid down the ways into the River Tyne. *Athabaskan* was towed to the fitting-out basin where she remained for more than a year. The regular fitting of engines, boilers and internal equipment was augmented with additions and modifications resulting from the British wartime experience with RN Tribal destroyers.

The company that crewed the *Athabaskan* did not arrive in one fell swoop. Some were posted to her as soon as the keel was laid and stayed with her as she grew. Others arrived later. Slowly and steadily, as the ship took shape, so did her crew. The builders crammed all sorts of equipment into the crew's quarters while the fittings were waiting to be installed. Consequently, many of the crew were billeted ashore in private homes where they quickly became members of a new family. Members of the crew came from all parts of the Dominion. Some were experienced hands; some were setting foot on a ship's deck for the first time. On one of the earliest drafts was 25-year-old Leading Writer Stuart Alexander Kettles, shivering on shore and waiting to go aboard.

Kettles was born on September 1, 1917, and raised in Ottawa. After graduating from Ottawa High School of Commerce, he completed a one-year course in mechanical drawing at Ottawa Technical High School. He then went to work as a clerk-stenographer with the J.R. Booth Ltd. Lumber Company in Ottawa. On February 21, 1942, he joined the RCN Volunteer Reserve, HMCS *Carleton*, a shore-based training ship at Ottawa, as a probationary writer (clerk). Because he was already trained in a trade that the navy could use, he was promoted to writer and transferred to the RCN. He was posted to HMCS *Stadacona* in Halifax on February 26. Kettles stayed ashore in Halifax, doing clerk's duties and learning to be a sailor, until October 28, 1942, when he went to England to join the crew of HMCS *Athabaskan*.

Finally, the workers completed the final installation of pipes, wires and machinery. The *Athabaskan's* guns and masts were installed. The modern warship was ready to receive the men who would bring her to life. A brief commissioning ceremony was held on February 3, 1943. The crew from HMCS *Niobe*, the RCN Shore Establishment at Greenock, Scotland, formed up by divisions on the pier.

The first lieutenant brought them to attention to hear the Bishop of Newcastle bless the ship, and all who would serve in her, to the care and the keeping of God. The ship's first commanding officer, Commander George R. Miles, waited on the quarterdeck. The shrill bo'sun's whistle piped the first hoisting of the White Ensign and the Commissioning Pennant. Both snapped from the ensign staff, heralding that HMCS *Athabaskan* was commissioned into the Royal Canadian Navy.

With the arrival of ammunition, stores, fuel, victuals and fresh young seamen, the ship became home to 250 Canadians and a ginger-coloured cat that followed them aboard. The ship had 10 officers, including the captain, two engineer officers, one paymaster, one medical officer and one gunnery officer. Below decks, *Athabaskan* had 110 sailors, 30 stokers, 15 engineer artificers and mechanics, nine telegraphists, nine signalmen, three coders, four cooks, four stewards and 50 others with varying specialities. Their level of expertise was varied, ranging from old seasoned hands to young novice sailors. For most, going to sea was a totally new experience and the beginning of new lives. They had the makings of a cohesive crew, these Athabaskans.

There was a dry canteen on board that was open three times a day to sell basic items such as cigarettes, candy, soft drinks, postage stamps and sewing materials at low prices. Beer and liquor were not available, but between 11:00 AM and 12:00 noon each day the crew received a ration of rum. This issue of rum, a "tot," was a holdover from a long-standing RN tradition dating back to when rum was considered a cure for scurvy. The chief gunner's mate, under the watchful eye of the officer-of-the-day when in harbour and the officer of the watch or the supply officer when at sea, doled it out in the supply assistant's office. Sailors under age 21 were not allowed to participate. In lieu of the rum, six cents per day was added to their pay.

Athabaska's commander, George Ralph Miles, was one of the most experienced Canadian naval officers, both at sea and ashore. He was born in St. John, New Brunswick on February 26, 1902. At the age of nine, he went to Rothesay Collegiate Institute as a boarder. He was an exceptional student and developed extra-curricular interests in shooting and fishing. In 1916, at age 14, he entered the Royal Naval College of Canada at Halifax. The Halifax explosion of 1917 destroyed the Naval College, and flying glass injured young Miles. He and the rest of the student body travelled to Kingston, Ontario to complete their studies at the Royal Military College (RMC). Upon graduation, Midshipman Miles was transferred to England and attached to the Royal Navy. This practice gave some RCN officers a variety of experience that was not available in the small Royal Canadian Navy.

Miles first went to sea on the battleship HMS *Malaya* in the spring of 1919. In 1921, he was promoted to sub-lieutenant and sent ashore to take a number of technical courses. Promoted to lieutenant, he was back at sea in 1922, serving in the sloop HMS *Clematis*. He returned to Halifax in 1924 and was assigned various shore appointments. He returned to the Royal Navy in 1926 to serve in the battlecruiser HMS *Repulse*.

In 1928, the RCN added the destroyers *Champlain* and *Vancouver* to its fleet. Miles returned to Canada to be the first lieutenant in *Champlain*, where he continued his career until 1930. Again sent to England, he did a tour of duty aboard the battleship HMS *Royal Oak*. In 1932, he was back in Halifax as a reserve training officer, and in 1934, he was appointed assistant director of Naval Reserves, Navy Headquarters, Ottawa.

Two years later, he was named first lieutenant of the Canadian destroyer HMCS *Saguenay*. One of Miles' midshipmen on *Saguenay* in 1936 was J.A. "Dunn" Lantier, a Montréal boy who was also a graduate of RMC. Lantier served with Miles again, as a lieutenant in *Athabaskan*. He too was one of her first officers on commissioning. Also on board *Saguenay*, and destined to join Miles on *Athabaskan*, were two brothers from Amherst, Nova Scotia. Lieutenant F. Caldwell was *Athabaskan*'s executive officer, and Lieutenant J.B. Caldwell was her engineering officer.

Transferred from *Saguenay*, George Miles served ashore in Halifax for the first six months of 1939. He returned to *Saguenay* in July, this time as her commanding officer. *Saguenay*'s wartime career began when she escorted HX-1, the first convoy from Halifax to Britain.

In October 1939, *Saguenay*, in company with the RN light cruiser HMS *Orion*, was cruising the West Indies, tasked with intercepting any interned enemy merchant shipping attempting to escape to Germany and detecting any enemy craft operating in the area. On October 23, they intercepted the German tanker *Emmy Friedrich* in the Yucatan Strait off Tampico, Mexico. When another light cruiser, HMS *Caradoc*, arrived on the scene, the Germans scuttled their ship to avoid its capture.

The following January, Miles was promoted to the rank of commander. He and *Saguenay* then engaged in convoy-escort duties in the North Atlantic.

On October 20, *Saguenay* was escorting a convoy southwest of Iceland when U-boat *U-124* struck. The submarine torpedoed and sank the British merchant ship *Sulaco*. Commander Miles ordered his ship to the scene but found only one survivor. *U-124* then turned her attention to the Norwegian ship *Cubano*, which she also sank. Searching through the debris, *Saguenay* found and rescued 29 crewmembers. On December 1, 1940, *Saguenay* escorted Convoy HG-47 to the UK. During the night, the Italian submarine *Argo* targeted *Saguenay* some 600 kilometres west of Ireland and put a torpedo into her bow.

Saguenay's bow was destroyed, and fire broke out in her forward lower mess deck. *Saguenay* remained afloat, but the fire was almost out of control. Commander Miles evacuated the bridge and moved control of his ship to the after steering position, located on the searchlight platform. By daybreak, the fire was out, and the damage control party had shored up the forward watertight bulkhead. Miles ordered most of his crew onto a British rescue ship and with a skeleton crew headed the crippled *Saguenay* west. Four anxious days later, she crawled painfully into the Isle of Man. Twenty-one ratings did not answer roll call. The captain gave his crew full credit for their heroic efforts that allowed him to steer her safely to port. For this feat of seamanship and endurance, the King decorated Commander Miles with the Order of the British Empire (OBE).

In the spring of 1941, Commander Miles took over the desk of Captain (D)—the D stood for destroyers—in Halifax and remained there for most of the year. This put him in charge of all escort vessels operating out of Halifax. Itching to get back to sea, Miles pestered the admirals until he received appointment as commanding officer designate of Canada's second Tribal Class destroyer, HMCS *Athabaskan*.

By February 1943, *Athabaskan* was a fully commissioned Tribal Class destroyer, but she still had yet to undergo a working-up period and complete a number of exhausting sea trials. The first priority for Miles was fire-fighting drill. This was no surprise to those who knew of the *Saguenay* saga. Then came the loading of ammunition. More than 2000 shells of different sizes were hoisted aboard and stowed below in the magazines. Fourteen thousand rounds of two-pounder ammunition and 10,000 rounds for the six 20-millimetre Oerlikon guns were loaded and made ready. Forty depth charges completed the loading procedure. Every sailor, no matter what trade, participated in the myriad duties required to get a ship ready for sea.

Athabaskan then went to the ranges where depth charge throwers were tested and most men saw an underwater explosion for the first time. Gun tests contributed noise and smoke to the proceedings. In the engine room the twin Parsons turbines whined through the full-power trials. Forward in the boiler room, stokers went about their duties, checking and adjusting numerous dials and instruments. Three boilers, working at 327°C temperatures, provided steam to the turbines. At the end of the trials, the ship returned to the yard where all machinery and equipment was double-checked and defects remedied.

After a final trial at sea, Commander Miles signed the acceptance papers and HMCS *Athabaskan* joined her sister ship, *Iroquois*, in the RCN, ready to do battle against the enemy.

On February 15, 1943, *Athabaskan* headed down the Tyne into the North Sea. Turning north under grey skies, *Athabaskan* dug her bow into the rolling seas as she made for the historic RN anchorage of Scapa Flow. Arriving the next day, the young Canadians were none too impressed with the bleak and treeless hills merging into the sea. The cold wind drove snow squalls into their faces as they moored their ship amid the impressive array of Allied warships. Under the direction of the admiral commanding the Home Fleet, *Athabaskan* began a training routine that continued until the end of March. The men practised drills until their efficiency was acceptable for a fleet destroyer.

CHAPTER EIGHT

An Unlucky Lady

HULL PLATES CRACKED AND rivets sheared when *Athabaskan* rubbed against the oiler *Danmark* in Scapa Flow in March 1943. The need to go to Greenock for repairs interrupted the training schedule. After this, the Canadian Tribal began her first mission on March 29, in company with the cruiser HMS *Bermuda*, patrolling the Faero–Iceland gap. Their task was to stop German ships trapped in foreign ports at the start of the war from slipping back to Germany. A violent storm brewed up, and the green ship and crew battled strong winds and high seas. Once again, her hull was stressed, and the bottom plates began to separate. The Canadian destroyer took a tremendous beating and had to return to port after about four days to repair damage caused by the storm.

After temporary repairs were made in Scapa, *Athabaskan* sailed for South Shields, Durham, where she went into dry dock for hull repairs and strengthening. The hull refit was an inauspicious beginning for the ship. Her weary seamen, however, welcomed the break from tossing on stormy seas. Problems with seasickness had only exacerbated the discomfort and annoyances of shipboard life.

On May 29, *Athabaskan* was assigned to the 3rd Destroyer Flotilla and the next day sailed for Greenock on the Clyde with the cruiser *Scylla*. On May 31, she headed north again with the aircraft carrier HMS *Furious,* the cruisers *Cumberland* and *Bermuda*, and the British destroyers *Eclipse, Echo* and *Middleton,* members of Force R. Force R's job was to relieve and resupply the Norwegian garrison at Spitsbergen, above the Arctic Circle. This voyage was the crew's initiation to the remote seas of the Arctic. Sudden storms and cold winds buffeted them and slowed the ship's passage. Snow squalls often obliterated their view. Massive grey-green waves consistently rolled over their bow. The ship's movement and position had to be carefully planned and monitored to keep the enemy ignorant of their presence. Most of the crew themselves had not known the ship's destination, but finally it was revealed.

While *Athabaskan* and *Eclipse* maintained anti-aircraft and anti-submarine patrols off the entrance to the fjord on June 10–11, *Cumberland* and *Bermuda* anchored off the jetty and transferred people and stores. Time was limited, as enemy aircraft regularly overflew Spitsbergen between 0340 and 0840 hours every morning. The ships landed 180 tons of stores and 116 Norwegian troops; 101 soldiers were embarked to go home. At 1:15 AM, the force cleared the fjord well ahead of the enemy aircraft's arrival. After an uneventful homeward passage, the small force returned to Scapa on June 14. HMCS *Athabaskan* had completed her first operational voyage, and she had crossed the Arctic Circle, two firsts for her green crew.

A few days later *Athabaskan* suffered more damage and greater embarrassment. Returning to Scapa from a torpedo-firing exercise, she was moving slowly towards the gate in the boom across the harbour mouth when the order "Full Astern" was signalled to the engine room. But *Athabaskan* continued forward and the gate cables sliced her bow. The destroyer's stern swung around and clipped the boom defence ship, HMS *Bargate*. In a unique occurrence, her engine room controls had jammed so the ship did not respond to the attempt to stop her. She was starting to earn the appellation "Unlucky Lady"! However, the crew welcomed the news that the ship was to proceed to Devonport Dock, Plymouth, for a refit to replace her leaky bow plates. On June 22, a cold, windy day, *Athabaskan* left the rough waters of Scapa and headed south to warmer climes. *Athabaskan* arrived in historic Plymouth Sound on June 24 and nestled in to Devonport Dock. While she was repaired, her crew went on leave.

By the time she was ready for action the war at sea had shifted somewhat. Aggressive Allied action was planned to catch the U-boats soon after they left French Atlantic ports. *Athabaskan's* operational area moved to the Bay of Biscay. On July 19, 1943, she sailed, leading Force "W" made up of her sister ship *Iroquois*, the Polish destroyer *Orkan* and the cruiser HMS *Glasgow*.

On July 24, the little force was sailing for home when *Athabaskan* found and rescued five German survivors of *U-558*, which had been sunk five days earlier. The next morning a Coastal Command Sunderland radioed that another submarine was sinking nearby. Force "W" responded and found 37 survivors of *U-459* and one Allied aviator, the tail gunner of the Wellington bomber that had participated in sinking the U-boat. *Iroquois* picked up the flyer, and *Orkan* rescued the enemy sailors. They returned to Plymouth on July 26.

During August, *Athabaskan* participated in three more patrols in the Bay of Biscay area. By the time they returned to Falmouth on August 19 for a boiler cleaning, the crew had become quick in responding to sea and air enemy activity. U-boat contacts became rare. Allied vessels began operating much closer to the French and Spanish coasts where the U-boats were travelling. The Royal Air Force flooded the area with radar-equipped aircraft, ready to attack any U- boat on the surface. The new strategy forced the German submarines to remain submerged during daylight hours but also brought Allied surface hunters within range of shore-based enemy aircraft.

Commander Miles conned *Athabaskan* out of Falmouth Bay on August 25 to join up with HMS *Grenville*. The British and Canadian destroyers were paired for operations in the Bay of Biscay. They headed for a patrol area off the northwest tip of Spain, further south than their normal area. The ships were floating above the Continental Shelf. The water depth there, an average of about 75 fathoms (135 metres), restricted the submarines' ability to manoeuvre and made them vulnerable as they did their constant surfacing and diving. On August 27, *Athabaskan* and *Grenville* joined HM sloop *Egret* and two frigates, *Rother* and *Jed*, to form the First Support Group. Their task was to prevent German submarines from returning to their underground base at Brest, France.

The ships formed a line abreast off Cape Villano and headed southwest. *Athabaskan* was to port, closest to shore. On this beautiful day (August 27), the sun shone gloriously on the translucent blue water that was like a sheet of glass. Many of the crew were on deck and had doffed their shirts in hopes of a suntan. RAF Liberators and Beaufighters flew overhead then returned to their base. At 1300 hours, a formation of Dornier 217s appeared. The 18 bombers of Kampfgeschwader 100, based at Toulouse, were led by Major Bernhardt Jope. Each bomber carried the newly operational HS 293 glider bomb. An operator in the aircraft guided this radio-controlled missile. The missile travelled at a speed of 600 kilometres per hour and had a warhead weighing 295 kilograms. On *Athabaskan*'s bridge, Commander Miles ordered the "Action Stations" alert to sound as the enemy formation swooped to attack.

Each crewmember, no matter what his normal duties, had a specific duty when "Action Stations" sounded. In seconds, each sailor raced for his position, and immediately the 4.7-inch and the four-inch guns opened up on the attackers. The ship's Oerlikon anti-aircraft guns joined the chatter. The enemy airmen picked their targets carefully. *Egret* turned and avoided a bomb that passed just astern, but then the bomb swung around and tore into the ship's starboard side. She sank in a matter of seconds, taking 200 officers and men with her. Only 35 survived.

From his station on the *Athabaskan* bridge, Kettles saw five aircraft above the port side of the ship. Three of them released their glider bombs at the same time. One tore through *Athabaskan* at the junction of "B" gun deck and the wheelhouse. It passed through the chart house and the chief petty officers' mess and came out the starboard side to explode about seven metres from the ship. The concussion flattened Kettles, Miles and everyone else on the bridge. For a brief second, intense heat from the explosion enveloped them, and a flash of flame blinded them. As well, bomb and ship fragments wounded several. When Kettles got to his feet, he saw that the starboard side of the ship from the bow to the fo'c'sle was crushed. "A" and "B" guns were completely out of action. The barrel of the starboard Oerlikon was twisted "like a wet rag."

As the missile had gone through the ship, its fins had sheared Telegraphist Charles Kent's feet off at the ankles. He stayed conscious long enough to apply tourniquets. (When Kent was sent home, he went to the Colonel Belcher Veterans' Hospital in his hometown of Calgary. While he was getting used to his new feet, shipmates on leave took him out to visit local taverns. The more Chuck drank, the more his stumps swelled and became uncomfortable. Pedestrians on streets near the hospital often were treated to the macabre sight of two sailors carrying Kent home, with their arms forming a chair, as he cradled his artificial feet on his lap.)

At B gun, the petty officer in charge was mortally wounded; Able Seaman William Pickett of Lower Bars, New Brunswick, was instantly killed. Blown overboard, Able Seaman Thomas Smith, of New Westminster, was never seen again. Leading Seaman John Gordon, of Hamilton, although injured and in severe pain, took charge and, with other injured men, got the gun into operation again.

Several members of A gun's crew were burned and wounded. Sub-Lieutenant Jack Scott, of Halifax, left the bridge and took command of that gun.

All communication with the bridge ceased, and confusion reigned for a few moments. Every light on the ship had gone out. Kettles and five others went below to shore up the caved-in side of *Athabaskan*. They slipped and swished around in a mix of dirty heavy black fuel oil and salt water up to their waists. They shoved anything they could get find into the hull's holes—hammocks, overcoats, underwear and boots, broken lockers, splinters from the mess tables, socks and hats. Everything was soaked in oil.

Much later, Kettles wrote this in his diary:

> *As you got down to plug a hole, the ship would take a slow, weary roll, and a shower of cold, salt water would hit you, almost taking your breath away, but*

you couldn't quit, you had to go on in order to get back to port. You worked until you were ready to give up. Reach for something, lose your balance and down you would go. Get up, wipe the oil off your face and salty taste off your lips and try again. It seemed so hopeless you felt like crying. Officers worked with the men for it was a case of all or nothing, and it is at times like this when the officers really forget their ranks and get to know the worth of the men, of the real honest-to-goodness everyday guy.

Occasionally the narrow beam of a flashlight penetrated the gloom as Surgeon Lieutenant William B. Wallace, of Toronto, and his medical orderly, Able Seaman Eric Mengoni, of Dartmouth, Nova Scotia, moved about treating the wounded. Some of the wounded were laying on the mess tables and others on benches, but most littered the deck outside the small cramped sick bay. Commander Miles turned his day cabin into a surgery and dressing station. The stench of mingled antiseptic, blood, smoke and oil was nauseating. Torn flesh and deep gaping wounds from flying shrapnel were prominent. Some men had broken legs and abdominal wounds. The concussion had blown out some of their teeth.

Damage control reported that the ship was in bad shape. Both forward magazines, the torpedo mess and number one boiler room were flooded. Most electrical equipment was unserviceable, and only emergency lighting was in use. The central fire control station, radar communications, ASDIC, compass and the B gun mounting were useless. *Athabaskan* was on fire, down at the bow by 10 degrees and listing 15 degrees to starboard. Able-bodied crewmen leaped to the task of saving their ship.

Gibraltar was the closest British base, but Commander Miles knew Plymouth, their homeport, was better equipped to handle the damaged destroyer. His crew struggled to keep the ship afloat and to raise steam to get her moving home. They succeeded in getting her under way at 14 knots. The remaining ships of the group were ordered to maintain the screen so no U-boat would slip through to the Brest U-boat base. *Athabaskan* received permission to "proceed independently" home. The ship took aboard *Egret's* 35 survivors and turned north.

The Luftwaffe was jubilant in announcing the success of their new weapon. Major Jope received the Knight's Cross from Hitler personally.

The stricken ship struggled through the day and, in the crimson rays of the setting sun, Commander Miles committed the bodies of five dead seamen to the waters. The next day, contaminated fuel forced *Athabaskan* to slow and stop three different times. Drinking water became fouled; food was scarce and cold. Meals were potluck as water had washed the labels off the canned goods so the contents remained a mystery until the can was opened.

In the afternoon of the third day after the bombing, three destroyers sent to escort *Athabaskan* home met her off the Scilly Islands. Commander Miles refused a tow and took his ship home under her own power. By 2130 hrs, she was secure alongside No. 1 jetty in Devonport Harbour. Her crew presented a sorry spectacle. To prevent oil burns, those who had been working shoring up the ship's side had discarded their shoes and socks and cut their trousers off at the knee on the doctor's orders. When the ship tied up at the dock, her men were filthy, oil-stained and unshaven. Their eyes were bloodshot from the hot August sun, dirt and lack of sleep.

Commander Miles, Engineer Lieutenant J.B. Caldwell, of Victoria, Chief Engine Room Artificer E.G. Mills, of Saanich, BC, and Acting Petty Officer F.R. Harbour, of Montréal, were mentioned in dispatches "for courage and seamanship in bringing their ship safely to port after she was damaged." Surgeon Lieutenant Wallace was also mentioned in dispatches "for service in caring for the wounded of HMCS *Athabaskan* after his ship was attacked by enemy aircraft."

Athabaskan was in dry dock for two months. During her refit, *Athabaskan* was treated to the installation of new equipment. A new foremast carried the latest radar that gave a continuous visual presentation of the area around the ship. Twelve new Oerlikon 20-millimetre guns on six twin mountings replaced the six single-barrel Oerlikon guns. A high-frequency direction-finding (H/F D/F) set enabled the accurate taking of a bearing of any high-frequency radio transmission. The latest very high-frequency (VHF) radios were installed which allowed immediate voice communications between ships.

Faces changed. Some men were drafted to other ships, and new drafts of sailors arrived. Most significant was the transfer of *Athabaskan's* Commander G.R. Miles to Ottawa as director of plans.

The following year, George Miles went to Halifax to become chief of staff to the commander-in-chief, Canadian North Atlantic. On March 26, 1946, he was promoted to the rank of commodore and appointed chief of naval personnel and a member of the Naval Board. He retired to Victoria and died on February 19, 1951, at age 48. He was cremated, and his ashes were spread over Esquimault harbour.

⊰◆⊱

Lieutenant Commander John H. Stubbs, DSO, 31 years old, replaced Miles as commander of the *Athabaskan* in late 1943. Stubbs was born on June 5, 1912 in Kaslo, BC, a small mining town on the shores of Lake Kootenay. On this lake, as a youngster, he honed his sailing abilities. The family moved to Victoria where, at age 18, he joined the RCN as a cadet. Like most young RCN officers, he went to England to train. He later served in the RN's Mediterranean Fleet. When the war broke out, Lieutenant Stubbs was the navigation officer on the RCN destroyer HMCS *Ottawa*. He joined the River Class HMCS *Assiniboine* as first lieutenant and later was given its command.

On August 6, 1941, Stubb's ship, *Assiniboine*, was one of six corvettes escorting convoy SC-94 towards England. A wolf pack of U-boats attacked them. The Canadians engaged *U-210*, under the command of

Kapitanleutnant Lempke, and they fought a long hard battle lasting more than two hours. *Assiniboine* took a hit on the starboard side of her bridge. A furious fire started. The destroyer found itself riding parallel to the submarine. The destroyer's guns hammered away at the sub. One shell hit the conning tower and killed the U-boat's commander. *Assiniboine* fired depth charges, which exploded under the sub, ripping it open. The U-boat began to settle beneath the waves. Her crew plunged over the side just as she slid stern first to the bottom.

Acting Lieutenant Commander Stubbs received the Distinguished Service Order for this action.

> *…[for] gallantry, devotion to duty and distinguished service under fire….in the face of enemy fire and with the bridge structure on fire, [Stubbs] handled his ship with dauntless resolution and courage, and pressed the attack with great determination to a successful conclusion.*

This was the background of the new commander of the *Athabaskan*. *Athabaskan*'s Leading Writer Stuart Kettles made the following entry in his diary for September to November 1943:

> *Underwent extensive refit, due to bomb damage in August. From September–mid-November we had radar,* ASDIC *and gun trials followed till the end of November, then based at Scapa Flow. Operated off the Norwegian coast in attack against enemy merchant shipping in convoy with Royal Navy Battleships HMS* ANSON *and the French Battleship* RICHELIEU, *Aircraft Carrier* ILLUSTRIOUS, *Cruisers HMS* NIGERIA,

HMS ALGERIA *and 18 Destroyers. Proceeded to KULA BAY RUSSIA, on convoy duty with American "Liberty" ships. Speed of convoy—six knots. Picked up convoy off FAERO ISLANDS. German Cruiser* SCHARNHORST *sunk about 60 miles from us on return voyage with empty merchant ships. We were dispatched to escort the cruisers in the* SCHARN-HORST *battle, but owing to engine room trouble, continued on to FAERO ISLANDS where Christmas was celebrated. Round trip took 28 days. One possible enemy submarine to our credit on this trip.*

Athabaskan returned to Scapa Flow on December 10 and rejoined the 3rd Destroyer Flotilla to begin her second Arctic tour. The first convoy she escorted was JW-55A, departing on December 12 for Murmansk.

On December 18, in the Barents Sea between Bear Island and the northern tip of Norway, the H/F D/F operator determined the bearing on a U-boat radio transmission. *Athabaskan* turned onto the bearing and raced to the suspected location. On arrival, she fired star shells. The magnesium flares lit the black Arctic night as effectively as if the sun had suddenly risen. Clearly visible from the bridge was the unmistakable silhouette of a submarine's conning tower. *Athabaskan* charged in at full speed. Well before the destroyer got close, a swirl of white water and foam was all that was left as the U-boat dove. The *Athabaskan* dropped a full pattern of depth charges. The ASDIC operator searched the area, but the sub had disappeared. Later an intercepted radio transmission indicated the U-boat had been damaged. Thus Stuart Kettles' claim was likely valid.

Athabaskan and her sister escorts left Kola Inlet on December 23. They shepherded RA-55A, a convoy of 19 empty cargo ships west to the United Kingdom. As the ships ploughed through the searing wind and spray of rising seas, men on deck strained their eyes in the stygian Arctic night for any sign of the enemy. Christmas Day, 1943, was just another day bucking giant waves at sea. Men had trouble staying on their feet as the ships' bows rose and crashed down into the onrushing seas. Northwest winds shrieked continuously through the rigging, coating gun mountings, bridge and the deck with a heavy layer of ice.

Early on December 24, the weather eased and the crew were afforded precious hours of rest. At 0615 hours, clanging alarm bells signalling "Action Stations" roused the sleeping sailors. The captain read a message from the Admiralty stating that the great German battleship *Scharnhorst* had left Altenfjord, Norway, was at sea and probably looking to attack the convoy. This was bad news as the convoy's escort was no match for the enemy battle cruiser and the five destroyers escorting her. However, the RN's Force 2, consisting of the cruisers *Belfast*, *Norfolk* and *Sheffield*, was within range. RN's Force 1, with the battleship *Duke of York*, cruiser Jamaica and destroyers *Saumarez*, *Savage*, *Scorpion* and *Stord*, was also close by.

On Christmas Day, convoy JW-55B nearby reported several contacts with enemy aircraft and U-boats.

These contacts left no doubt that it would be attacked soon. The convoy altered its heading to the north, and Force 2 received orders to close. Force 2 rendezvoused with the convoy at 0815, and at 0840, *Belfast* detected the German battle cruiser on radar. *Sheffield* reported that *Scharnhorst* was in sight at 12 kilometres. When *Scharnhorst* tried to engage the convoy, *Norfolk* shelled her. The German ship drew away to the northeast, and Force 2 lost contact. *Scharnhorst* closed on the convoy again at 10:00 AM. At 12:15 PM, *Belfast* regained contact with the battle cruiser, and *Sheffield* came into visual range of the behemoth. *Scharnhorst* broke off, getting no closer to the convoy than nine kilometres, and turned away.

All hands aboard *Athabaskan* were frustrated. A fierce naval battle was in progress nearby, but the ship had not been ordered to detach from the convoy it was protecting and join in. Her duty remained—to escort and protect the merchantmen of RA-55A. At 1615 hours, *Duke of York*'s radar found the *Scharnhorst* and rapidly closed the 35-kilometre gap. The four destroyers accompanying her were told to get into position to launch torpedoes. At 1650 hours, *Belfast* lit the sky with star shells, and *Duke of York* and *Jamaica* opened fire from 18 kilometres away. *Scharnhorst* returned fire, and the big ships hammered away at each other.

At 1829 hours, *Scharnhorst's* guns fell silent, and she turned away, using her superior speed to escape. The destroyers hung on, like terriers after a huge rabbit, and fired their torpedoes. The tin fish hit the German ship, which slowed. *Duke of York* and *Jamaica* kept up their fire from nine kilometres away. Four cruisers raced in to finish off the target. At 1945 hours, the German battle cruiser sank, taking almost all her crew of 1968 men with her. Only 36 survivors were picked up. The RN lost neither warships nor merchant ships, a stunning victory.

A few days later *Athabaskan* berthed with HMS *Ashanti* in a small cove of the Faeroe Islands, just north of Scapa Flow. The two commanders decided that, even late, a Christmas celebration would be "just the ticket." To make the celebration festive, crews shared food. Singing and laughter rang out from both ships. In Plymouth Lieutenant Commander Stubbs laid in a supply of beer and liquor. Both flowed freely. In proper navy tradition for the Christmas meal, the youngest sailor, Able Seaman John W. Fairchild, of Québec City, was named commanding officer for the day and paraded through the ship wearing Stubbs' uniform jacket. Merriment subsided as the day wore on. By evening most of the men were catching up on lost sleep.

On December 31, 1943, Convoy RA-55A arrived safely at Loch Ewe. On New Year's Day, *Athabaskan* went into a floating dry dock at Scapa Flow for minor repairs to the hull.

On January 8, 1944, *Athabaskan* and *Ashanti* sailed southward to a destination unknown to most of the crewmembers. They joined three more Royal Navy destroyers and set up a screen protecting the battleship

HMS *King George V.* The weather warmed and became tropical. At daybreak on the January 11, land dotted with white buildings appeared ahead. *Athabaskan* and *Ashanti* were alone in the Azores. The rest of the group had gone to Gibraltar. Half the Canadian crew was granted shore leave in Ponta Delgrada, but Stuart Kettles was not among them. He had to content himself with soaking up the sun on the foredeck and bartering with Portugese men in dories and bumboats that pulled alongside. Purchases in various currencies and trades were made for oranges, pineapples, bananas, grapes and wine, Chateau Mateus being a favourite.

The two Tribal destroyers refuelled, weighed anchor and sailed east towards Gibraltar. On January 15, *King George V* glided out of Algeciras Bay, joined her escorts and pointed north. She was carrying British Prime Minister Winston Churchill home from talks with the other Allied leaders. The special fleet arrived safely in Plymouth on January 18, and the two destroyers tied up at Devonport Dock to await their next assignment.

The English Channel continued to be problematic. German E-boats darted here and there. They created a great deal of havoc, sinking coastal convoy and navy ships, even though Allied motor torpedo boats savagely harassed them. The Channel itself was very dangerous for maritime traffic. It was strewn with mines, wrecks and menacing shoals. Officers of warships needed to use exceptional navigational skills to ply these waters.

Athabaskan became valuable in convoy-interception patrols designed to destroy enemy seapower in the Channel. These patrols continued throughout January and February. An exception to this pattern happened when *Athabaskan*, with *Haida* and *Iroquois*, took part in a large raid on German shipping along the Norwegian Coast.

In mid-February, the three Canadian Tribals returned to Plymouth and the 10th Destroyer Flotilla to form Force 26. Channel patrols resumed, but most were quite uneventful as the enemy chose to remain in port. More and more, the Canadian destroyers participated in night operations to improve their night-fighting efficiency. On March 24, Vice-Admiral Percy Nelles, Chief of the Naval Staff, inspected a clean and polished *Athabaskan* and her crew.

In the spring of 1944, Force 26 was a highly trained unit ready for the invasion of France. Its patrols, exercises and operations against the enemy intensified significantly. Every time the force returned to Plymouth they found more destroyers and landing barges gathering for the assault on Northwest Europe.

The night of April 25–26 started out as just another routine patrol for Force 26. It was quite uneventful until radar echoes revealed a force of German ships rapidly approaching. In the Allied formation were the destroyers *Black Prince*, *Athabaskan*, *Haida*, *Ashanti* and *Huron*. The opposition was three Elbing Class destroyers, known to the Germans as Fleet Torpedo Boats, *T-24*, *T-27* and *T-29*. The Germans turned about and raced to safety, but Force 26 increased its speed to more than 30 knots and closed the gap.

At 0223 hours, at 10 kilometres, the Allied destroyers opened fire. *Ashanti* claimed a hit. The enemy began laying a smokescreen. The gun turret B on *Black Prince* jammed and the ship fell back, removing itself from the action. The other four Tribals continued the hectic chase, perilously close to minefields and the rocky coast. At a range of about two miles both formations began trading shots. *Haida* and *Athabaskan* engaged one of the enemy Elbings, *T-29*. Both destroyers registered telling hits. *Athabaskan's* hits set fire to *T-29's* bridge and bow.

Huron and *Ashanti* joined the fray, and all four destroyers cornered *T-29* a few kilometres off St. Malo, Brittany, from where Cartier had sailed to discover Canada many years earlier. The other two Elbings fled. Despite the furious fire on their ship, *T-29's* gunners did not let up. *T-29's* after magazine blew up, but her gunners made a last-ditch fight. The Elbing was aflame from bow to stern but still refused to sink. The Tribals manoeuvred into position for torpedo launches. During these twists and turns, *Ashanti* rammed *Huron* amidships. One of *Haida's* torpedoes scored on the German warship, which suddenly rolled to port and sank. She took the CO of the flotilla, Lieutenant Commander Kohlauf, her own captain, all officers and most of her crew with her. Because of the Canadians' collision, *Ashanti's* bow was split, and *Huron* had much damage to her port side. Some of her hull plates buckled. Under inaccurate fire from German shore batteries, the Tribals departed. They entered Plymouth Sound in triumph.

Burrow and Beaudoin, in their book *Unlucky Lady*, report that shortly after this action *Ashanti* requested to be withdrawn from the 10th Destroyer Flotilla. Its captain claimed the Canadians were savage in their attacks and described them as "wild Indians" and "very bloodthirsty."

After the destroyer-destroyer collision, *Athabaskan* and *Haida* were the only seaworthy Tribals in Force 26. Three days later, they were berthed side by side on the same mooring buoy when they were ordered to sea. Neither crew were sufficiently rested from the past few weeks. At 2000 hours, April 28, 1944. *Haida* lead *Athabaskan* out the harbour mouth. Their task this night was to support the 10th Minelaying Flotilla as it laid a minefield close to the coast of France. The moon rose in a clear sky. The smooth water with a low swell barely rippled in a force-three wind. Visibility was about three kilometres.

At 0200 hours, the ships reached their assigned position and began patrolling at 16 knots. Captain Stubbs on the bridge discussed the possibility of enemy action with his First Lieutenant, Ralph M. Lawrence, of Glasgow, Scotland, and his Navigation Officer, Lieutenant Robin B. Hayward, of Duncan, BC. Meanwhile, the two surviving vessels of the 4th Torpedo Boat Flotilla, *T-24* and *T-27*, were proceeding at 20 knots towards the Canadians. Ships on both sides had their crews at Action Stations. At 0400 hours, both Tribals confirmed radar contacts at 22 kilometres. Twelve minutes later, star shells were fired, and the sky lit up like daytime. The two Elbings were brightly illuminated. At 6.4 kilometres *Haida* and *Athabaskan* opened fire with their guns. The Germans turned away, and each launched a spread of six torpedoes toward the Canadian ships. Inexplicably, the tin fish veered from their course. The Canadians altered course to avoid the torpedoes and maintained their rate of fire. *Athabaskan* seemed to be the enemy's prime target. Radar picked up two new fast-moving objects, on her starboard side, while the Elbings were on her port side. One of the starboard boats, probably a German motor torpedo boat, fired a torpedo that hit *Athabaskan* astern on her starboard side. The damage caused by this hit, added to that already suffered, made the future bleak for that unfortunate ship.

Kettles' diary recorded the tragic last hours of the *Athabaskan*:

> *0410 hours[April 29]—Range for third salvo "dead on" but before it could be fired, received direct hit aft attributed to shore battery and 21-inch torpedo fired from undetected E-Boats. "X" and "Y" guns were blown overboard; the four-barrel Pom-Pom was demolished; "A" gun was blown loose from its mounting. All communications from the Bridge to the guns was severed; Diesel oil fire breaks out at the tubes enveloping entire after canopy and stern. Flames fourty [sic] to fifty feet high. Pom-Pom ammunition explodes in all directions. Both propeller shafts were smashed and* HMCS ATHABASKAN *stopped dead. In spite of*

"A" gun having been knocked off its mounting, she continued to engage the enemy while "B" gun lighted up the target with Star-shell. HMCS HAIDA laid a smokescreen to enable us to try and escape.

0420 hours—Orders from the bridge passed by word of mouth, "Stand by to abandon ship." Magazine supply crews and remainder of personnel not killed by first torpedo and shore battery shell explosion, secure Action Stations and proceed to abandon ship stations. Attempts are made to secure towlines to HMCS HAIDA.

0425 hours—Received second torpedo hit at the break of the forecastle on the Port side from Destroyer. No. 1 Boiler Room exploded. Fire breaks out anew, this time enveloping entire Starboard side. Ship takes a very bad list to Port and crew takes to the water and whatever Carley Floats and floatanets [sic] remain.

0435 hours—The end of a short but thrilling career...

Haida pressed home her attack on the enemy craft, even after the *Athabaskan* signalled she was badly damaged. The enemy, as it fled, fired at the burning *Athabaskan* in an attempt to finish her off. *Haida* positioned herself between them and laid a thick, white smokescreen. *Haida* hit and badly damaged one of the Elbings, *T-24*, which dashed east. *T-27* raced south with *Haida* close behind.

Meanwhile, *Athabaskan* drifted helplessly. She was a highly visible target for E-boats and shore batteries, but her sailors did not panic as they went about the business of damage control. She was quickly settling in the water, and Stubbs gave up any hope of *Haida* taking her in tow. The men scarcely believed their ears when Stubbs gave the order from the bridge: "Prepare to abandon ship."

Then came the *coup de grâce*. A German torpedo ripped into *Athabaskan*'s starboard side just behind the forecastle. First Lieutenant Ralph Lawrence was killed instantly. A split second later, the ship's after magazine, fuel tanks and high-pressure steam supply created a roaring blowtorch. Men were blown into the water as they dashed for the decks. Crew on *Haida*, eight kilometres away, saw the bright light and heard the explosion. Hearts dropped as they realized it had come from the *Athabaskan*. Amid the devastation on the bridge, at 4:30 AM Stubbs gave his final command "All hands abandon ship." While others went overboard and were eventually rescued, Stubbs went down with the *Athabaskan*.

Stuart Kettles later recalled what he did after the order to abandon ship:

> *I looked over the side at that cold uninviting water of the English Channel, by now covered with thick, dirty, fuel oil. My first thought was "Gee, I can't jump into that," but when I turned around and looked at the burning ship, which was beginning to settle to her watery grave. I suddenly decided, "Hell, I can't stay here neither." There was no shock when you hit the water, but it wasn't very doggone long until we soon realized that it was no Turkish bath.*

I swam to where George and Glen were, and it was quite a wet reunion. However, it certainly didn't lack any enthusiasm. A short time after, George said "Roll me over on my back and hold me there 'til I see if I can get this damn light going." The light he was referring to was attached to a small hat which was part of a new type of life jackets we had just recently been issued. His only remark was "Well, I'll be doggoned, the darn thing works." We got a laugh out of this, in spite of the grim situation we were in. We suddenly spotted a ghost-like form approaching us from out of the false dawn. There were cries of "Good old Haida." Our sister ship had come to pick up what survivors she could.

I started to swim to the directed place. I had just about 12 more feet to go when the Haida threw her engines into reverse, the force of the water from her propellers washed me away from her side out about a quarter mile [half kilometre] from the bow. I now found myself entirely alone, and my legs and arms were growing numb as the minutes passed. The tide, which was going out at the time, came in long slow rolling waves. This caused a very nice sensation, like rocking a child to sleep in a cradle, and it wasn't very long before this motion began to make me very sleepy. There were none of the other lads around to talk to to help stay awake. I felt myself going to sleep, and knowing I couldn't stay awake much longer, pulled up the head rest on my life jacket, and was quite prepared to take whatever lay ahead of me, even though I should fall asleep, which is exactly what happened. The next time I saw the welcome rays of sun was quite different. I lay on a wooden table naked as

the day I was born, shivering from the cold immersion.
I asked where we were, the answer, "On a German
destroyer."

The weight of water pouring into *Athabaskan* dragged her down by the stern. Soon her bow was pointing straight up. Machinery tore away, and all loose gear and equipment hurtled downwards. One survivor said, "The sound was almost human—like watching a friend dying in agony." Seconds later, there was no more to be seen. There was not much debris. Only the haze from her fire and the bobbing lifejacket lights marked her final resting place. Her captain and 128 men were lost. Elbing *T-24* picked up 83 and took them prisoner. *Haida* rescued 44.

T-24 was the very ship that had torpedoed the *Athabaska* and caused her destruction. Her captain, *Kapitanleutnant* Wilheim Meentzen, was awarded the Knight's Cross, First Class in recognition of his successful engagement with the enemy.

The Canadian POWs, including Stuart Kettles, spent the rest of the war in prisoner of war camps. After a four-day train trip to Germany, the POWs were taken to an interrogation camp. They were herded into small cells. Each of these cells held one prisoner and had one small window with iron bars on it. In a corner was a wooden bunk with a straw mattress on it. The mattress cover was made of burlap. Each man had two thin blankets, which were far from adequate when the weather turned chilly during the night. Around 8:00 AM the next morning, the long-awaited first breakfast finally arrived. Along with it came bitter disappointment, for the meal consisted of two slices of black bread, with jam but no margarine, and a cup of ersatz tea, barely enough to tease a good appetite. For the next 28 long days, this menu was served for both breakfast and supper. Lunch consisted of a small bowl of soup and maybe two or three potatoes with their skins on.

After 10 days, a Gestapo officer interrogated Kettles for two hours. After three weeks, the Germans gave them a toothbrush and some kind of toothpaste. It was a real treat for the POWs to feel their teeth and mouths clean after not brushing for nearly a month.

On June 3, Kettles was moved to a nearby *dulag* (displacement camp). Two days after his arrival at the *dulag*, he received his first Red Cross parcel. On June 17, he moved to Marlag und Milag, a prisoner of war camp for naval and merchant seamen, one kilometre down the road from the *dulag*. The POW camp was at Westertimke, 50 kilometres southwest of Hamburg and 16 kilometres north of Bremen. At this regular naval prisoner camp, each room housed 12 men. Two-tier wooden bunks, with straw mattresses and few blankets, lined the rooms' walls. The POWs were forced to muster outside on parade three times a day, at 9:00 AM, 2:30 PM and at 7:00 PM. Rain, snow, sleet or blow they stood, often for more than half an hour, while the guards counted them.

In the early days of captivity, the Germans employed ferocious, trained police dogs to guard the prisoners.

Canadian POWs surreptitiously used food and petting to melt away the dogs' ferocity. One day, German guards entered the barracks and were shocked to find several of their "man-eating" dogs lying under the bunks. The guards promptly posted a notice in English that the dogs were absolutely forbidden to accept food from the prisoners.

As Germany's manpower dwindled, aging World War I veterans replaced young guards who were sent off to the army. When food packages for the captured seamen arrived at a village five kilometres distant, a detail of POWs escorted by these guards went to fetch them. The walk frequently was too strenuous for the decrepit jailers, so the POWs carried their rifles for them and let them ride in the carts. Before arriving back at camp they helped the guards down from the carts, buttoned their tunics, cleaned them up and handed back their rifles. The prisoners wanted to make sure hard-boiled *Hitlerjugend* recruits did not replace the compliant guards.

The advancing Allies liberated Kettles' camp in early 1945. He arrived in Scotland on May 14. At his medical examination, he reported receiving only a small laceration on his right shin during the sinking of *Athabaskan*. It had healed in four or five days. A ship landed him in New York on May 28. Trains carried him to Ottawa where he was discharged from the RCNVR on November 21, 1945. Kettles joined the Ottawa City Police Force and reached the rank of sergeant. He served until his death in Ottawa on May 20, 1966, at age 49.

CHAPTER NINE

Tribals Sail On

WITH THE LOSS OF *ATHABASKAN*, CANADA was left with only three Canadian Tribal Class destroyers. Although four more ships of this type were ordered, none of these were commissioned before the end of the war. *Iroquois*, *Huron* and *Haida* continued to sail with the 10th Destroyer Flotilla, based in Plymouth, England.

This mixed force of British, Canadian and Polish warships kept the Channel clear of enemy ships in the days leading up to the D-Day landings. They were given the task of securing the western approaches of the English Channel from enemy submarines, surface raiders and smaller escort vessels. *Haida* distinguished herself as Canada's most effective warship by sinking no less than nine German ships in the period from April to September 1944.

HMCS *Haida*

On June 9, 1944, three days after the D-day landings, four German ships were detected heading toward Normandy to harass the Allied invasion force. HMCS *Haida*, with other members of the 10th Destroyer Flotilla (HMCS *Huron*, the British ships HM Ships *Ashanti*, *Eskimo*, and *Javelin*, and two Polish destroyers, the *Blyskawica* and *Piorun)* were sent to intercept the Germans. In a long, confusing engagement, the German destroyer *ZH1* was sunk. *Haida* and *Huron* heavily damaged two other German ships, *Z24* and *T24,* but they escaped. The Canadian ships then turned on *Z32,* setting her ablaze and forcing her to run aground on Ile de Bas.

On Saturday, June 24, 1944, HMCS *Haida* and HMS *Eskimo* patrolled off the French coast just north of Ushant Ile in support of the 2nd Escort Group. At 1545 hours, the *Haida* observed a Liberator reconnaissance aircraft, dropping bombs or depth charges eight kilometres astern. Course was immediately altered towards a smoke float the aircraft had dropped. On arrival, speed was reduced to seven knots. An anti-submarine search commenced. *Eskimo* gained first contact at 1625 hours, and *Haida* located the sub nine minutes later. During the next two hours, nine deliberate attacks were carried out, seven by *Eskimo.*

Eskimo lost contact at about 1900 hours and was searching at slow speed. At 1917 hours, nearly an hour after the last depth charges had been dropped, *Haida* was stopped about 800 metres from the target, bows on, waiting for movement, when the ASDIC operator reported that the target was moving. *Haida's* captain, Harry de Wolf, prepared to attack. Suddenly, at 1921 hours, the submarine surfaced. *Haida's* B gun opened fire and hit the U-boat's conning tower with the second shot. High explosive penetrated the submarine and started a fire. Flames were clearly visible through the hole. The Canadians stopped shelling the sub as soon as they saw the enemy did not intend to fight. The U-boat crew started abandoning ship. *Haida* and *Eskimo* both closed on the sub, with ideas of boarding. *Haida* lowered a whaler and motorboat and *Eskimo* a whaler, but the U-boat went down before the boats reached her. All boats then recovered survivors. They saved 52, including the captain and four other officers. Six of the survivors were injured, three seriously. The prisoners were landed at Falmouth the next day.

On August 6, 1944, HMCS *Haida*, accompanied by HMCS *Iroquois* and HM Ships *Ballona*, *Tartar* and *Ashanti*, engaged a six-ship German convoy south of St. Nazaire and Ile de Yeu in the Bay of Biscay. The Allied flotilla daringly manoeuvred between the German convoy and the coast and sunk all six German ships. The convoy did not realize that it was under attack until the first German vessel was sunk, at first thinking the sounds of shellfire were from nearby German shore batteries. *Haida* has been confirmed conclusively as the ship that sunk *M486*.

Haida and HMS *Kalvin* were on patrol in the Bay of Biscay again a month later. On September 6, 1944, they surprised two small German patrol boats five kilometres off the coast of Les Sables D'Olonne. The Allied ships quickly opened fire and forced the German ships to surrender. *Haida* captured the *Vedette*, but the prize sank while in tow.

Following a refit in Halifax, *Haida* rejoined the British Home Fleet in Scapa Flow in early 1945 and spent the rest of the war operating in the Arctic and on the coast of Norway. After the surrender of Germany, the ship was overhauled to operate in the Pacific. The war ended before her conversion was complete.

Haida did two tours in Korean waters between 1952 and 1954. She was paid off and taken out of service in 1963. The ship was to be sold for scrap, but a group of Torontonians, recognizing that this was the most famous ship in the Royal Canadian Navy, raised enough money in the private sector to buy the vessel and have her towed to Toronto. In August 1965, she opened to tourists at the foot of York Street as a naval museum, maritime memorial and Sea Cadet training ship. In 2000, Heritage Canada acquired the ship, which was restored and permanently berthed in Hamilton, Ontario.

HMCS *Iroquois*

In July 1943, German aircraft attacked three troop-ships that HMCS *Iroquois* was escorting 500 kilome-tres off Vigo, Spain. Two of the troopships were sunk. *Iroquois* rescued 628 survivors from the *Duchess of York*. In early 1944, after a refit in Halifax, she joined the 10th Destroyer Flotilla in Plymouth to pre-pare for the Normandy invasion. After D-Day, she carried out patrols in the English Channel and the Bay of Biscay and provided escort service in British waters. From October 16, 1944, *Iroquois* served with the Home Fleet at Scapa Flow but returned to the 10th DF on November 6. Throughout the 1944–45 winter, she was on escort duty in coastal waters. On March 16, 1945, *Iroquois* rejoined the Home Fleet and for the rest of the month joined *Haida,* screening carrier strikes on Norwegian targets and escorting convoys to Russia. In April, *Huron, Haida* and *Iroquois* escorted their last convoy to Russia.

When the war in Europe ended on May 8, the crew of the *Iroquois, Haida* and *Huron* celebrated at Scapa Flow. The three ships sailed to Oslo, Copenhagen and Kiel. From Copenhagen, *Iroquois* escorted the German cruisers *Prince Eugen* and *Nurnberg* to Kiel for their surrender. *Iroquois* then returned to Halifax to prepare for war in the Pacific. With the war's end *Iroquois'* refit was halted, and she went into reserve on February 22, 1946.

Iroquois was pulled out of reserve for the Korean War. She left Halifax on April 21, 1952 for the first of two tours of duty in Korea. Her main duties were attacking coastal defence batteries and destroying trains. *Iroquois* was the only Canadian ship to suffer casualties during the Korean War. On October 2, 1952, she exchanged fire with a shore-based artillery battery near Songjin and sustained hits to the B gun mounting. The resulting explosion killed three and severely injured two others of her crew. Metal splinters lightly wounded eight crewmembers.

By November 26, 1952, she finished her first tour of duty. She arrived in Halifax on January 8, 1953. In June of that year, *Iroquois* returned to Korea with *Huron.* Their mission was coastal patrol along Korea's west coast. When the conflict ended on July 27, 1953,

Iroquois stayed behind to assist with evacuations of Allied troops from above or near the 38th parallel.

On New Year's Day 1954, she began her homeward voyage via the Mediterranean and arrived in Halifax on February 10, having circumnavigated the globe.

On October 24, 1962, *Iroquois* was paid off and went into Operational Reserve in Halifax. After being towed to Sydney, Nova Scotia, for disposal in 1966, she was scrapped at Bilbao, Spain.

HMCS *Huron*

Huron was commissioned July 19, 1943, and assigned to the 3rd Destroyer Flotilla of the British Home Fleet, located in Scapa Flow.

In October 1943, she sailed to Murmansk with special technical personnel and naval stores. For two months, *Huron* escorted convoys to Russia. In February 1944, she sailed south to join the 10th Destroyer Flotilla at Plymouth for pre-invasion duties. For the next seven months, she patrolled the Channel and the Bay of Biscay. On April 25–26, 1944, *Huron*, *Haida*, *Athabaskan* and HMS *Ashanti* encountered German Elbing Class destroyers in the English Channel. After the battle, *Ashanti* collided with the *Huron*, damaging *Huron*'s hull on the port side and her main bulkhead between No. 1 and No. 2 boiler rooms. The port cutter and its davits were smashed; the torpedo-davit damaged and deck guardrails and stanchions bent inwards. *Huron* returned safely to Plymouth. On May 7, repairs were complete, just in time for operations in support of the D-Day invasion.

HMCS *Huron* arrived in Halifax for a refit on August 13, 1944. By November 20, she was en route back to the United Kingdom. She called at the Azores and arrived in Cardiff for new radar equipment before proceeding to Scapa Flow.

During February and March 1945, *Huron* was assigned to escort duties in the Western Approaches. In April, she, with *Haida* and *Iroquois,* took their last convoy to Russia. After sharing in the liberation of Scandinavia, all three returned to Halifax for service in the Pacific. The RCN suspended refits when the war ended in August, and *Huron* went into reserve. She was paid off March 9, 1946.

Huron was recommissioned at Halifax in 1950 and sailed on January 22, 1951 for the first of two tours in Korean waters. Halifax was so cold that day that *Huron's* siren and Stadacona's band instruments froze. They had to be thawed before any sound was heard. *Huron's* first mission was screening aircraft carriers on Korea's west coast. Her second tour was in 1953–54. On her return, she reverted to her peacetime role of training until she was paid off on April 30, 1963, at Halifax. *Huron* was broken up at La Spezia, Italy in 1965.

~∞∞~

CHAPTER TEN

...And All the Ships at Sea

They that go down to the sea in ships, that do business in deep waters see the works of the Lord and His wonders in the deep.

Psalm 107:23

ON MAY 10, 1945, LORD LEATHERS, Minister of War Transport in the British government, sent the following message to all the officers and men of the merchant navies:

...For more than five and a half years side by side with the Allied Merchant Navies in the face of continual and merciless attacks by the enemy you have maintained the ceaseless flow of sea traffic on which the life and strength of this country depend. In this historic hour we think with special gratitude of the many merchant seamen who have fallen in the fight and whose service and sacrifice will always be a proud memory.

Thus, the British Admiralty and the Royal Navy expressed gratitude to those men, and a few women, who sailed the merchant ships across the hostile North Atlantic, keeping the supply lanes open and ensuring the very survival of Great Britain during the dark years of World War II.

According to Veterans Affairs Canada, from September 1939 to late May 1945, a total of 25,343 merchant ships carried 164,783,921 tonnes of cargo from North America to Britain. Sixty-seven Canadian-registered ships were lost, taking 1629 Canadian civilian sailors, including eight women, to the bottom with them. The coastal waters of North America and Europe, the Mediterranean, the North and South Atlantic, the Indian and the Pacific Oceans each took their share of the one in eight of the 12,000 Canadian merchant seafarers who were lost to the enemy's rapacious U-boats.

At the beginning of the war, Canada had only 37 deep-sea merchant ships. By war's end, Canada had the fourth largest merchant navy in the world. Her shipyards had produced 402 ships. They ranged from ponderous oil tankers and iron ore carriers to the usual cargo vessels carrying fuel, food, tanks, airplanes, beans, bacon, butter and flour. Ships had transported all the necessities to wage war and for the beleaguered British civilian population to survive.

In an effort to pinch off the slim sea bridge supplying Britain with the necessities, the *Kreigsmarine* moved U-boats in force to the western Atlantic. They swarmed the convoy sea-lanes and imposed a steady drain on Allied shipbuilding resources. For every new hull that slid down the ways, the deadly U-boat campaign claimed three others. RN and RCN escort service was only provided at each end of the convoy routes, leaving a 2400-kilometre gap of treacherous North Atlantic waters. Escort ships with long-range

Merchant ships under construction in Vancouver, December 1941

capability and adequate armament were needed. St. John's, Newfoundland, the large port that was the farthest east in North America, became key to providing effective convoy defence.

The convoy-and-escort system the Admiralty devised for ships crossing the Atlantic began with a 800-kilometre journey from Halifax to some point off Newfoundland. There, the escorts broke off and went in to St. John's for refuelling before shepherding another group back to Halifax. Mid-ocean escorts from St. John's took the convoy to the area of Iceland

and turned it over to British warships for the final leg. The escorts breaking off at Iceland refuelled there and picked up a westbound convoy to return to St. John's. This relay system enabled smaller destroyers and corvettes to carry out convoy escort despite their limited ranges of operation. The Royal Canadian Navy took over a wide sector of the North Atlantic, began commanding the Newfoundland Force and became responsible for all ships sailing in adjoining waters. This system, when it worked smoothly, ensured that convoys always had ship escorts.

The initial convoys leaving Halifax contained ships capable of speeds greater than nine knots. The first convoy, HX-1, left Halifax on September 16, 1939, a week after Canada's declaration of war. Soon two convoys sailed each week. As 1939 drew to a close, 14 convoys had left Halifax, with 410 ships, of which only three were lost. Mines destroyed two, and one was a victim of a U-boat attack. By August 1940, the dire need for vessels meant that older, slower ships were pressed into service. Convoy speed was reduced to meet these slower speeds, and Sydney, Cape Breton, was established as the assembly point for slow convoys.

Fast vessels, capable of 15 knots or more, sailed independently, although few were able to outrun an 18-knot German raider.

A typical North Atlantic convoy was 10 columns wide with four ships in each column. In the centre of the first line was the ship carrying the convoy commodore. Warships patrolled the convoy's outer flanks.

Often, a rescue ship trailed behind to pick up floating sailors from sunken merchantmen. Inside the convoy sailed the high-risk ships—those carrying ammunition and tankers loaded with oil or highly volatile aviation fuel. Some ships had World War I vintage deck guns mounted as defence against aircraft or surfaced submarines. Naval gunners were assigned to these ships, and they became known as DEMS gunners (Defensively Equipped Merchant Ships gunners).

The sea lanes were fraught with danger. Aircraft, surface raiders and submarines attacked the merchant ships, which were sailing blacked-out at night through the natural hazards of weather, ice and shoals. Men died at the hands of the enemy, from accidents in fog and from exposure to foul weather and winter gales. A complex organization governing ship movement, the positioning of vessels within the convoy and convoy defence by navy ships and crew ensured the successful flow of materiel to a desperate Britain.

CHAPTER ELEVEN

Lady Mariners

MERCHANT CREWS TRAVELLED back and forth across the hostile ocean. They were poorly paid, provided their own clothing and were subjected to fierce attacks with no protection or armament to respond. If their ship was torpedoed, they had only a 50 percent chance of survival. Death came from explosion, fire, scalding steam or drowning in unbelievably cold water covered by oil slicks that were often on fire. These people plied the oceans of the world repeatedly delivering whatever supplies were required for the war effort. Floundering sailors were frequently abandoned to the malevolent Atlantic as the convoy stayed its course. To heave to and attempt a rescue invited disaster.

Within hours of Britain's declaration of war on September 3, 1939, a German U-boat, *U-30*, sank a British ship. The 12,318-tonne Cunard liner, *Athenia,* en route to Montréal, was the first victim of Germany's unrestricted submarine campaign. *Athenia* was carrying 1000 civilian passengers; 118 died, including 22 Americans. Her loss was greeted with shock all around the world. Winston Churchill, the First Sea Lord, interpreted the action as a declaration of all-out U-boat warfare and ordered that henceforth, merchant ships would travel in convoy. In the United States, which was supposedly neutral, a groundswell of hostility towards Germany gathered momentum.

Canada declared war on Germany on September 10. The sinking caused Canadian shipbuilders to launch an unprecedented effort, which bore fruit in the following years when new ships were most needed.

In *Kreigsmarine* headquarters, *Großadmiral* Erich Raeder, commander-in-chief of the navy, and Admiral Karl Dönitz, commanding U-boats, greeted news of the sinking with consternation. Hitler had, at this stage of the war, ordered the navy to observe the Hague Convention Prize Rules. Few in the world saw the sinking as anything but deliberate, However, the commander of U-30, *Oberleutnant zur See* Fritz-Julius Lemp, pleaded that the large blacked-out ship he saw through his periscope zigzagging at high speed looked as if it was armed. Lemp was reported to have been reprimanded, but he was awarded the Iron Cross 2nd Class later that month, on September 27, 1939, and promoted to *Kapitänleutnant* on October 1. The next year, he was decorated with the Knight's Cross.

Lemp's U-boat exploits had a profound impact on the war. On his first patrol as commander of *U-110*, his boat was captured east of Cape Farewell. On May 9, 1941, HMS *Bulldog* and HMS *Broadway* forced his sub to surface. HMS *Bulldog* immediately went onto a ramming course, which Lemp noticed and ordered "Abandon Ship." Lemp figured that since the boat was going to be rammed (and presumably sunk), its secrets were safe within it. *Bulldog,* however, realized that a capture could occur and veered off, striking only a glancing blow on the sub. Only when he was in the water did Lemp realize that the boat was not sinking, and he attempted to swim back to prevent capture. That was the last seen of him.

The British tars made several journeys between *U-110* and HMS *Bulldog* to collect all they could get their hands on from inside the boat. Secret documents and an Enigma cypher machine with its code books were found in the control room. The day after the boat was captured someone realized that the Allies had the most important part of *U-110*. British Intelligence knew the German headquarters would soon find out the British had captured the boat and, assuming the worst, change their codes and cipher system. The captured U-boat thus "accidentally" sank when being towed to Britain. Fifteen submariners were killed in the initial action, and 32 captured. Lemp did not survive. Reportedly, British sailors shot him whilst he was swimming back to his boat. It is very likely that numerous U-boats were sunk using the information retrieved from *U-110*.

A young Canadian lady who did not survive the sinking of the *Athenia* was Hannah Baird, a stewardess from Verdun, Québec. She was the first Canadian casualty of the war and was among the first merchant mariners to perish in the war.

Women played a small part in the merchant navy, because seamanship was considered "man's work." Some women merchant mariners worked as stewardesses, and a few Canadian women pioneered as radio officers on Norwegian ships, the only fleet that at the time permitted women to serve at sea as wireless operators. Little is known of these women, mere girls really. Some of them died in service. Their lives were cut short before they established homes and families, so there are no descendents.

❦

Fern (Blodgett) Sunde

Fern (Blodgett) Sunde was the first Canadian woman to earn her wireless certificate and the first to go to sea. She was also the first woman to serve as a wireless officer in the Norwegian Merchant Navy. Fern sailed four years aboard the M/V *Mosdale* and made 78 wartime crossings of the Atlantic.

On the shores of Lake Ontario, a winsome young girl spent hours fascinated by the big lake boats sailing past her town of Cobourg, Ontario. It never occurred to her that she could not become a sailor. Fern Blodgett loved the sounds of the engines throbbing through the water and the shriek of the laker's whistles. She was not to be denied her dream. When war came, she saw a slim chance.

Fern was working in Toronto as a stenographer when she applied to three schools that gave wireless training. Two had no intentions of enrolling a female student, but the Radio College of Canada was far more open-minded and took her in to evening classes. After 18 months of study she graduated as a trained operator. There was no job available for a girl in any Canadian ship. Several days later the school principal phoned Fern with an offer she could not refuse. On Friday, June 13, 1941, 23-year-old Fern was on a train to Montréal.

When Norway was invaded on April 9, 1940, the Norwegian freighter *Mosdale* was en route to Santa Maria, Colombia, for a cargo of bananas for Oslo. The invasion changed her plans. She was taken over by the British Ministry of War Transport and put into regular service between Montréal and Liverpool. When Fern arrived at the Montreal dock, *Mosdale*'s captain, 30-year-old Gerner Sunde, was anxious to get away and had no choice but to take his new radio operator in a skirt. Norwegian authorities could find no prohibition against female crewmembers. On that warm June morning, the girl who wanted to be a sailor was on the high seas.

Mosdale usually sailed alone, carrying freight and often passengers. She became known as the "Bacon Ship" because she was on a regular service from Canada to England, with meat and bacon usually taken on board in Montréal and unloaded in Liverpool. During the war, *Mosdale* crossed the Atlantic 96 times, usually without a convoy. Running independently enabled her to make the crossings faster, unload and load her cargoes very quickly and go back across again. In the summer of 1943, while in Cardiff after her 51st crossing, King Haakon VII himself came on board to personally express his gratitude and admiration. The King was in exile in London during the war and often visited Norwegian ships.

On April 10, 1942, as reported in the USN Eastern Sea Frontier Enemy Action Diary, *Mosdale* was on a voyage from Halifax to Liverpool when, four hours out from Halifax at 1900 hours, its crew spotted a U-boat's periscope and part of its conning tower. Precautions were taken, including Fern sending a radio report to the USN Admiralty at Argentia. A little over an hour later another periscope was seen. The ship's deck gunners fired three rounds, and Fern sent another radio message to the USN radio station. The sub's periscope disappeared, and *Mosdale* got away at her full speed of 15 knots, quickly outpacing the U-boat.

Romance blossomed on board. Fern married the captain, Gerner Sunde, in 1942, and both served on board all through the war. This was not an unusual occurrence on Norwegian ships with Canadian female radio officers.

A Focke Wulf 200 attacked *Mosdale* in the morning of February 4, 1943, en route from England to Canada. Following some rounds from the ship's Oerlikon anti-aircraft gun, the aircraft departed without having caused any damage. In May that same year, she sailed in convoy HX-239. This convoy joined another that departed New York City on May 13. The convoy had a total of 43 ships and six to eight escorts, USN or RN destroyers and Canadian corvettes. *Mosdale* and 11 other ships joined the convoy near Halifax.

She had a general cargo for Avonmouth and was sailing in station 103 of the convoy.

During the first 24 hours out of Halifax, fog covered the meeting with the Halifax ships. When the fog cleared in daylight the next day, the Halifax ships took up their positions immediately. The convoy encountered heavy rain and patches of fog over the Grand Banks. Two large icebergs were sighted on May 20. That day the convoy experienced a heavy northwesterly gale with rough sea. A fair wind lasted for the next two days. Then they had fair weather for the rest of the voyage and arrived at Liverpool on May 28.

On April 24, 1944, *Mosdale* sailed from New York City with convoy CU-22. She was carrying general cargo for London. U-473 torpedoed the escorting destroyer escort USS *Donnell* on May 3. None of the remaining 31 ships was lost. The convoy arrived off Liverpool on May 6.

Apparently, *Mosdale* was involved in a collision in 1944. No further details exist except that the other ship, the British vessel *Kerry Coast*, sank following the collision, though she was later salvaged and repaired.

Mosdale was a lucky ship. She was one of a half-dozen Norwegian fruit carriers at the start of the war and the only one to survive. Fern and Gerner settled in Farsund, Norway after the war. Gerner died in 1962, and Fern died in 1991.

Maud Elizabeth Steane

Maud Elizabeth Steane, while working as an addressograph clerk at Toronto Hydro, enrolled at the Radio College of Canada to qualify as a Wireless Operator 2nd Class. She began her night-school training in June 1942 and completed her requirements 15 months later, graduating second in her class.

Women with their radio operator tickets were banned from joining Canadian ships as well as banned from joining foreign ships in Canadian ports. In May 1944, Steane joined the merchant ship SS *Viggo Hansteen* at New York. The *Hansteen* was an American-built Liberty Ship transferred to Norwegian registry for emergency war transport. Just 10 weeks after leaving home, at age 28, Maud was murdered aboard the *Hansteen* while it was anchored off Naples, Italy. A male crewmember shot her and then turned the gun on himself. She was the first woman from Toronto killed on active service. She is buried in the Allied War Cemetery at Florence, Italy. The Norwegian Consul General at Toronto expressed condolences to her family. Her Silver Cross remains unclaimed.

Both Baird's and Steane's names are recorded on the Women Mariners' Memorial in Langford, BC. This monument is the only freestanding memorial to women mariners in Canada. Located in Vancouver Island's Langford Veterans Park, it is a large gazebo used for musical concerts.

Other women mariners were lost in World War II. The Women Mariners' Memorial also commemorates Lillie C. Cook-Gorbeil, a stewardess lost aboard the SS *Lady Hawkins* on January 19, 1942. *Lady Hawkins* was carrying 212 passengers and 109 crew en route to the West Indies when she sank. The survivors escaped in three lifeboats. Two lifeboats were never found. The third lifeboat had 76 persons in it. Five of these died before S.S. *Coamo* rescued them on January 24 and landed them at San Juan, Puerto Rico. In total, 250 of the 321 persons on board were lost.

The Women Mariners' Memorial also commemorates Eileen Pomeroy, second cook aboard the Upper Lakes freighter *George L. Torian*. She died when *U-129* torpedoed the *Torian* off Guyana, on February 22, 1942. The German U-boat crew interrogated the survivors after the sinking and offered them directions, food and water.

During the war the Newfoundland Railway experienced its most tragic loss when German submarine *U-69* torpedoed and sank the NR ferry *Caribou* on October 14, 1942. *Caribou,* sailing from Sydney, NS to Port aux Basques, Newfoundland, sank 40 kilometres off Port aux Basques in the Cabot Strait. One hundred and thirty-seven persons (31 crew and 106 passengers) lost their lives. In honour of the passengers and crew who were lost, the Newfoundland Railway Employees Association had the entire workforce forego a day's wages as a donation to a public campaign that saw a memorial built near the Port aux Basques railway terminal.

Bride Fitzpatrick was a stewardess aboard the ferry *Caribou*. *U-69* sunk this ship in the Cabot Strait on October 14, 1942. Fitzpatrick was the only female member of the Newfoundland Merchant Navy known to have lost her life to enemy action during World War II.

Caribou's lone escort was HMCS *Grandmere*, a Bangor Class minesweeper commanded by Lieutenant James S.C. Cuthbert, RCNR. It rushed in to ram *U-69*. When the submarine crash-dived, *Grandmere* dropped a pattern of six depth charges. The U-boat remained submerged, while the ferry's passengers fought for their lives above. *Grandmere* picked up 101 survivors.

Two other women sailing aboard *Caribou* were RCN nursing sisters. Lieutenant Agnes Wightman Wilkie, a 30-year-old from Carman, Manitoba, became the only Canadian nursing sister to die due to enemy action during the war. Wilkie graduated as an operating-room nurse at Misericordia Hospital, Winnipeg. She is commemorated at Mount Pleasant Cemetery in St. John's, Newfoundland. A photograph of her was hung in all Canadian Naval Hospitals. In 1967, Wilkie Lake, in Manitoba, was named after her.

Wilkie's good friend and travelling companion, Sub-Lieutenant (Dietician) Margaret Brooke, was named a Member of the Order of the British Empire for her gallant efforts to save Wilkie as the two drifted through the night, struggling to hold on to the ropes of an overturned lifeboat.

~•X•~

CHAPTER TWELVE

Merchantmen

Joseph Gilbert Kenny was born in December 1923 in the small village of Saint Rose, New Brunswick. His father was the blacksmith for the farm community. Gil was 15 and still in school when war broke out. His two older brothers joined the army, but his teacher told Gil that his father and indeed his whole family needed him to help run the farm. However, Gil was determined to get into the war. He went to an army recruiter in Newcastle but was turned down because of his age. He went to an air force office at Moncton and was accepted. But three weeks later, at the depot in Fredericton, his age was revealed. They proposed to send him home.

Instead, Gil Kenny travelled to Halifax and joined the merchant navy. He had never been to sea, nor had he had any inclination to sail. He simply went down to the Halifax waterfront and started looking for a ship. In his pure naivety, he walked up a gangplank of a likely looking vessel and was snooping around. One of the petty officers spotted the youngster and asked him what he was looking for. "Looking for a job," he brashly replied. He was directed to the captain's cabin with the admonition not to annoy the officer. Admitted to the ship's inner sanctum, the captain quizzed him. "How old are you?" he asked and the boy replied "Sixteen." "You should be in school," said the captain and Gil responded, "I was— last week." A strapping young fellow, he was hired and put to work.

M/S *Amerika*, a Danish ship, sailed under orders of the British government's Ministry of War Transport from May 1940 on. Few Canadian boats were available, so Canadian merchant mariners, such as Kenny, sailed on whatever ship took them. Kenny's war service eventually took him on British, Danish and Norwegian ships. On the *Amerika*, a petty officer asked, "What do you do?" Gil answered that he had worked on a farm. "Ain't many farms on the ocean," said the sailor. "In the summertime," Gil said, "I worked in the woods at a lumber camp. I helped the cook." "Oh!" said the sailor, "So you are a cook. Go below to the galley and see the chef." The chef told him he would be the "gully boy." He would peel potatoes and generally make himself useful. "But you'll be a cook before I'm done with you!"

The ship pushed away from the dock at 11:00 PM that night, and Gil began the first of his 22 ocean crossings. The cook sent him up to the captain's office to make sure his name was in the log. Gil did not see the sense in that. "If the ship goes down, the log will go with it," was his thought.

A couple of destroyers and four or five corvettes accompanied the convoy leaving Halifax. The escorts warned all the ships in the convoy that there had been a U-boat sighted just outside the harbour. Gil was taken around the ship and told some of his duties. He was a cook, but he was expected to do anything else required.

Anti-submarine nets protected Halifax's harbour mouth. Small vessels opened the two gates in the nets so the convoy could pass through. Once at sea, the convoy spread out over about 30 kilometres and maintained a speed of seven knots. The convoy turned north for Newfoundland. There they met with ships coming from Montreal and New York and were organized into their transoceanic configuration. Seeing American ships in their convoy, Kenny and others hoped the U.S. Navy would help protect it. The convoy steamed north about 30 kilometres from shore through the Strait of Belle Isle and turned east towards Iceland and the "black pit" hunting ground of the U-boats.

On the open water, all the crewmembers became friendly with the young newcomer. They were mainly Danes, but the common language was English. They explained various jobs of a seaman. He began his work in the galley at 0400 hours. If he became seasick, he was allowed to stay in bed, but not during his turn on duty. During the winter months, the first task of all crewmembers was to chop ice away from the superstructure, the cables and the winches. Ice was a nemesis that made ships top-heavy, threatening capsizing. As the voyage began, the captain announced on the intercom that each trip was a matter of survival. It was every man's job to do whatever it took to ensure survival. For protection, they had a four-inch gun mounted on the stern, but it was old and ineffective and the crew was ill trained in using it.

Kenny's ship, the M/S *Amerika*, left Halifax in company with 14 other merchantmen. They joined convoy HX-234 at the H.O.M.P. (Halifax Ocean Meeting Point). At 1400 hours on April 15, 1943, they met the 22 ships that had sailed from New York and began maintaining an average speed of 8.7 knots. Four days later, *U-108* sank a ship in the convoy, the *Robert Gray*, a vessel under U.S. registry. There were no survivors.

A strong northerly gale sprang up with heavy snow blizzards. During the night the speed of the convoy was reduced to three or four knots. At about 1:00 AM, on April 22, a U-boat torpedoed Kenny's ship. It sank 190 kilometres south-southeast of Cape Farewell, Greenland. She was hit on the port side aft and amidships.

According to the convoy commodore, no rockets were seen, and no distress signals were intercepted. The only ship in the convoy that saw *Amerika* torpedoed was *Washington Express* sailing in the next column who reported seeing three flashes and hearing a siren. The *Express* did not fire white rockets, unfortunately. *Corner Brook* reported that the last time she saw *Amerika* was just before the alteration of course at 2130 hours on April 21, and that *Amerika* was then a long way astern of her station in the convoy. *Amerika* had a declared speed of 14 knots, but she was not good at keeping her station.

The M/S *Amerika* carried 75 to 85 crew and, as passengers, 53 RCAF aircrew officers, 26 bomber aimers, 12 navigators and 15 pilots. Altogether, 86 died, including 37 passengers. HMS *Asphodel*, a RN corvette commanded by Lieutenant H.P. Carse, D.S.C., RNVR picked up 16 RCAF aircrew survivors and approximately 40 crewmembers. When reports of the *Amerika* torpedoing circulated, *Asphodel* took immediate action, sailing straight through the convoy between its columns and across its front, then going through the convoy and out its tail to pick up survivors. Among those the *Asphodel* picked up was John H. Newland:

> *I was one of two survivors of the last boat to leave the ship, which sank out from under the boat, which was on chocks, not on davits. The lifeboat rolled over. I came up some distance from the overturned boat, which had a few survivors on it, and swam to the lifeboat that had been on the windward side of the ship and had also been on chocks. It was awash, so it was a case of getting out of the water and into the water.*
>
> *Eight RCAF aircrew officers were in the fore end of the boat and about the same number of ship's crew were in the other end. One teen-age seaman was in the bow of the boat. The third mate (or was it the bos'n?) was in the boat, but he jumped out and swam to a life raft and survived. The young sailor in our end of the boat was struck in the head by a floating timber and killed. Two of the RCAF aircrew officers aboard died, one of exposure, the other by a six-by-six timber, which came over the boat on a wave, hit him and carried him far beyond where we could reach him. By that time*

none of us were able to handle anything that could have helped him since we were stiff with cold, to the point where we were imagining we would probably have to have our hands and feet amputated if we were rescued. The ship's crewmen in the other end of the boat were carried away by the seas that swept over the boat.

I lay down on one of the boat's seat with my head on the gunwale to rest, only to be awakened by waves coming over me. The last time I was awakened I saw Asphodel. The man next to me woke up when I shouted "corvette!" and we both waved our survivor lights and shouted. The RCAF types in the bow didn't believe it until they smelled the smoke from the corvette. Then they joined the chorus.

The Asphodel *came alongside the boat. I remember we complimented whoever was handling the corvette when she arrived at the lifeboat. I believe it was Lieutenant Carse on the bridge and a veteran seaman at the wheel. Not a bump! We couldn't grab a rope. All we could do was hold up our arms for help, and they pulled us aboard. I was grabbed by a sailor and came close to pulling him overboard because he was a little guy. But one of the other RN men grabbed him, and here I am.*

Fifteen-year-old Gil Kenny survived but was not among those the *Asphodel* picked up. The explosion of the ship knocked Kenny senseless and left him forever partly deaf. When he revived, the ship was on fire, sinking. All the boats were gone. He found a raft, threw it overboard and followed it. He was alone on the five-metre-by-four-metre raft for about 72 hours. He had food but was afraid that he would not survive the cold to be rescued. A westbound American ship eventually fished him out of the briny. The ship was sailing for New York and deposited Gil on Ellis Island. He was there about 30 days healing his injuries, including severe bruising. Then he went back to Halifax and another ship.

The senior officer of the escorts estimated that 12 U-boats were concentrated on the convoy on April 22. "The loss of such a fine ship as *Amerika* is very much deplored," he wrote. "It is, however, felt that had she been in her proper station, she might quite easily have escaped. The signal 'submarines known to be in vicinity—keep well closed up' had been made twice to the convoy."

Kenny was assigned to another merchantman. In total, he completed 22 North Atlantic crossings. Eventually he enlisted in the Royal Navy as a cook on HMS *Sheffield*, a Town Class light cruiser. This ship made a trip to Australia, transporting troops and supplies. They were routed down the coast of Spain and through the Mediterranean, the Suez Canal and the Indian Ocean to Burma. On the way back, they did supply stops in North Africa and Sicily. The ship also participated as a supply ship to the landings in Normandy.

Gil Kenny survived the war, returned to Canada, settled down in New Brunswick and raised a family.

CHAPTER THIRTEEN

Andrew Beattie's War

IN THE LITTLE SCOTTISH FISHING VILLAGE of St. Cyrus, 50 kilometres south of Aberdeen, George and Jessie (Petrie) Beattie celebrated the birth of their second child, a son, Andrew, on September 19, 1912. He was named after his maternal grandfather. From his bedroom window, Beattie often gazed out to sea. As a lad, he spent many hours sailing up and down the coast of the North Sea near the Firth of Forth. He began school at age four under a headmaster who taught his charges seamanship, how to use a sextant and plot a course. Andy's siblings included his brother Bill, two years older, another brother, Allan, and a sister, Nan.

St. Cyrus had no electricity but did have an excellent library. Andy found a book with a description of how to make a battery-powered crystal radio. He coaxed his grandfather into giving him the money to order the parts to build it. His grandfather considered it money well spent when the boy's creation picked up the BBC. This was Andy's introduction to radio communications. At age 14, Andy left school for a job on a farm but was encouraged to leave this job when he saw a poster advertising land and opportunities in Canada. Much against his mother's wishes, his father signed for him to go. On April 1, 1928, 15-year-old Andy sailed on the SS *Athenia* from Glasgow down the Clyde and out to sea.

He landed in Halifax on April 9. Canadian authorities issued the migrant farm worker with a food voucher and train tickets to Tweed, Ontario. The coach-class car had bare wooden seats and a stove at each end. Travelling through New Brunswick and Québec to Montreal all he saw were rocks and trees. Beattie was to work for farmer Earl Alexander, near Roslin. Beattie farmed for Earl's brother Norman in Roslin for seven or eight years. Norman introduced the boy to maple sugar gathering and manufacturing.

In 1931, Beattie's spirit of adventure resurfaced. He and a friend rode the rails west, staying in hobo jungles. For six months, he worked in Churchill and The Pas, Manitoba. He did odd jobs on prairie farms for 20 cents an hour. His wanderlust sated, he returned to Belleville, Tweed and Roslin. By this time, he was seeing Kathleen Carter, a local dark-haired beauty.

In the late 1930s, Beattie applied to the Department of Transport for a position with a weather station. To get the job, he needed a radio licence and a Morse-code capability of 25 words per minute. He enrolled at the Radio College of Canada in Toronto and made ends meet with a part-time job at a Canadian Tire warehouse. He achieved his diploma and licence but instead of a job was offered only a place on a Department of Transport waiting list.

War broke out, and Beattie tried to join the air force as a pilot. Poor reflexes in his right foot disqualified him. The British Merchant Marine was in desperate need of radio operators and offered him a position. The British consul in Toronto gave him a voucher for two meals and a train ticket to New York City. There, at the British consulate, he received orders to join the ship *Duquesne*. The British government's Ministry of War Transport had taken over the U.S. ship in 1940. The *Duquesne* was later renamed *Empire Kudu*.

Andy Beattie joined the *Duquesne* in Mobile, Alabama. Waiting in a hotel for the *Duquesne* to be loaded, he met six Australian navy gunners who had signed on as its gun crew. However, the ship had no guns except a World War I Ross rifle.

The ship's senior radio officer, Mr. Roberts, made sure Beattie knew all he needed to be a good operator. His responsibilities included copying all instructions, course changes, enemy positions and change in destination. To miss one message was to jeopardize the safety of the ship.

The stevedores loaded cargo, stores and bunker oil, then *Duquesne* went to Tampa to load explosives before heading to Halifax. The ship had two radio officers, who stood six-hour watches. Every night en route Beattie listened to distress signals from ships at sea. The distress signals, accompanied by ship call letters and position in latitude and longitude, varied depending on the threat: "SSS" indicated a sub was attacking

the ship, "RRRR" indicated a surface raider was shelling the ship.

Surviving a nasty sea off Cape Hatteras, Beattie
learned he was not prone to seasickness. Approaching
Halifax, he learned to use the Aldis lamp to signal the
gate vessels. They opened the barrier, allowing his
vessel to enter the harbour and go into Bedford Basin
to join 100 other ships anchored there. His ship, now
loaded with steel and scrap iron, was assigned to convoy HX-102, which sailed from Halifax to Liverpool,
January 11–29, 1941.

During the winter of 1941 the U-boats' "Happy
Time" continued in the western approaches as they
sunk ship after ship from the poorly defended convoys. Bad weather in January and February fortunately kept the number of sinkings low. Approximately
22 U-boats were operational out of the 90 in commission. Also long-range aircraft, including Focke-Wulf
Kondors, roamed the skies off Ireland, spotting for
the U-boats and sinking ships on their own. Even the
Italian navy was involved in the U-boats' "Happy
Time." On January 7, the Italian submarine *Nani*
attacked a convoy in the North Channel. The corvette
Anemone sank it before it did any harm.

Fifty-nine British, Allied and neutral ships total-
ling 248,000 tonnes were lost from all causes in the
Battle of the Atlantic. To counter the U-boat threat,
the navy organized the merchant ships into two categories. Those ships capable of making more than
10 knots were considered "fast." Convoys composed

of these ships were identified with the letter "F." Ships sailing slower than 10 knots were put in "slow" convoys, each of which was identified with an "S." Usually 50 ships, escorted by two corvettes, formed a convoy. Before each convoy sailed, the convoy commodore, usually a retired admiral, called the merchant captains and senior radio officers ashore to attend a convoy conference. The convoy commodore told the ships' officers what types of evasive action their ships should take, warned them to maintain station and admonished them not to make any excessive smoke and not to show any lights. The captains got sealed orders with times, special codes, call letters and radio frequencies to monitor and use. Merchant captains were old sea dogs who had wrung more saltwater from their socks than the navy staff had seen.

Beattie's *Duquesne* was among the 30 ships in HX-102, which left Bedford Basin, line astern, on January 11, 1941. Any spies watching could see the ships were sitting low in the water, so it was obvious they were heading east. At first, the sea was calm. The ships plugged along at nine knots. After one day, the weather turned into a pea soup fog. Then gale-force winds and snow pummelled the ships. One escort developed boiler trouble and had to go to St. Johns, which left only one escort, HMS *Voltaire,* as protection for the convoy. She could stay with them only as far as the Black Pit, the area in mid-ocean where the merchant ships had no protection from escorts. There German U-boats enjoyed their "Happy Time." At the extreme limit of its endurance, *Voltaire* left, sending a "Good Luck" signal. The convoy sailed 800 kilometres without escort until it met warships from the UK, who protected the convoy for the rest of its journey.

At the Butt of Lewis, HX-102 split: east coast ships went through Pentland Firth; the rest sailed south through the Minches to Glasgow and the Mersey ports. Next morning, through glasses, Beattie saw the spire of the church at St. Cyrus as his ship entered the Firth of Forth and tied up at Leith. He got a week's leave and so headed home to his parents. His father had died the previous month, but Beattie's mother, Jessie, was waiting. Smuggled in his duffle bag were sugar, tea and ham because wartime rationing severely curtailed the availability of consumer goods. Families were allowed only one egg a week.

When he returned to his ship six days later, he was wearing a new uniform with two wavy rings (signifying Royal Naval Reserve) on the sleeves. The *Duquesne* cruised upriver to Grangemouth to have its guns installed and for its crew to take gunnery school, then joined a westbound convoy off Loch Broome. This crossing was certainly no picnic. Their destroyer escort lasted three days, then they were left on their own. The next night two ships were torpedoed. In the morning, two more went down. The convoy commodore gave the order to scatter. Every ship continued on its own, plugging ahead at full speed. Soon no other ships were to be seen. Lookouts were doubled, gun crews stood by their guns, and the crew checked and double-checked the ship's lifeboats. No one had to be told to wear his lifejacket. The radio room was busy as radio operators tried to get bearings on ships that were transmitting distress signals. These bearings allowed his captain to change course to avoid the U-boats. They were expressly prohibited from going to help the crew of sinking ships. However, many ships did stop, or at least slow down, to pick up survivors or render other assistance to stricken vessels.

One by one, the convoy's ships straggled into Halifax. Of 31, they had lost 12. Everyone knew the navy was not to blame, but rather the politicians who had let the navy deteriorate.

From Halifax, *Duquesne* joined a southbound convoy of mostly tankers headed to Aruba and Venezuela. The crew spent Christmas in Beaumont, Texas, feeding on tinned Spam, potatoes and rice pudding produced by a drunken cook. The crewmembers threw the drunk overboard, and American pleasure boaters rescued him. He was carried home on another ship as a Distressed British Seaman. (The Merchant Shipping Act, section 48, covers this: "The master of every British ship shall receive on board his ship, and afford a passage and maintenance, to all distressed seamen whom he is required under this Act to take on board his ship.")

With a new cook in charge of the galley, *Duquesne* went to Tampa to load explosives and then north again to Halifax. After a week at anchor in Bedford Basin, Beattie's ship began her long, slow crawl east to the UK.

The Germans were using a new tactical formation called the wolf pack. When a convoy was spotted, a scout submarine stayed well back and shadowed the ships at night on the surface. It informed the "wolf pack" of the convoy's course, speed and escorts. The U-boats then patiently waited and pounced. It was slaughter.

Beattie left the *Dusquesne* early in 1941. Later that year the *Dusquesne*, by then renamed *Empire Kudu*, was lost, running aground in Canada's Straits of Belle Isle on September 26, 1941. Her convoy passing through the Straits was alerted that a submarine had been sighted. Amid panic and confusion, four ships ran aground. Among the four were the *Empire Kudu*, carrying a load of scrap iron, and the *South Wales*, with a load of grain.

Beattie was assigned to another British freighter, which headed to England in a convoy. The name of his ship and the convoy is not recorded, but the convoy was quite likely HX-126, which lost nine ships in May 1941.

Just east of Newfoundland, convoy HX-126 got word to change course and head north for Denmark Strait, a narrow strip of water separating Iceland and Greenland. Changing to the new route north of Iceland was an effort to avoid marauding U-boats. However, north of Newfoundland and east of Labrador, a wolf pack of 11 U-boats was waiting.

May 19 was a cold, clear night. The merchantmen were keeping station with the convoy's pitifully few escorts ahead. An armed merchant cruiser, HMS *Aurania,* and a submarine, HMS *Tribune*, were the only escorts for the convoy. Beattie, on the 4:00 to 8:00 PM watch, came on duty. A sailor brought him the usual cup of ki (a weird mixture of cocoa, sugar, condensed milk and boiling water). He settled in for a routine night of receiving weather reports and Admiralty bulletins.

Then all hell broke loose. Beattie heard and felt a terrific explosion. He looked out the door. All he saw of the next ship was its funnel as the ship went down. Radio officers kept extra clothes in the radio room, so Beattie scrambled into his and put on his lifejacket. The chief officer came in and gave him the ship's latest recorded position, so he could radio that information in case they were sunk themselves. A steward brought him a mug of coffee. Beattie expected that the coffee would have a shot of rum in it and took a swig, but it was so potent that he thought the steward must have filled it with rum and put in a shot of coffee.

U-94 spotted the convoy on May 19 and before losing contact sank two ships. *U-556* found the convoy the next day and in two attacks sank two ships and damaged a tanker. During the evening of May 20, *U-111* and *U-98* joined the attack; the next morning *U-93* joined in. The next day, *U-66*, *U-46*, *U-557*, and *U-74* also attacked HX-126.

Two other ships on the side of the convoy away from Beattie's ship went down. Depth charges exploded all around. Their shaking rattled everything on the ships. The escorts were running around like a pack of hounds. Unrelenting, the subs attacked from both sides and the rear. Chief Radio Officer Roberts came in to see if Beattie needed any help, then went to test transmitters in the lifeboats as they were being swung out on their davits.

In the radio room, Beattie listened to ship after ship sending "SSS torpedoed" distress signals. He heard another station repeat each message along with the name of the ship and its location, and then heard Cape Race repeat the information again. Soon, Beattie's own turn came to send this signal.

Wham!

A torpedo got them right in the engine room. All the ship's power went off. Beattie switched on the emergency battery power for his transmitter and sent a distress signal. He sent it a second time, got an acknowledgement from an escort and waited to hear it repeated. Thinking of the ship's explosive cargo, he clamped his telegraph key down and hustled out to the boat deck to find everyone, except the captain and first mate, already in the lifeboats and the lifeboats standing off from the ship. The captain and Beattie ran along the deck towards some swung-out boats when the ship made a violent list to port. The lurch capsized the boats and threw the two running men down on the deck. The captain yelled for Beattie to jump. He did. While under the water he heard two splashes and saw that the other two officers had followed him. The water was so cold you could only survive in it for a few minutes.

Beattie spotted a raft nearby and swam the few metres to it. Sailors aboard hauled him in. Beattie passed out and did not see his ship go down.

Someone spotted a British gunner, who had come on board in Halifax, in the water, hanging onto a lifeboat next to the sinking ship. He was apparently too frightened to let go to swim to the safety of the raft. One of the lifeboats moved over to assist him when another torpedo hit the ship. The ship settled lower in the water and slowly sank. The gunner died.

Beattie regained consciousness on board a destroyer, stark naked and wrapped in blankets. An English voice asked if he wanted a drink. He gratefully accepted. An hour later, they brought him his clothes, all nice and dry. He felt good until he learned that only eight of his ship's entire crew had survived. Both other sparks (radio operators) were gone. The captain and the entire engine room staff were the only other ones that survived. The engine room staff were the people on the raft who had pulled him out.

The *Aurania* took the survivors to Liverpool. They were given the customary survivors' leave—one month off. During his time off in May 1941, Beattie experienced the air raids of the Liverpool blitz. Andy Beattie spent two nights under a cement stairwell in the train station trying to get a train home to Scotland. The whole city seemed on fire. Women were operating fire hoses. He just felt helpless and wished he was back at sea. His family was surprised to see him. He was travelling light, having lost all his gear including the new uniform, in the sinking. At the end of three weeks, not a month, a telegram marked "urgent" arrived, telling him he had been promoted to the position of chief radio operator and to report to Liverpool at 10:00 the next morning to sign on the *Olivebank*.

The "Bank Line" is part of Andrew Weir Shipping Ltd., founded in 1885 in Scotland and established in London. Weir formed the "Bank Line" in 1905 and since that time has been operating regular steamship service between Europe and the South Pacific (especially the Orient and India).

Beattie reported to the shipping office, met the captain, signed the articles and went to the ship. She was as nice as he expected. The ship had teak planking for the main deck, freshly holystoned with not a mark anywhere. Its brass work was polished to a tee. A steward, looking smart in his uniform, met Beattie at the bottom of the gangplank, took his gear and led him to his cabin around the corner from the captain's. The captain told him "Lunch will be served in 30 minutes, and then we will get underway."

The dining salon was panelled in mahogany. Since they were still tied up at the dock, everyone ate at once. Beattie was seated beside the chief engineer, who was, as usual, a Scot. Everyone was in uniform, including the cadets who had been painting one of the masts when Beattie came on board. The two junior radio operators seemed to be likeable lads. One was from Belfast. He had been studying for the priesthood but had taken leave from college for the duration of the war. The gun crew was all Royal Navy.

The lines were cast off, and *Olivebank* proceeded to her convoy staging area. The new chief radio operator, Andrew Beattie, tested the ship's radio equipment. The ship cleared the Mersey, entering the Irish Sea, and its crew commenced a regular watch keeping schedule. The captain opened his sealed orders. They directed the ship to stay in the convoy for three days, until far enough west that German bombers could not reach them, then to turn south, travel unescorted to Capetown then to Alexandria, Egypt, to help supply the Eighth Army. They endured three days of rough weather until they turned south and the seas became calm.

Their job for the next six months was taking supplies from Port Sudan, partway up the Red Sea, to the beleaguered troops at Tobruk. They sailed at night to avoid bomber attacks. On their third voyage, they were hit 80 kilometres west of Alexandria. A bomb demolished part of the bridge and the radio room. Beattie was trapped in rubble. His legs were smashed, and a piece of shrapnel had entered one eye. Ten others also were badly injured. Back at Alexandria, ambulances took the injured to hospital. Beattie's eye was operated on immediately When he woke up both eyes were bandaged, and he thought he had become blind. He struggled, but both arms were tied down. The nursing sisters calmed him down, and a British

Army doctor said they would be operating on his legs in the morning. The surgical team hoped to be able to save one.

Near morning, two explosions awoke him. A nurse and two orderlies lifted him onto a stretcher and into an ambulance. Cursing because the hospital was being bombed, they took him to a Swiss hospital in Alexandria, where an old Swiss surgeon operated on his legs. Beattie was forever grateful to this doctor, who took a mess of tangled bones and flesh and gave him the means to walk again. After three weeks he was put aboard a hospital ship and taken to Haifa, Israel, to an army hospital on Mount Carmel. *Olivebank* was repaired in the Haifa docks. After two months' recuperation, Beattie rejoined his ship at Port Said.

After the December 7, 1941, Japanese attack on Pearl Harbour, the U.S. entered the war. The U.S. Navy began to use the Suez Canal frequently, and *Olivebank*'s ferry days were over. *Olivebank* was ordered to Calcutta to dry dock so that her bottom could be scraped. The crew spent Christmas Day, 1941, in the 49°C temperatures of the Red Sea. In Calcutta, the ship was fumigated to get rid of the many bugs and insects it had acquired in the Middle East.

At the end of January 1942, Royal Navy headquarters ordered *Olivebank* to proceed with utmost haste to Singapore to evacuate nurses and civilians. Japanese forces were rapidly closing in on the city. *Olivebank* sped through the Malaga Straits with the ship going faster than it ever had before. *Olivebank*'s crew could see the intense bombardment as enemy land batteries lobbed shells at Singapore. The crew wondered if they would get there in time. They tied up at the Singapore dock beside two P&O liners and a hospital ship, nearly done loading refugees. Singapore was well fortified, but its big guns faced seaward. The Japanese army was marching in the back door through Malaya. Beattie and the second engineer were sent with a truck to pick up nurses in a military hospital near the Raffles Hotel. By the time the group arrived at the dock, the sound of the fighting was loud. The evacuees were herded aboard, and *Olivebank* followed the other three ships out to sea at dusk on February 7. Enemy bombers attacked but missed the ships by a long ways. The next day, Japanese soldiers stormed into the island of Singapore itself.

The nurses disembarked in Columbo, Ceylon, where *Olivebank* was loaded with general cargo destined for Buenos Aires and Montevideo, Uruguay. Approaching those ports, the ship went past the remains of *Graf Spee*, her masts above water. HMS *Ajax*, HMS *Exeter* and HMS *Achilles* had heavily damaged this surface raider, and her crew scuttled her. *Olivebank* loaded coffee in Brazil and set sail for Freetown, Sierra Leone, where the Royal Marines put navy ratings on board as DEMS gunners (Navy gunners assigned to defensively equipped merchant ships) for the four-inch gun and the ship's anti-aircraft guns. A convoy was formed with ships from Capetown, India and South America.

It sailed for Britain, keeping well off the coast and out of range of shore-based bombers

A year and a half after leaving the Mersey, the *Olivebank* tied up at the same pier she had left. Her crew had covered thousands of kilometres, sailed on seven different oceans and seas, some of them twice, They had lived, slept and ate with millions of bugs; experienced yellow fever, dysentery and malaria; nearly lost the ship in the Mediterranean; dodged enemy bombing off Burma; and survived bombing and shelling by shore batteries off the coast of the Malaysian Peninsula and Singapore. Some crew had been badly wounded. Three had died: two lascar sailors and one engineer who died of malaria.

Beattie took a three-week holiday to visit his folks in Scotland then went back to the depot in Liverpool, to ask the superintendent for a ship to Canada. There was a ship going to New York for refit. She had been bombed but was deemed seaworthy. Beattie jumped at the chance, which was a mistake. She was the *Empire Stour*, laying at Salford at the end of the Manchester Canal. The *Stour* was a Ministry of War Transport ship. She had been launched as the *Harpenden* in 1930, and the Ministry had taken her over in 1941. After the elegance of the *Olivebank*, this ship was a mess. Her engine room and radio rooms were okay, but the bridge was temporary and her steering was jury-rigged. There was no refrigeration but lots of salt beef, bread and jam. All her guns had been taken off, and she was a sorry sight.

In late afternoon, the *Stour* started down the canal. She had gone about halfway when an air raid began on Liverpool. They pulled to the side and tied up because if the ship got hit and went down it would block the canal, a disaster for canal traffic. In the morning, they joined a convoy bound for New York. The first few days were fine, then they hit a wicked storm. The ship had water ballast but not enough to keep her stable. She pitched and rolled, stood on her head and then stood on her stern. The crew could not walk above or below deck. Lines were strung everywhere as handholds. There was no cooking—the men lived on bread and jam. They wedged themselves into bunks to sleep. South of Newfoundland the storm abated, and ships going to Halifax split from the convoy. The remainder altered course southwest for Long Island Sound and New York harbour.

Once the ship was tied up at the repair docks, the captain told Beattie he could have nine days' unrecorded leave to go to Canada. Beattie left immediately on a Saturday afternoon. He caught the night train to Toronto and then travelled to Belleville where the Alexanders met him and drove him to Roslin. It had been two years since he had seen Kathleen. There was no telephone service so he went to her farm. That night, he gave her an engagement ring that he had bought in Scotland, and it has not been off her finger since. At the end of a great week he went back to a repaired ship in New York. *Stour* was carrying 40 ambulances and six road rollers on board as deck cargo.

Once again, they sailed north and just off Newfoundland joined a convoy from Halifax. Two days
later, a U-boat wolf pack attacked the convoy and
picked off ships one by one. Just before daylight,
a torpedo tore a hole in the number one hold of Beattie's ship. The torpedo did not explode, but the ship
took on water from the hole the torpedo had made.
The chief officer and bos'un took some crew below
and blocked the hole with tarps nailed to a wooden
frame. The ship's speed was reduced, and the convoy
soon outdistanced them. The ship started to go down
at the head, and the crew swung out the lifeboats. To
lighten the load, the crew removed the ship's railings
and began running the ambulances overboard. The
sea became very rough. Two road rollers broke loose
and started careening up and down the deck. All
night they thundered back and forth and about daybreak finally went over the side. One of the pumps
quit. As water in the hold rose higher, the crew
pushed the rest of the ambulances overboard.

Beattie worked 30 hours straight in the radio room,
monitoring the radio network. The captain asked
him to break radio silence and send a request for a
salvage tug to meet them Their ship was only making
seven knots, and the 300 kilometres to Oban would
take their ship more than a day to cover. The captain
declared he doubted if they would float another day
without help. The captain also asked Beattie to
request air cover, because every sub in the ocean
would take a bearing on his radio transmission and
come to get them.

Beattie sent the transmission and hoped the promised help would arrive soon. The ship, growing lower in the water, wallowed through another long night with waves breaking over the bow. Finally, the lookout aloft spotted approaching vessels. Two tugs arrived! The first tug lashed alongside and started her huge pumps working, fighting the rising water. Another lashed itself to the other side. That afternoon a Sunderland flying boat provided air cover, and they sailed into Oban harbour.

A barge came out and using underwater welding put a plate over the hole. Pumps sucked the hold dry. Torpedo artificers then went down and disabled the torpedo. A crane lifted it out. The ship rejoined her convoy the next morning and sailed through the Pentland Firth down the east coast to Hull.

A bombing raid had hit the *Empire Mouflon,* and a skeleton crew was required to take her to the Tyne shipyards. *Stour* was going into dry dock, and the crew was signed off so Beattie signed on the *Mouflon* on November 3, 1942. He signed off on November 7, 1942, his shortest voyage. (These are the dates in the referenced Beattie diary, but it is more likely the year he signed on was 1941.)

Next day in Hull, Beattie joined the *Empire Tide* (6329 tonnes, built in 1941). She was a brand new CAM (Catapult Armed Merchantman) ship equipped with a Hurricane fighter plane that launched itself from a catapult on the bow. There was no way for the aircraft to land again on the ship, so the pilot had to find land or ditch in the ocean near a ship in hopes of being picked up. The ship's Hurricane was launched once, on their second trip to Murmansk. The plane was lost, but they picked up the pilot.

Empire Tide had everything: two transmitters, two receivers, an auto alarm direction finder, a complete radiotelegraph system and a radar system. This radar was the first set installed on a merchant ship and the first Beattie had ever seen. Fortunately, it came with a navy technician to operate it. The ship was designed to accommodate a convoy commodore and his staff who would have command of the convoy. They were responsible for setting the course, zigzag patterns and evasive actions using their own signallers for the Aldis lamp and the flag halyards. A musician noted that her whistle blew in F-sharp.

The convoy formed and had an uneventful voyage to Halifax and back to Birkenhead on the Mersey. Conditions for the merchant mariners were getting better. Escorts were more plentiful, and the convoys were guarded all the way across the North Atlantic and back.

For Beattie, then came a run through the Arctic to Murmansk that remains seared in the memory of those merchant sailors and Navy seamen who participated. There was some argument to postpone the convoy until the autumn or winter, but political considerations overruled caution.

The convoy departed Reykjavik, Iceland, on June 27, 1942. Convoy PQ-17 consisted of 35 cargo ships, six destroyers and 15 other armed vessels. It carried tanks, plane parts, ambulances and food from Britain and the USA to Russia. It suffered the heaviest losses of any Russia-bound convoy.

German reconnaissance aircraft sighted Convoy PQ-17 on July 1, and starting the next day torpedo bombers attacked repeatedly. Late on July 4, the convoy was ordered to disperse because the German battleship *Tirpitz* was believed to be closing (actually, she was not). The merchantmen were slaughtered. Combined air and submarine attacks cost the Allies 24 merchant ships, one rescue ship, 450 tanks, 200 fighter planes, 300 Army vehicles and one hundred thousand tonnes of war supplies; more than £450 million worth (at present-day values), all at the bottom of the Barents Sea. Enough to equip a whole army! *Empire Tide* was one of the few to make it through, and she distinguished herself by rescuing many survivors from other ships that were sunk. Her master, Captain Frank Willis Harvey, received the Distinguished Service Order for his rescue of so many survivors.

On the northern route, losses to German aircraft and U-boats had been increasing. In May, PQ-16 had lost seven ships, but PQ-17 was the largest and most valuable convoy to date with military equipment valued at more than $700 million. The Germans were prompted to reinforce their efforts to break the convoy route to Archangelsk and Murmansk and began Operation *Rösselsprung*, meaning "Knight's Move," the assembling of naval surface forces to achieve this objective.

Convoy PQ-17's 35 merchant ships and escorts assembled at Hvalfjordur, Iceland, and were bound for Murmansk. *Empire Tide* sailed from the Mersey up the west coast of Scotland to rendezvous with PQ-17 southeast of Iceland. The close escort, sailing from Scapa Flow, was the First Escort Group (EG-1) under Commander Jack Broome. It included four destroyers, 10 corvettes and two anti-aircraft auxiliaries. In a more distant covering role was the First Cruiser Squadron (CS-1) under Rear Admiral Hamilton, with four cruisers and four destroyers. As additional protection, Home Fleet battleships HMS *Duke of York* and USS *Washington*, two cruisers, eight destroyers and the aircraft carrier HMS *Victorious* tracked the convoy at about 300 kilometres' distance until it was past North Cape. The route took the convoy close to Svalbard, north of Bjørnøya, and skirted the edge of the ice pack before turning south and following the coast of Novaya Zemlya before turning southwest across the Barents Sea and entering the White Sea, turning almost due south.

U-456 sighted and tracked the convoy shortly after it entered the open sea. Luftwaffe BV 138s soon joined the U-boat. The German airfields all along the Norwegian coast put the convoy within one hour's flying time, within easy bombing range. German torpedo-bombers began their attacks at daybreak of July 2. Every ship went into a pre-arranged zigzag pattern, and anti-aircraft fire kept the enemy planes high. Every man who was not on watch was on the guns or loading magazines. It started getting dark about 5:00 PM, and every sailor prepared for a long, long night of submarine attacks.

The first losses did not come until July 4, when two steamships, *Christopher Newport* and *William Hooper*, were lost. For four days and four nights, planes by day and subs by night battered the convoy. By the time the convoy reached North Cape it was in shambles. Only 16 ships were still afloat. For self-preservation, *Empire Tide* led three American ships into the small Moller Bay southwest of Spitzbergen. Two more ships followed them in and anchored near a bombed-out Norwegian weather station.

On the night of July 4, the Admiralty received intelligence that German capital ships *Tirpitz*, *Admiral Scheer* and *Admiral Hipper* with some destroyers had left Trondheim to intercept the convoy. First Sea Lord Sir Dudley Pound, after agonizing for several hours, eventually made the fateful decision to scatter the convoy, reasoning that *Tirpitz*, with its high speed and 38-centimetre guns, was capable of inflicting massive losses on closely bunched merchant ships travelling in convoy. *Tirpitz* and her escorts were not in fact heading for the convoy—their movement that day was merely a change of berth. Two days later they steamed out to attack the convoy. From his damaged ship the commodore ordered the convoy's ships to scatter and make for the icefields as the U-boats did not venture into ice.

So convoy PQ-17, its hopes rising, to the sound of depth charges exploding and the thud-thud of anti-aircraft guns, continued on its way. The convoy had now left behind the treacherous drift ice and dangerous seas of the Denmark Straits and was entering the strange, becalmed summer world of the Arctic Ocean, with its mirages, its refractory images of upside-down ships upon a calm iridescent sea, in a rarefied, almost intoxicating atmosphere in which the sun at midnight burned sailor's faces in spite of an air temperature well below zero. Ships began to pass majestic icebergs, and crews saw polar bears basking themselves upon ice floes, which sailed silently by like giant water lilies.

In Moller Bay the next morning, a Russian seaplane landed, and its pilot held a conference with the sea captains from a few ships that had sought refuge in the bay. They were instructed to assemble their ships and proceed on a given course. The Russians promised to provide air cover and send two destroyers to meet them. The American captains were sceptical, but there seemed to be no better choice. The *Empire Tide* had 260 survivors on board, mostly Americans, and they were running out of food. The *Tide* led the way back to sea in poor visibility and heavy snow. They never saw any air cover, but the two destroyers met them about 30 kilometres out and escorted the group to Polyarnye Zori, a town some 224 kilometres south of Murmansk.

The German naval force, including *Tirpitz*, *Admiral Scheer* and *Admiral Hipper*, was ordered to sea on July 6, but following reports of the successes of the Luftwaffe and U-boats it was soon ordered back to port. Meanwhile, the majority of the convoy's escorts returned to Scapa Flow, leaving only the anti-aircraft auxiliary and a few armed trawlers. The scattered merchant ships were easy prey for U-boats and aircraft. Twelve vessels were lost. The Luftwaffe sunk six, and four U-boats sunk the remaining six.

On July 6 two more ships were sunk. The Luftwaffe sunk SS *Pan Atlantic*, and *U-255* sunk SS *John Witherspoon*. On July 7–8 five more ships were sunk—two by *U-255*. The remaining escort vessels withdrew into the Arctic Ocean on July 9, but the merchant ships suffered no more losses that day. The last to be lost were SS *Hoosier* and SS *El Capitan* on July 10. The Luftwaffe had flown 202 sorties against the convoy.

Two surviving ships made port at Archangelsk on July 10. Another nine arrived there or at Murmansk over the following week. Tom Bigmore of Sheffield, England, was the leading seaman radar in charge of the radar set on the SS *Empire Tide*. Later he recalled:

> *"We were the convoy dispersed by the Admiralty in the mistaken belief that the German battleship Tirpitz was at sea intent on destroying our convoy. In the event, of course, out of nearly 40 merchant ships that left Iceland we were one of four merchant ships that survived the journey to Archangel and back. I regard myself at the age of 90 as one of the lucky ones."*

In the demise of convoy PQ-17, 129,000 tonnes of shipping were sunk and 153 merchantmen perished. Material losses included 3350 motor vehicles, 430 tanks and around 85,000 tonnes of other cargo.

The night that the *Empire Tide* landed in Russia, Beattie and the second engineer, ashore at the British Club, proceeeded to get drunk on rum and vodka. It was a release of pent-up tension. Two of their stokers had already cracked and tried to jump overboard. They were put in irons and locked in the infirmary. Both officers woke up the next day, absolutely convinced that drinking was not a good idea. Except for the occasional social drink, that was the end of Beattie's approach to alcoholism.

Two of the surviving ships, SS *Silver Sword* and SS *Bellingham* were sunk on the return journey, convoy QP-14, which departed Archangel on September 13, 1942 and arrived in Loch Ewe on September 26. One of them became the fifth victim of *U-255*. Convoy QP-14 consisted of 15 ships, including eleven that had survived the outward-bound PQ-17. The other four had been left there previously awaiting a return convoy. Since Russia had nothing to export, all the ships had no cargo except ballast. Joining them were the two rescue ships, *Zamalek* and *Rathlin*, and a fleet oil tanker, *Gray Ranger*. The weather into which they steamed was typical for that time of the year, thick fog patches and heavy snow squalls, and it was bitterly cold again.

Later in the day, the weather started to freshen up. By nightfall, there was a heavy sea running. The wind began to howl in the rigging, and soon a fierce gale engulfed the scattered ships. The *Empire Tide*, proceeding at only five knots, dipped, rolled and plunged into the heavy seas. Spray and, at times, snow swept her decks. This gale really stirred up the convoy and lasted for two days and nights, before abating to a more normal kind of blow. The following day the winds dropped away almost completely, and the sea gradually flattened itself out, with blue skies and the sun overhead. The few ships remaining of the convoy and escort gathered themselves again and made all speed towards Loch Ewe, where they finally dropped anchors in those glassy-looking waters on September 26, 1942. It had been three months since they had left that port.

Despite Soviet protests, the sailing of the next outward-bound convoy to Russia, Convoy PQ-18, had been postponed until September 1942. Although the convoy had more than 50 escorts, 16 ships were sunk. All future convoys were suspended until the darkness of winter. PQ-19/JW-51 sailed in December.

The British ships left Convoy QP-14 north of the Shetlands, headed down through the Hebrides and sailed up the Clyde to Glasgow. Beattie took a week's leave to visit his hometown then returned to the depot at Glasgow to sign on with a tanker crew. His new ship left for the western ocean, down the eastern seaboard of North America to the Caribbean. After loading 14,000 tonnes of high-octane fuel she sailed north. At the assembly point east of Halifax she joined 20 other tankers for the 8000-kilometre trip to the UK. A USN destroyer, USS *Lea*, led the escort force of four Canadian corvettes.

They had no sooner tied up in Grenock when the depot superintendant boarded to assign the two radio officers to another ship departing within hours. She was the Norwegian freighter *Nordeflinge*. En route to join a convoy she had been strafed. Her chief officer, senior radio officer and his second had been wounded and needed to be replaced. Beattie and his comrade had no option and were packed into a waiting car to go to Ardnossan, 30 kilometres away. On the dock waited the captain and the shipping master. Articles were signed, and the lines were cast off. *Nordeflinge* sailed westbound. Beattie got a pleasant surprise when the captain informed him that their destination was Three Rivers (Trois Rivières) in Canada.

After an uneventful crossing, Beattie had six days' leave and took the train to Montréal and Belleville, stopping just long enough to telephone Kathleen. They had a glorious week together before Beattie returned to his loaded ship. The crew sailed down the St. Lawrence into the Gulf and joined a convoy at Sydney for a pleasant trip back to England. On reporting to the depot he learned that he was to be sent to Iceland to be the radio officer in a replacement crew for the fleet oiler *Cowrie*, stationed in Hvalfjord, 64 kilometres northwest of Reykjavic. This 7436-tonne tanker was used to oil (refuel) escorts at sea. That was no big deal in calm water, but in the Arctic, in a blizzard, with winches, cables and flotation equipment frozen, it was a formidable task.

For the refueling, two ships positioned themselves a half kilometre apart, and the oiler floated a line to the receiving ship. The line, with a hose attached, was winched aboard. Steam pipes running through the hose heated the oil and kept it liquified. Otherwise, in Arctic temperatures, the oil became practically solid. The speeds of the ships had to be synchronized, and it fell to the radio officer to maintain communications with an Aldis lamp while crouched in the lee of the bridge. In heavy weather, with both ships plunging and rolling, maintaining slack in the hose was difficult. A broken hose pumped tonnes of oil into the sea before the flow was stopped.

The replacement sailors left Liverpool in comfort aboard a Norwegian liner. In Reykjavic they were transferred to a destroyer where the shivering men huddled on the lee side of the deck for the 60-kilometre trip to Hvalfjord. The country was bleak, with mountains of black volcanic rock all around from sea to sky. Also based in the fjord were a large British maintenance ship and two American tugs. Ships awaiting a convoy often joined them in the anchorage. The oiler's crew was constantly on watch, and her engine room always kept steam up so they could quickly put to sea. It also kept their cargo of oil heated.

One black December night, during a westerly gale, the *Cowrie* was ordered to proceed at top speed to a rendezvous about 150 kilometres off the island's east coast. For 10 long hours they bucked and rolled with the gale at their back. At the meeting place, they saw nothing except a distant light flashing the message "Well done!" Navy ships had been watching their approach on radar. Soon a massive battleship and two destroyers hove into view. The *Duke of York* took 1088 tonnes, and each destroyer took 180 tonnes. They left at full speed, and the oiler fought its way back to its nest.

On Christmas Day 1943, *Scharnhorst* and several destroyers put to sea to attack a convoy northwest of Norway. Fortunately, the British decoded their orders and sent a superior force to intercept. Royal Navy cruisers *Belfast*, *Norfolk* and *Sheffield* effectively kept *Scharnhorst* away from the convoy until reinforcements arrived. Realizing the futility of their mission, the German ships attempted to return to their base, but the British battleship *Duke of York* and her escorting cruisers and destroyers cut off the *Scharnhorst*. In a three-hour battle in the frigid Arctic seas, the Allied naval forces battered the German battleship with gunfire and sank it with torpedoes. Only 36 survived of her crew of some 1968 men. The captain of the *Cowrie* broke out the rum to celebrate. They had done their job!

Late in 1943, Beattie and his crew went with an eastbound convoy around the north of Scotland to the North Sea port of Middlesboro where they were paid off. Beattie discovered that the Canadian service was taking experienced radio officers so he transferred. Passage to Canada was provided on the *Mauritania*.

Beattie decided five years' wait was long enough— he and Kathleen should be married. His trip across the ocean was novel in that *Mauritania* sailed in a straight line at 25 knots. Her fast speed was thought enough protection from U-boats' torpedoes. Beattie took his usual trip by train from Halifax to Montréal and Belleville. Kathleen was waiting at the station.

December 21, 1943, dawned bright but cold. Beattie ploughed thorough a snowbank to get to the back door of Holloway United Church in Belleville. His heart swelled when the organist began playing and the lovely Kathleen paraded down the aisle. Beattie had made reservations at the grand King Edward Hotel in Toronto for their three-day honeymoon. On New Year's Day, he packed up again and on January 2, 1944, he travelled to Montréal to learn that he was assigned to the *Metwata Park* as her chief radio officer. The ship was one of the Victory Class, new to the Canadian Transport Company Limited, and not yet in service.

For the sixth time, Beattie went on a gunnery course while he waited for a ship to get her finishing touches. On completion, he collected a pass, food vouchers and train tickets to Vancouver. The *Metwata* was in the Burrard yards in North Vancouver. Each day he had to report on board to check the progress of the radio station installation. Most afternoons he and his two junior officers went sightseeing and strolling in Stanley Park. Finally, the day for the ship's final trials arrived. They left the Ballentines pier with a list of a hundred and one things to check. Compasses needed calibration. Boilers, engines and steering gear all had to function flawlessly. Beattie had to test all of the radio equipment, transmitters and receivers and direction finders. The ship did speed trials up and down Howe Sound. Government inspectors checked communications equipment and sealed it because it was not to be used until the ship was at sea. The secret codes were only delivered when the ship was ready to sail.

At 32 years of age, Beattie had already lived one lifetime at sea. Next morning the crewmembers signed off at the Manning Pool and signed on their brand new ship. Stores were loaded, fuel and water taken on, and a partial cargo loaded. On February 1, under command of Captain Russell Jones, they took *Metwata Park* to sea on her maiden voyage. En route to San Francisco they encountered the edge of a hurricane that Beattie remembered as being the worst storm he ever encountered. Both the ship and her new hands weathered the conditions well.

Their first port of call was Auckland, New Zealand, then Darwin, Australia, a war zone that was swarming with U.S. soldiers. Heading east, back across the Pacific to Vancouver, they arrived on May 31, 1944. After a week in port it was down the west coast, through the Panama Canal to Halifax and across the Atlantic to Liverpool. Although the Royal Canadian Navy had become a considerable deterrent to prowling German U-boats, the North Atlantic was still very dangerous water. The merchant navy had withstood the worst of enemy attacks and suffered tremendous losses in ships and men, but they had kept the lifeline to Britain and all of Europe open.

After a good crossing, *Metwata Park* sailed into the Mersey, up Manchester Canal and tied up at the Salford docks in Manchester. Beattie promptly took off for Scotland with his kitbag full of smuggled goodies. Customs presented no real problem. During the next four days, Beattie saw all his family then returned to the *Park*. They loaded machinery for a paper mill in Powell River, BC then joined a convoy in Liverpool. It went west around the northern tip of Ireland, then south to the Caicos Islands. Their cargo from here was a load of salt destined for Tacoma, Washington. Navigating the Panama Canal was interesting. They entered it from the Atlantic and traveled 80 kilometres to the Pacific, only to emerge from the canal 19 kilometres further east than where they had started.

After Tacoma and Powell River, they tied up in Vancouver where they stayed a month for needed maintenance. Beattie had written Kathleen from the Canal Zone to advise her of the layover and encourage her to travel out by train. They had three wonderful weeks before the ship had to be moved to New Westminster. It was also the day Kathleen was to go home. As the *Park* left the pier, Beattie looked back to see her standing at the end of the dock, watching and waving.

With the exception of the bos'n and the carpenter, the deck crew was all new. In the engine room most of the engineers had been replaced. The new crew had seen no action, and none had much sea time. However, the chief steward, cook and the five DEMS gunners had returned.

They took on cargo at Port Alberni. Then it was back through the Panama Canal to the United Kingdom. Their route was through the dangerous English Channel to Plymouth, Portsmouth and up the Thames to London. In the Caribbean, they joined a convoy made up mostly of tankers loaded with high-octane and bunker fuels. The *Park*'s load of explosives made it a volatile mix. During the deathwatch hours of an early morning off the east coast of North America, a terrific explosion shattered the calm. The tanker two ships ahead of the *Park* had been torpedoed and split in two. Then the one directly ahead, loaded with high octane fuel, just seemed to disappear, and the ocean was on fire. With the conflagration licking up the ship's sides, *Park*'s speed was increased to the maximum. Again, it was sailing through the horror of a fiery sea, debris and burning bodies. Again, its crew was helpless to assist seamen struggling in waves and fire.

It was a tough initiation for the younger seamen. Even the experienced sailors never forgot the sights, sounds and smells of that day. The convoy lost three ships, and the escorts claimed two kills.

They met an eastbound convoy south of Newfoundland and enjoyed trouble-free days until they entered the Irish Sea. There, the convoy split as ships headed for their destination ports. The *Metwata Park* and two others were bound for the Channel. On a lovely spring morning, the ship rounded Lands End and headed for Plymouth. After three days in this town, steeped in English maritime history, they left for Portsmouth, a premier base for the Royal Navy. The next morning, just before dawn, they followed navy minesweepers out into the Channel. Overhead an armada of aircraft towing paratrooper gliders en route to the Rhine area provided an umbrella. Entering the mouth of the Thames, the radio room received a message to heave to and wait for another ship to leave their intended dock. As the other ship passed, air-raid sirens began to wail. The deck crew heard the motor of a V-2 rocket. The German missile blew up *Metwata Park*'s intended dock. Ordered to another dock, the ship tied up and its crew debarked to visit the city and celebrate their close shave with death.

London, even in wartime, was a great place to be. Andy Beattie met his brother, Allan, on leave from the army in Normandy, and the two enjoyed a reunion and nice steak dinner that Andy enjoyed, even after Allan told him it was horsemeat.

Metwata Park had a load of tanks on her deck when they set sail for Normandy. They unloaded at the manmade mulberry piers off the French coast and took on ballast to go to Falmouth. They joined a convoy destined for the Panama Canal via the Caribbean. It was the first time Beattie sailed past the south coast of Ireland. Previous wartime convoys always headed north around the island.

In the lower Caribbean, the convoy split up, with each vessel going off on its own. *Metwata Park* cleared Panama Canal and headed south for Lima, Peru. Down the west coast of South America they went to

Coquimbo, Chile, then headed north for Vancouver. Somewhere off the coast of Ecuador came the news that the war in Europe had ended. All submarines were ordered to surface, head for an Allied port and surrender. Early one morning a U-boat, sailing under a surrender flag towards San Francisco, cut across the *Park*'s bow and dipped its flag in salute. Captain Jones responded with a couple of blasts of the steam whistle. For both crews, the war was over.

On February 2, 1946, in Vancouver, Andy Beattie's seagoing days ended. He signed off his last ship and off the Manning Pool. He collected his salary and headed home. Beattie arrived in Belleville on Valentine's Day, February 14. After a few false starts, he took a job with Canadian Tire, and he and Kathleen moved to Toronto. After five and a half years aboard ship, it took some time for him to adjust to living ashore.

Their daughter, Heather, was born on February 5, 1947, in the Women's Hospital, Toronto. Merchant seamen did not collect veterans' benefits, resettlement benefits, housing assistance under the Veterans' Land Act, education nor job-seeking support. In short, the Canadian government and veterans' groups did not even consider them veterans. In spite of this, Beattie never wanted for employment. Because of his experience in electronics, he often worked for electric services. Eventually, he and a friend started their own business in Toronto installing water heaters for Ontario Hydro.

Their family grew. Heather became a teacher, married and produced two daughters. Andy and Kathleen also had three sons. George, born in 1950, drives tractor-trailers, is married and has two sons. Graham, born in 1952, is married and has a daughter and a son. He has his own electrical business. Allan was born in 1958, is a technician for business machines, married and has one son.

Andrew Petrie Beattie died in his 93rd year on January 24, 2005. He was an active member of Scarborough's Highland Creek branch of the Royal Canadian Legion and the League of Merchant Mariner Veterans of Canada. He and Kathleen had been married 61 years.

CHAPTER FOURTEEN

Frigates

THE TERM "FRIGATE" WAS LOST from the lexicon of the Royal Canadian Navy until 1941. At that time, corvettes were being used for mid-ocean convoy escort, a role for which they were not designed. The corvettes' flaws became obvious with the first trials at sea. To get a better ocean escort vessel, shipyards built an improved corvette. It had an extended forecastle, improved bridge and heavier armament. However, the RCN was anxiously waiting for a newly designed and revised patrol vessel. Naval engineer William Reed designed it to have two engines and twin screws and to be 30 metres longer than the corvette. Admiral Percy Nelles, chief of the Naval Staff, dubbed these new ships "frigates."

The fleet of River Class frigates proposed in 1941 was the Canadian navy's replacement for the corvette as mid-ocean escorts. The frigate was faster, more comfortable and better armed than the corvette. It could sail 12,000 kilometres at a speed of 12 knots. Its range was thus twice that of a Flower Class corvette.

As frigates were too large to sail down from the Great Lakes, Canadian WWII frigate contracts were given to shipyards in BC and along the deeper waters

HMCS *Chebogue*, March 17, 1944, after commissioning

of the St. Lawrence. Sixty Canadian-built frigates were ordered for the RCN starting in 1943. The RCN received 10 additional frigates built in Great Britain and originally destined for the Royal Navy. Unfortunately, frigates took one full year to complete. Only in spring 1944 did the first Canadian-built frigates join the RCN. Meanwhile, Britain offered 10 River Class frigates to the RCN. Frigates were used mostly to escort convoys and became the most valuable warships ever built in Canada for anti-submarine warfare.

One of the first Canadian-built RCN frigates, HMCS *Chebogue*, named for a river near Yarmouth, Nova Scotia, had a brief but exciting RCN career of only seven months. She was a River Class frigate built at the Yarrows Limited dockyards of Esquimault, British Columbia. Her keel was laid on March 19, 1943, and she was launched on August 17 with the pennant K-317. She was commissioned on February 22, 1944. Following her workups and trials in Nanoose Bay on the east coast of Vancouver Island, she turned to Vancouver on March 6, ready for full duties. Her first commander was Lieutenant Commander Thomas McDuff.

Typical of a River Class frigate, *Chebogue* displaced 1310 tonnes. She was 92 metres long and had a beam of 11 metres. Powered with reciprocating steam engines, she had twin screws that drove her as fast as 19 knots. At 12 knots, her endurance was 12,000 kilometres. She had a four-inch gun forward and a two-pounder aft. For close range, she had four 20-millimetre Oerlikons. She had four depth-charge throwers and a 24-tube hedgehog with 200 bombs. The hedgehog was an anti-submarine weapon mounted on convoy-escort warships to supplement the depth charge. The weapon fired a number of small spigot mortar bombs from spiked fittings. Rather than having a time or depth fuse, as depth charges had, the mortar bombs exploded on contact and had a higher sinking rate against submarines than depth charges. The hedgehog device received its name because when unloaded, its rows of empty spigots resembled the spines of a hedgehog.

Chebogue was assigned to convoy duty in the North Atlantic, and she left for Halifax on March 2, 1944. In the engine room, deep in her belly, she carried Able Bodied Seaman Stoker Ed Slater. Slater turned 18 years old in December 1940 and joined the navy in June 1941, directly after finishing most of grade 12 at Vancouver Technical High School. His basic training was at HMCS *Discovery*, the old yacht club in Vancouver. Mostly, the recruits were taught to march in step around Stanley Park. After six weeks of training there and at Esquimault, Slater elected to be trained as a stoker and went to Comox, BC, for six weeks' engine room training. In Comox he learned how to operate and clean ship boilers. He was also introduced to the intricacies of reciprocating and turbine engines. On graduation the navy sent him back to Esquimault to a holding unit.

A memorable event in any sailor's life occurred when he was marched to the supply building to be "kitted out." Each recruit was issued two of everything, which went with the old saying "One on and one in the wash": black boots, two pairs; thick navy blue woollen socks, two pairs; white underpants and shirts, two sets; one woollen navy blue jersey; two white shirts; two serge uniforms; two black caps and one white cap, sailors, for the use of; a cylindrical metal box in which two of the caps were stored; two blue collars on which were three white, narrow tapes, origin unknown; two large, black, silk squares, to be made into scarves as mourning for Nelson; one lanyard to be worn if ever allowed liberty; two boiler suits, known as overalls; one woollen, navy blue jersey; one navy belt with a pouch pocket; and one long, black, oilskin coat.

Then followed the ancillaries: one ditty box made of white wood which, under penalties of severe displeasure, had to always remain in that condition; a housewife (a package containing necessities for the repair of service clothing: needles, wool, a piece of beeswax, some essential buttons and a block of wooden type comprising carved wooden letters on a holder, making the name and initials of the owner); two white cotton towels; two brushes for boots and one for clothes. Then last of all, each sailor was issued with a kit bag, into which he stuffed the whole issue. How the supply assistant gauged the sizes was something of a miracle. Added to the issue were two black cap ribbons, emblazoned with the name HMCS *Discovery* (to be changed accordingly whenever he was assigned to a new ship). These ribbons were tied around two of the three caps. In the summer, the white cap was worn, and the two black caps were stowed in the metal hatbox.

Slater and his buddies were sent to Royal Roads on guard duty, which mostly meant raking leaves and more marching. He recalled one instance of real guard duty—on December 7, 1941, after the bombing of Pearl Harbour. He and others were armed with Lee Enfield rifles and ordered to patrol a BC beach. However, they were provided with no ammunition. In mid-January 1942, his whole draft of recruits arrived in Halifax. Still they were not assigned to any ship and instead put in two weeks shovelling snow.

One morning on parade, the petty officer called for volunteers for a special job. Slater had not yet learned to volunteer for nothing. Hoping to go to a ship, he stepped forward. With great excitement the volunteers were loaded aboard a train for New York City. Sent to the Brooklyn Navy Yard, they were herded aboard the Royal Navy cruiser HMS *Phoebe*. The ship was in for repair, and the Canadians were soon put to work. Months later, when *Phoebe* sailed for the United Kingdom, the Canadians went with her. When at sea, the name of the game was "Exercises." The stokers' particular part in the Engine Room Department was to learn to combat flooding and fire, known as damage control. Being on a training voyage, as expected, exercises were frequent, both day and night. On watch in the boiler room, tending to sprayers and learning various pipe systems was not too bad, but at damage control stations, the sailors had to hop about a bit, shoring up pretend damaged bulkheads and fighting imaginary fires. When the practices included the assumption that the lighting had failed and they had to be carried out in darkness, they were a different kettle of fish!

On arrival in Britain, the Canadians were sent to the Canadian land base in Scotland, a converted mental hospital renamed HMCS *Niobe*.

Command shunted the Canadians from *Niobe* to Londonderry, Ireland, where, in groups of four, they found places aboard Royal Navy sloops for more engine room training. Being a trainee stoker, one of Slater's shipboard duties at sea was in the boiler room, tending sprayers that sprayed hot oil into a furnace. The hot oil immediately burned. The pumping in of air, under pressure, ensured complete combustion so that the boilers did not smoke. The furnace cones, through which the oil was sprayed, collected a ring of carbon, and one of Slater's jobs was to prevent the ring from growing. Using a long metal rod with a chisel end, Slater scraped the ring. Mirrors allowed the watch keeper to see into the boiler uptakes and see if any light from outside was visible. If the watch keeper could not see any light coming down the uptake, smoke was being generated. Smoke had to be avoided at all costs for a couple of reasons. Firstly, smoke meant fuel was being incompletely burned. Secondly, any enemy forces nearby would see the smoke and use it to locate the ship. Slater learned why overalls were worn over thin work clothes, not over a uniform: the heat in the boiler room was intense. There was no hope of sitting while on watch. At time, the four-hour work shifts seemed endless.

One evening an RN petty officer confronted Slater with the question: "You're a stoker, aren't you?" Receiving an affirmative reply, the petty officer said, "You are needed on an RN ship at once!" "You can't send me," naively replied Slater. "I'm Canadian!" Within hours, he was at sea aboard the RN destroyer HMS *Venomous*, bound for Iceland to escort a convoy on the Murmansk run. For the next three days Slater was so seasick that he didn't care where he was, he only wanted to be on firm land. *Venomous* developed boiler problems and had to return to Londonderry. The RN sailor Slater had been replacing was out of hospital and went back to duty.

Clearly, Slater could not be left ashore. He was drafted to a RN Hunt Class destroyer, HMS *Zetland*, which was escorting convoys to and from North America. On September 4, 1942, it escorted RMS

Queen Elizabeth to England with a load of U.S. troops. On October 28, *Zetland* sailed with a load of troops for the invasion of North Africa. *Zetland* arrived at Algiers on November 8 and was the second Allied ship to enter the harbour. She debarked her soldiers and began patrolling the North African coast. That same day, *Zetland* fired on the Vichy French fort at Cape Matifu, putting its guns out of action. Nearby HMS *Broke* was landing infantrymen under fire in Algiers. Vichy French artillery damaged *Broke*, which withdrew after landing her troops. *Zetland* took *Broke* under tow, but the enemy artillery hit *Broke* again and again. *Broke* collided with her rescuer, then sank. *Zetland* successfully saved her crew.

On January 30, 1943, the Italian submarine *Platino* torpedoed and sank HMS *Samphire,* a Flower Class corvette off Bougie, Algiers. *Zetland* sped to the scene and rescued the crew. Damage from her collision with *Broke* and from an air attack required *Zetland* to head for Plymouth for repairs. Navy Headquarters ordered Slater back to HMCS *Niobe.* Imagine his dismay when Canadian comrades took him to be RN because of his acquired British accent and lack of "Canada" shoulder flashes. He was sent to Chatham for further stoker training, qualifying him for the rank of petty officer, and then sent to Canada on leave. In January 1944, he joined the crew of the soon-to-be-commissioned HMCS *Chebogue*, one of the first Canadian-built RCN frigates.

Knowing *Chebogue* was nearing the end of her workups and trials and would be going to sea soon,

Slater proposed to and married Betty (Parkes), on March 4, 1944 in St. James Church, Victoria. His ship then went to Vancouver to undergo degaussing (demagnetizing). Betty also went there, but on a Princess ship. She was somewhat dismayed to see that *Chebogue* had women on board. Slater had neglected to tell her that the ship would be transporting the cast of the Navy Show. Slater sailed for the Panama Canal on March 10. After a five-day wait in Colon, she cruised through the Canal.

Chebogue cleared the Panama Canal on April 2, escorted an aircraft carrier, HMS *Ruler,* to Norfolk, Virginia and arrived in Halifax on April 12, 1944. She was assigned to the Escort Group C-1 of the Mid-Ocean Escort Force for convoy duty between St. John's and Londonderry. But first the ship had to be fitted out in Halifax as a senior officer's ship, with additional accommodation for an escort group commander and his staff. On May 21, it went to Bermuda for three weeks of continuous exercises to bring her and her crew up to operational readiness.

The new Canadian frigate, now battle ready, cleared Bermuda on June 10. En route to her station in St. John's, she stopped at Yarmouth, Nova Scotia. Yarmouth had grown to include the village of Chebogue, the ship's namesake. Petty Officer Ed Slater was proud to be at attention with the ship's company lining *Chebogue*'s deck as she sailed, flags and bunting flying, into the harbour. For four days, the ship's crew enjoyed the hospitality of the town, then it was time for the ship to go to work. She sailed around the tip of

Nova Scotia and headed north, and on June 23 entered the narrow gut of St. John's harbour.

Convoy HXF-296 (Halifax-to-Britain Fast) began its voyage on June 19, 1944, in New York City. Ploughing north, it passed Halifax on June 21, when 18 ships sailed out of Bedford Basin and joined the convoy. The next day five ships joined from Sydney and then one more came from St. John's with the escort group C-1. Leading the group was Slater's ship HMCS *Chebogue*. She was followed by another frigate, HMCS *New Glasgow*, carrying the senior navy officer, and the corvettes HMC Ships *Orangeville, Fredericton, Giffard, Halifax* and *Chambly*. They were herding 91 merchantmen. The convoy commodore, F. Ratsey, RN was in S.S. *Mataroa* and the vice commodore, J. J. E. Barclay, RNR, was in *Waterland*. They encountered no U-boats, and the crossing was completely uneventful. With the exception of two ships that turned back due to engine problems, the entire convoy arrived safely in Liverpool on July 3.

Their return passage was just as uneventful. Escort group C-1 took convoy ONF-244 (Outbound Fast) to sea from Liverpool on July 10. Eight days later, they arrived at St. John's. After each crossing and before entering harbour, *Chebogue*'s hedgehog was fired and the bombs replaced with new ones. Once fired, the ship was supposed to veer off to one side so as not to be above the projectiles should they happen to hit something and explode. Before entering St. John's on July 18, *Chebogue* fired her hedgehog. The ship did not change its course, and unfortunately, it was in shallower water than expected. When the hedgehog bombs struck the ocean floor and exploded, the ship was directly over the point of explosion. The explosions lifted and severely shook the ship. Many of her riveted plates loosened. *Chebogue* went into a floating dry dock for the necessary repairs, but the metalworkers could not tighten all the plates. From then on, the ship leaked in heavy seas. In the engine room mess there was often five to eight centimetres of water. The sound of its swishing across the deck kept many a sailor from a good night's sleep.

During this time in St. John's, Lieutenant-Commander Maurice F. Oliver, RCNR, took command. *Chebogue* became the senior ship of the Escort Group, and the senior officer, Commander George S. Hall, RCNR, moved from the *New Glasgow* to new quarters in *Chebogue*. A new face in the engine room was Engine Artificer (Fifth Class) Frank J. Murphy.

Murphy was born in June 1924 in Canmore, Alberta, but the following year his family moved to Leduc, about 30 kilometres south of Edmonton. In September 1939, he started high school at St. Joseph's in Edmonton. Although he had never even seen the ocean or a ship, in March 1943, he joined the Royal Canadian Navy as a second-class stoker. He took his basic training at HMCS *Nonsuch* in Edmonton and then went on a five-month-long electrical artificer's course at the University of Alberta. His next posting was to a five-month-long machine shop course in Windsor, Ontario. Three months' torpedo training in Halifax followed. The navy promoted him to fifth class electrical artificer, for which he earned $2.25 a day. After a short time in the Halifax dockyard's electrical workshop, the navy ordered him aboard the new frigate HMCS *Chebogue*. In July 1944, a ferryboat carried Murphy to St. John's to join his ship, which was finishing repairs after the hedgehog incident.

On July 31, 1944, *Chebogue*, the senior ship of Escort Group C-1, slid outbound through the narrow mouth of St. John's harbour to begin protecting Convoy HMX-301. The only change in the escort group was that the corvette *Frontenac* had replaced *Chambly*. HMX-301 was a huge convoy, consisting of 134 ships, 12 of which were USN LSTs (Landing Ship Tanks) carrying military equipment to Europe. Most of the ships left New York on July 25, with 17, including the rescue vessel *Dewsbury*, joining at Halifax and another 10 joining at Sydney. The convoy reached Oversay, off Liverpool, without incident on August 8.

This was the 15th voyage for *Dewsbury* as a convoy rescue ship. Also in HMX-301 was the Dutch ship *Curacao* (Captain Meynderts). On board the *Curacao* were several service wives, travelling as passengers to join their military husbands. *Curacao* began her voyage in Montreal. One of the wives was Rose Eldridge returning to England to join her RAF husband, Flight Lieutenant George R. Eldridge, who had been posted back to England.

After sailing, Rose Eldridge and other passengers on *Curacao* awoke to find ships as far as the eye could see in most directions. There was an aircraft carrier on their left with sailors playing hockey on the flight deck. They were close enough for the sailors to whoop, whistle and wave to the young women whenever they ventured out on deck.

As soon as *Chebogue* cleared the harbour, one of Frank Murphy's jobs was to lower the electro-log. This device was a brass pipe about 10 centimetres in diameter. It protruded about a metre out of the ship's hull. On the bottom was a small propeller. As the ship moved through the water, the propeller rotated and sent speed and distance-travelled information to the captain and the navigator. This data was important information for the officers navigating the ship. Despite his best efforts, Frank could not get the log out. It hit something solid and refused to go down through the ship's hull. There was nothing he, the navigating officer, the electrical officer and several other specialists could do to lower the log. They continued east without it. In Londonderry, a diver went down to determine the problem. He found that an overzealous welder during the repairs in St. John's had spotted the hole and welded a plate over it. Once removed, all was well again.

Slater and Murphy shared the most dangerous workplace aboard a ship at sea—the engine room. U-boat commanders aimed their torpedoes at the centre of their targets. The engine room was located in the centre of the ship far below the waterline. It was criss-crossed with steam pipes that could rupture from the force of a torpedo explosion. Climbing to safety after a torpedo hit was perilous. After a torpedo

hit, the stokers would have to climb steep metal ladders from the depths of the engine room, in total
darkness, with steam hissing and water swirling
around their feet. The ship would be listing and lurch-
ing. As the sea would force its way in behind the torpedo, the ship would be rapidly sinking. Not a cheery
prospect!

Chebogue's crew was quite efficient since their
"workups" in Bermuda in May. However, a Royal
Navy officer had replaced their first lieutenant. Bringing British discipline aboard, he made wholesale
changes, especially for battle station assignments. He
created problems constantly, and the crew became
more discontented each day. Approaching Londonderry, in the River Foyle, a tanker came alongside to
refuel the frigate. When finished, the crew refused to
disconnect the ships. Seventy-nine of the crew locked
themselves in the seamen's mess and refused to sail
until the first lieutenant was replaced. Of course, this
was a mutiny. The first lieutenant hightailed it to
headquarters in Londonderry, resulting in a visit by
the British commodore, who came out and gave the
crew a tongue-lashing. Resentment ran high, but the
Canadian crew went back to work. RN officers did
not realize that the discipline and routine of their
large ships did not work on the small, overcrowded
escort ships with their egalitarian crews.

As a form of punishment, *Chebogue* was taken
off Atlantic convoy duty and sent, on September 1
with a seven-day supply of food, to patrol duties in
the North Sea. They joined Force 32 in continuous

anti-submarine sweeps across the mouth of North Minches between Cape Wrath and the Butt of Lewis. This was a good spot for U-boats to wait for convoys to North Russia. *Chebogue* was at sea for 21 days. After the first week, food was rationed. By the end of the patrol, the crew was on emergency rations. Resentment towards the British and in particular, the Royal Navy, grew. The only excitement occurred when a covering aircraft reported a German U-boat on the surface on September 4. However, *Chebogue* made no contact.

About this time, Slater thought about his future and employment after the war, and decided that he would make the navy his career. To do this he, transferred from the RCNVR to the RCN.

Two days after the reported submarine sighting, *Chebogue* and *Orangeville*, with the carrier HMS *Implacable*, covered the convoys EN-31 and WN-30 from the Firth of Forth to Loch Ewe. After another 10 days patrol in the Minches, *Chebogue* rejoined Escort Force C-1 at Londonderry.

On September 30, she was westbound as the senior ship escorting 60 empty ships of Convoy ONS-33. The ONS series had been suspended because of the withdrawal of escort groups because of the invasion of Normandy. It started up again with ONS-33. As well as the *Chebogue*, Escort Force C-1 was composed of HMC Ships *Giffard*, *Frontenac*, *Orangeville*, *Arnprior* and *Chambly*. Escort groups EG-12, 15 and 31 reinforced the convoy for the first two days, providing a cover of

24 warships. These three escort groups left the convoy at 0400 hours on October 2.

A general withdrawal of U-boats from the North Atlantic to home waters had occurred in September 1944. This was partly because of the loss of French coastal bases the month before and partly because of the introduction of the *Schnorkel*. The German invention provided considerable success in the shallower waters of the English Channel, the Irish Sea and harbour approaches. Some boats, however, continued to stalk the convoy routes.

In the early morning hours of October 4, 1944, HMCS *Giffard* reported a radar contact, evaluated to be a surfaced submarine. *Arnprior* was ordered to join the search. No further contact was gained. At 1147 hours, *Chebogue* intercepted the signal of a submarine transmitting a message. She turned to investigate the signal. At 1225 hours, the masthead lookout spotted a surfaced submarine bearing 180 degrees at 12,000 yards. The U-boat altered course sharply and submerged. The senior officer ordered *Orangeville* to join the search. Little was accomplished. The presence of a large group of whales considerably hampered the search. *Chebogue* carried out two hedgehog attacks but with no results.

Cruising silently under the waves was *U-1227*. She was a type IXC/40 boat, in commission since December 8, 1943. The submarine was on her first patrol under the command of *Oberleutnant* Friedrich Altmeier. She had sailed from Lorient, France, just days before Allied ground forces overran the base. The boat had a surface speed of 29 knots and a submerged speed of 7.3 knots. She carried 22 torpedoes. She could launch four from her bow and two from her stern, simultaneously. She had a deck gun, 44 mines and a crew of 48 to 56 men.

Chebogue was the only "kill" credited to this U-boat. Twelve hours after the hunt started, the sub crew got a fix on *Chebogue*'s location. The sub's log revealed that at 2259 hours it fired one GNAT (German Naval Acoustic Torpedo) and immediately submerged. The Germans did not expect a hit because the frigate had her CAT (Counter-Acoustic Torpedo) gear out and because the German torpedoes were unreliable. However, over the circular saw sound the CAT gear was making, the German submariners heard explosions. An hour later, the submarine climbed to periscope depth. Altmeier saw that the escort had stopped and that they had indeed hit the frigate.

Joined by *Chambly* and *Frontenac*, *Chebogue* had continued the hunt until 1700 hours, when she gave it up and turned to return to the convoy, by then some 60 kilometres away. The crew relaxed, and Murphy went to the electrical workshop to write a letter to a young woman, Patricia MacDonald of Edmonton. He wanted it to be ready for posting as soon as they arrived in St. John's. At about 2057 hours, Frank finished his letter and was walking to the mailbox. At this time, *Chebogue*'s radar operator reported a contact bearing 290 degrees at 8000 metres. He evaluated the target as a surfaced submarine. *Chebogue* altered course to intercept and fired star shells, but nothing was seen. The "Action Stations" bell rang, and Slater and Murphy ran to their posts. Slater went to the forward four-inch gun and Murphy to the gyrocompass room amidships. Had they been on duty in the engine room, the torpedo would have killed them both.

Chebogue continued to alter course, following the radar contacts, in an effort to head the submarine off from the convoy. At 2130 hours, expecting an acoustic torpedo attack, she streamed her CAT gear. This towed device gave off noise to attract the torpedo away from the ship's propellers.

It was a still night, with almost no breeze and a full moon rising astern of the warship. Her captain was painfully aware of the visual target she presented. Star shells fired again, but nothing was seen again. The radar signal began to fade. Speed was reduced to 11 knots, but at 2302 hours, radar contact was lost.

Two minutes later, a muffled thunderous explosion assailed everyone's ears. According to the signals officer, Lieutenant Jack Benson, RCNVR, of Toronto, flying debris filled the air as high as the mast. The explosion killed two sailors immediately and wounded 15, with four dying of their wounds the next day. *Chebogue* was heavily damaged, her stern folded over onto itself. With a convulsive shudder, she began to rapidly settle at the stern. The chances of saving the ship appeared slight indeed, and the captain ordered the crew to emergency stations.

HMCS *Chebogue* after she was torpedoed by *U-1227*

On the bridge at the helm, was the ship's coxswain, Petty Officer James Cumming, RCNVR, of Toronto. His first thought when he heard the crash was that depth charges had fallen overboard and exploded beneath them. When the lights went out and the secondary lighting immediately came on, instinct told him they had a serious problem. He relayed the captain's order to "Stop Engines" to the engine room.

U-1227 torpedoed HMCS *Chebogue* on October 4, 1944 while she was escorting Convoy ONS-33. *Chebogue* was towed to harbour in Wales. Her short career was over.

Shaken but not physically injured, Slater helped wrap the seriously injured in blankets and placed them in the motor launch under the care of the sick bay attendant. The less injured were sent away in the ship's whaler. Then he returned to his post at the gun, vigilant for the U-boat to surface and try to finish off her victim. Damage control parties hurried to shore up interior bulkheads, which were not designed to withstand the enormous pressure of the ocean rushing to fill the ship.

Torpedomen Leading Seaman Peter Newlands, of Fort William (now Thunder Bay), and AB Walter Ayres, of Winnipeg, crawled through the wreckage of the stern to remove the primers to render the depth charges "safe" so they would not explode if the ship sank.

The explosion knocked out Murphy. He regained consciousness in pitch-black surroundings. Realizing the power was out, he tried to get to the main switchboard. Stepping out on the main deck, he was amazed to see so many lights on the surface of the ocean. For the ship's safety, no lights should have been showing on the upper deck. As comprehension returned, he learned that the lights were on the ship's lifeboats and Carley floats bobbing up and down. In the dark, a shipmate grabbed his arm just before he stepped into a huge hole in the deck. A piece of propeller shaft, weighing several tonnes, had blown about 50 metres and landed amidships. It went through the upper deck and the emergency diesel generating room and stopped on the bottom of the ship. It narrowly missed the gyro room where Frank had been, as well as the ammunition locker, diesel supply tanks and high-pressure boiler. Murphy arrived at his "abandon ship" station, only to find that the Carley float there had been cut loose and was far out at sea. He had no choice but to stay with the sinking ship.

The complete destruction of the electrical workshop where he had written his letter shocked Frank. Steel bulkheads were crumpled like newspaper. Steel deck plates were bent into unrecognizable form. The ship was an unbelievable mess of twisted wreckage. The stern was heaved up and bent over; the rear section of the quarterdeck was flung ahead and above, flat against the gun deck.

Chebogue's telegraphist radioed their distress call. An hour and 15 minutes later, out of the gloom, rode the shadowy form of *Giffard,* commanded by Lieutenant G.H. Matheson, RCNR, of Victoria. Its crew immediately did what they could to save lives. Husky, redheaded AB Kenneth Holloway, 19, of Brantford, and dapper Engine Room Artificer (ERA) Jules Yvon, 27, of Montréal, leaped fully clothed from the deck of HMCS *Giffard* into the ocean to rescue *Chebogue's* ERA Larry D. Smith, of Brantford. Smith was administered first aid and rallied briefly, but he died of his injuries several hours later. On March 26, 1945, Alfred Jules Yvon, A/ERA 4, RCNVR, was commended with a Mention in Dispatches.

For courage and initiative beyond the ordinary requirements of service, in diving overboard from a moving ship, with a line made fast to him, and rescuing a badly injured, helpless survivor from HMCS Chebogue.

Soon *Arnprior* too arrived at the sinking ship. *Giffard* signalled *Chambly* (commanded by Lieutenant Stephen D. Taylor, RCNR, of Duncan, BC) to carry out an anti-submarine search in the area of the "wreck." *Chebogue's* captain interrupted with the message: "We ain't no wreck!" *Chebogue's* injured were taken on board *Arnprior* from the whaler and the motorboat. With them went the senior officer of the Escort Group and all those not required for duty. Six officers and 37 men remained with their ship, hoping to keep her afloat. Both Slater and Murphy stayed.

Engine Room Artificer (ERA) William Fysh, RCNVR, came to Murphy and asked him to help free Chief Shipwright Harry Booth, RCN, and Cook Eric Long, RCNVR, trapped under some wreckage. Just as they began, another engine room artificer told Murphy they were ordered to go to the diesel room to try to provide emergency power, especially for communications. When they arrived, they found the flying piece of propeller shaft had severed fuel lines. The damage was too extensive to be repaired. They returned to the upper deck to find that the two sailors had been freed and that part of the ship was under water. Booth, only slightly hurt, stayed with *Chebogue* all the way to the United Kingdom and was commended for his work in securing the ship en route. Long, with a broken arm and other injuries, was taken aboard *Arnprior* and brought to Canada for treatment.

On deck, both Slater and Murphy were offered a "tot" of dark Jamaican rum. A keg of rum had been blown onto the upper deck and had developed a leak. One enterprising sailor, appalled at the thought of losing such good drink, retrieved an aluminium cooking pot and some ladles from the galley. Being stuck aboard a sinking ship seemed as good a reason as any to have some drinks. The rescue ships found some had had more than a few.

HMCS *Arnprior,* under the skilful manoeuvring of Lieutenant D. Thom, RCNVR, slid alongside close enough for survivors to jump. As well as improving morale, the rum also seems to have improved their jumping skill, for none missed. To do so meant certain death as the two ships rubbed together. Frank Murphy was one of the last to jump to safety. The rest chose to stay on board the sinking ship. *Arnprior* hurried to rejoin the convoy. Overhead, an RAF Liberator and a USAAF Flying Fortress provided air cover.

Ed Slater stayed aboard *Chebogue,* and that afternoon, *Chambly* took her in tow. Although *Chebogue*'s afterdeck was constantly awash, the two, under HMS *Primrose*'s protection, travelled at 7.5 knots. That evening, one more officer and 30 ratings, including Stoker Ed Slater, transferred to *Chambly*. Although most men took nothing with them, Slater grabbed his ditty bag containing toiletry essentials and a few spare clothes. He stayed on *Chambly* until she arrived in St. John's.

Ships of Escort Group 15 met the tow at 1930 hours on October 6, and HMS *Mounsley* took the damaged ship in tow. *Chambly, Giffard* and *Primrose* departed at 2100 hours. The weather held fair, and the tow proceeded without problems until 2210 hours the next night, when the eight-centimetre towing line snapped. The ships of EG-15 left, and *Chebogue* became the ward of HMC ships *Ribble* (another frigate) and *New Glasgow* and *Jonquiere* (corvettes). *Ribble* took the tow and maintained 5.5 knots. Fine weather continued. At 1730 hours on October 9, they met the ocean tug *Earner* and handed over the tow in calm seas.

The barometer began falling on the afternoon of October 10, and storm clouds gathered over them the next day. Even so, the remaining men on *Chebogue* began to relax. She had been towed some 1400 arduous kilometres without incident. At 1215 hours, they were abeam the Mumbles Light off Swansea Bay, in Wales. In the shallow waters of the bay *Chebogue* put out two anchors, and *Earner* dropped the tow in anticipation of the arrival of local tugs to take the injured warship into harbour.

In the early afternoon of October 10, the weather conditions deteriorated rapidly. Winds approaching gale force lashed the stricken frigate. By 1530 hours, squalls of hurricane intensity had whipped the sea into a foaming green monster. *Chebogue*'s stern began to drag over the sandy bottom. Weather damage forced *Earner* to stand off in deeper water. The Canadian survivors on *Chebogue*, according to their commanding officer "...were completely out of visual touch with the world, and feeling very lonely indeed." At 1900 hours the following evening, the flag officer in Cardiff ordered the crew to "abandon ship forthwith." The question was "To where?" Going overboard was completely out of the question, so the crew was forced to stay on board. For six hours, the ship drifted in blinding rain and sleet.

Suddenly, a searchlight played over *Chebogue*. The crew of the derelict ship saw a lifeboat on the crest of a wave beside them. The lifeboat was from the Royal Lifesaving Society station at Mumbles. Because of the foul weather and huge waves, the lifeboat could not anchor to windward and drop down to the vessel on their cable. Instead Coxswain William Gammon's only chance to rescue the crew was to go down sea and swing back into the storm, barge into the turbulent green waves and make a pass alongside to allow crew to jump onto his lifeboat. One moment the lifeboat was high above the warship's forecastle and the next below her waterline. The frigate's bow was swinging into wind, and Gammon could not keep the lifeboat alongside for more than a few moments at a time—only long enough for three or four men to jump. This courageous act was not done once but 12 times, allowing all 42 survivors to jump to the safety of the lifeboat.

Lieutenant Ian McPhee, RCNVR, of Toronto, stunned upon landing in the lifeboat, fell over the side. Lifeboat coxswain Gammon, already injured when a falling man hit him, reached into the boiling sea, grabbed McPhee and pulled him aboard to safety before he was crushed between the lifeboat and the frigate. A rating broke a leg leaping into the boat. With courage and skill the lifeboat's eight-man crew, which included four men more than 60 years of age (two older than 70), carried out this hazardous work. For his gallant actions, Coxswain Gammon received the Royal National Lifeboat Institution's gold medal for bravery. This rescue, according to many official sources, was the highest point of achievement during the long history of the Mumbles lifeboat station.

The storm drove the hapless *Chebogue* ashore. Next day, the fury of the storm abated, and the Canadians reboarded their badly wounded ship. The tide rose, and the stern floated off the sand bank. The bolstered bulkheads were holding. At 1400 hours, two tugs took *Chebogue* in tow. An hour and 15 minutes later, she was secured alongside Port Talbot Dock in County Glamorgan, Wales. The torpedo damage and the battering from the elements dictated that, for *Chebogue,* the war was over.

On September 21, 1945, *Chebogue* was towed up the Bristol Channel to Newport to be made ready for a transatlantic crossing under tow. Four days later, she was paid off from the Royal Canadian Navy. She was later sold to ship breakers.

Frank Murphy survived the *Chebogue* disaster. He was among those who jumped on board the HMCS *Arnprior.* The corvette proceeded at full speed to catch up to Convoy ONS-33. She was quite crowded, but her crew could not have been more generous with food, blankets and clothing. On the first night, Murphy slept on the deck in the seamen's quarters. He found this spot to be dangerous because, when the "Action Station" bells rang, men sleeping in the hammocks above leaped to the deck and ran to their respective stations. He found it safer to sleep under the table. Next night he found a safer, but not softer, place under a stairwell.

Five or six days later the ship arrived at St. John's, Newfoundland where ambulances and Red Cross workers met them dockside. St. John's was noted for its kind consideration of escort ships, and *Chebogue*'s survivors received a warm welcome. They were a grubby-looking lot with a week's growth of beard. They mostly had only the clothing they happened to have on their backs at the time of the torpedoing. The ambulances took them to HMCS *Avalon*, the shore establishment. They found housing in barracks, ate at the mess hall and went to clothing stores for new uniforms and kit.

Everyone was granted 56 days' leave—28 days annual and 28 days survivors' leave. After travelling to Halifax, each man scrambled for a train for home. With no berths available, Murphy spent four days and nights travelling to Edmonton, sitting on a wooden bench.

When the 56 days were over, Murphy went back to St. John's to do electrical repairs on ships sailing from

Newfoundland. In the summer of 1945, the navy placed him on the frigate HMCS *La Hulloise*, which was being refitted and loaded to join the war in the Pacific. Given a short embarkation leave, he was home in Edmonton in August 1945 when the USAAF dropped the atom bomb, ending the war with Japan. He still had to report to his ship, berthed in St. John, New Brunswick. On arrival, he applied for and was granted leave to return home to help with the harvest. Frank Murphy ended his navy career where he started—on the HMCS *Nonsuch* in Edmonton.

Murphy had injured his back in the torpedoing. There was no doctor on *Arnprior*, and he was too busy getting on with his life until recent years to ask for compensation. Finally he did and now receives a permanent disability pension from Veterans Affairs.

Petty Officer Ed Slater, another survivor of the *Chebogue* disaster, stayed with HMCS *Chambly* to St. John's. He was then flown to Halifax and then sent on annual and survivors' leave for 56 days in Vancouver. Thankfully, he spent Christmas with Betty and his family. In January 1945, Slater returned to the navy at HMCS *Scotian* in Halifax. From there he went to HMCS *Peregrine*, also in Halifax, the draft depot where processing for discharge of naval personnel was taking place at the cessation of the European War. He convinced Betty to join him in Halifax and settled into married life ashore. He began to develop a cough but simply attributed it to his smoking habit.

The end of April 1945, Slater was scheduled to go back to sea on a corvette. On a Friday, he had a chest x-ray as part of the routine medical examination. That Saturday, he and his mates took their wives to a dance in Bedford. On Monday morning, Slater was called to attend the medical officer. He was admitted to sick bay, and his draft to the ship was stopped. After a score of tests, he was diagnosed with pulmonary tuberculosis. He was hospitalized at HMCS *Stadacona*, the main east coast navy hospital. Slater was in hospital on VE-Day. Betty came to visit him, and they went for a walk in the city. Appalled at the celebrants' rioting and destruction and learning that martial law had been declared, they retreated to the hospital.

Three weeks later, Slater travelled by train to Vancouver and to treatment at a chest center. By August 1945, Slater was medically discharged for bilateral pneumothorax treatments. Every week he was subjected to a needle being poked into his collapsed lung. Their son, Michael, was born on December 9, 1945. Slater was still unable to work. In December 1945, he joined the Vancouver Tuberculous Servicemen's Branch of the Royal Canadian Legion. In February 1946, Slater qualified for low rental CMHC housing in the Fraser district of Vancouver. He and Betty lived there until 1953.

In 1946, he was elected to the Legion executive and about the same time began taking bookkeeping courses at the Western Business College. It was not until 1948 that he was cleared to work. The Department of Veterans Affairs sent him to apply for a job with a federal department as a clerk. However, as soon as he mentioned that he had tuberculosis, he was quickly ushered out the door. On May 18, 1948, second son, Kenny, was born. Slater finally landed a job typing for the Legion Tuberculous Association key tag program. Slater was granted a permanent disability pension for his tuberculosis from Veterans Affairs.

In March 1953, Slater was interviewed and selected to be the provincial command service officer for the Legion. His youngest son, Douglas, was born on March 1 of that year. Slater began earning $2400 a year, which was barely sufficient to raise three children. On February 1, 1960, Legion's Dominion Command in Ottawa hired Slater as a service officer to assist veterans with their applications and appeals to Veterans Affairs for disability pensions. He was appointed director of the Service Bureau in 1980, and he retired in 1988. With their children gone, Ed and Betty Slater left their Manotick, Ontario, home to retire in Penticton, BC. On April 24, 1995, Ed Slater died of pancreatic cancer and is buried on the hill overlooking the city and the lake.

~⊃C⊱

CHAPTER FIFTEEN

Battle for the Gulf

THE EUROPEAN WAR FORCEFULLY CAME TO Canada on July 6, 1942, when three ships from a convoy were torpedoed and sunk in the mouth of the St. Lawrence River. Two weeks later, another merchantman went down off Cap-de-la-Madeleine. The battle at sea was no longer a disembodied radio report from the mid-Atlantic. Now the Battle of the Atlantic was in plain sight of Canadian fishing ports along the north shore within a day's drive from Québec City. The U-boat threat became real to Canadians, who had not had enemy warships spewing death and destruction in inland waters since the War of 1812, when American warships roamed the Great Lakes. Suddenly, the Gulf of St. Lawrence was no longer relatively safe for international traffic. However, these were not the first ships to be lost in what came to be known as the Battle of the Gulf of St. Lawrence.

By 1942, *U-553*, a VIIC U-boat built in the Blohm & Voss yards in Hamburg in 1939, had prowled the Gulf of St. Lawrence and the St. Lawrence River. Its captain, *Kapitänleutnant* Karl Thurmann, commissioned *U-553* in December 1940 and had completed nine North Atlantic patrols before venturing into Canadian waters. The German navy's attention had been attracted to the east coast of North America, the Cabot Strait and the Strait of Belle Isle in their quest to decimate convoys carrying materiel to Britain. On May 11, 1942, crew 28, on the deck of *U-553*, enjoyed the spring sunshine. They were far enough off the northern Gaspé coast to be undetected by curious Canadian eyes. It was a special treat for the crew as they rarely surfaced during daylight hours.

Late in the afternoon, Thurmann submerged the boat to periscope depth and lay waiting 13 kilometres off Gaspé just north of Pointe-à-la-Frégate. Shortly before midnight, he was rewarded with the silhouette of a merchantman steaming northeast outbound towards the Gulf. Thurmann's crew had had considerable success on their previous North Atlantic patrols, so scrambling to attack positions was little more than routine. It took only one well-placed torpedo to destroy the 3000-tonne ship. Forty-one crewmembers and passengers of the SS *Nicoya* reached the shore, near the village of Cloridorme and the hamlet of Anse-à-Valleau. Six merchant seamen were lost.

In the early hours of May 12, less than three hours after the SS *Nicoya* went down, *U-553* claimed another ship. Loaded with airplane engines and other cargo, SS *Leto*, a Dutch ship chartered by the British Ministry of War Transport, was headed for England. She was torpedoed offshore of Rivière-la-Madeleine. Twelve died in the attack. The Dutch ship *Titus* recovered *Leto*'s survivors two hours later. Some were clinging to small rafts and wreckage because they had had time to launch only one small boat. Some of the crew waded ashore at Pointe-au-Père at daybreak. Among them was Wilhem Koëning, one of *Leto's* officers, who did not survive his wounds. He was laid to rest in the cemetery at Pointe-au-Père.

Thurmann's *U-553* made his way undetected from the gulf to the safety of open ocean. On August 24, Thurmann was awarded the Knight's Cross for this sinking. (*U-553* made her last radio transmission on January 20, 1943. She was never heard from again, lost with her entire crew of 47.)

Only days earlier, on May 1, the naval base at Gaspé, HMCS *Fort Ramsay,* opened with only one vessel—the *Venning*, an examination ship—in her port. Fear, anger and dismay fell on the heads of senior navy officers. On May 12, Canada's naval minister told Parliament that one ship had been torpedoed. However, he said that any future sinkings would not be announced. Navy reasoning was that German submarines were possibly lying somewhere under the waters of the St. Lawrence and could get valuable information from the news of sinkings.

Gaspesians, who knew that two ships had been sunk, found this meagre report less than satisfactory. They knew that the only RCN ships on anti-submarine duty in the St. Lawrence were one Bangor minesweeper and two Fairmiles. Residents along the Gaspé coast, the St. Lawrence River and the Gulf of St. Lawrence were terrified at the sight of maritime warfare off their shores, with ships on fire and explosions rattling their communities, while debris and bodies floated ashore. The Canadian government's wartime secrecy forbade media reports of St. Lawrence sinkings, so the only news was gossip.

The government took some measures to defend the gulf. Blackouts were strictly enforced. Army units were sent out on coastal patrols along roads and railway lines.

Eastern Air Command established anti-submarine patrols over the Gulf and began operations on May 11, the day the *Nicoya* went down. When news of the sinking of *Nicoya* reached them, the RCAF deployed Curtiss Kittyhawk fighters of No. 130 (Panther) Squadron to the air gunner-training base at Mont-Joli, Québec. Eventually, a squadron of Canso and Catalina aircraft, No. 117 (Bomber and Reconnaisance) Squadron, went to North Sydney, Nova Scotia. The squadron sent a detachment to Mont-Joli. No. 113 (Bomber and Reconnaisance) Squadron took their Hudson aircraft to Yarmouth, Nova Scotia, and by 1944 had made the majority of anti-submarine attacks in the Gulf. Before the end of the war, 13 other RCAF squadrons provided air cover over the St. Lawrence.

Summer 1942

Two months after Thurmann's exploits, *U-132*, commanded by *Kapitänleutnant* Ernst Vogelsang from Frankfurt, invaded the Gulf. In July, *U-132* sank three freighters and damaged another off the Gaspé coast. Each time she escaped attack by the corvette HMCS *Drummondville*.

Kapitänleutnant Vogelsang had been in command of the Type VIIC boat since its commissioning in Bremen on May 29, 1941. On July 6, *U-132* was silently submerged just off Cap Chat on the north coast of Gaspé. Laying quietly deep in the water her underwater sound detector operator reported an approaching convoy. Vogelsang began tracking this convoy when it was about 50 kilometres away. He had enough time to determine that there were at least 12 merchant ships escorted by at least one warship. Passive sonar wasn't able to determine the range of the target ships, but Vogelsang's operator was experienced enough to make an educated guess. *U-132* was equipped with the standard electric T-2 torpedo that had a range of 5000 metres. With all her own equipment turned off to prevent any interference, she quietly waited until the convoy passed overhead offshore Sainte-Anne-des-Monts.

Vogelsang peered through the periscope and took a range and bearing on the nearest ship. He passed the information to the torpedo control room. They fired torpedoes. The British-registered SS *Dinaric* was the first ship in Convoy QS-15 to sink. Vogelsang's second target, SS *Hainaut,* quickly followed. HMCS *Drummondville* turned back to search for the U-boat. But before *Drummondville* got to the scene, *U-132* fired a third torpedo, this one into the bowels of the Greek freighter SS *Anastassios Pateras.*

Drummondville was a new Bangor class minesweeper. She was launched on May 21, 1941, in the Canadian Vickers yards at Montréal. She was commissioned on

Rescued merchant sailors aboard HMCS *Arvida*, September 1942

October 30. Her first commanding officer, Lieutenant James Philip Fraser, RCNR, of Halifax was still the commander on the day of this action. Using her top speed of 16 knots she quickly arrived over the suspected position of *U-132*. On the run in, her crew of six officers and 77 sailors were brought to readiness at action stations. Once over the estimated position of the submerged vessel they carried out several depth charge runs. They got no hits, but *U-132* was forced to the bottom where she waited for 12 hours before Vogelsang considered it safe to slowly leave the area.

Once sure that their prey had escaped, *Drummond-ville* and her crew turned their attention to where the SS *Dinaric*, the worst case, was sinking. Barely keeping their heads above the cold, oily water were a number of her crew who had abandoned the sinking ship. *Drummondville* threw scramble-nets over the side and tossed lines to the desperate men. The Canadian warship saved 34 merchantmen from a watery grave. The *Dinaric* slid under the waves on July 9, three days after the sinking.

Meanwhile, No. 130 Squadron at Mont-Joli scrambled four of its Kittyhawk I fighters to join in the attack. At their maximum speed of 583 kilometres per hour, they quickly arrived over the suspected site. After a fruitless search of the area they turned their noses for home. But only three landed. The flight leader, Squadron Leader J.A.J. Chevrier, and his aircraft disappeared, and neither he nor any part of his aircraft have ever been found. He was the only operational casualty of the squadron during the whole war.

Two weeks later, on July 20, *U-132* rose to periscope depth west of Pointe-à-la-Frégate. She took a range and bearing on the British ship *Frederika Lensen* and torpedoed the merchantman. Ten seamen lost their lives, and the ship was so damaged that she was declared a total loss. (Four months later, on November 4, 1942, *U-132* radioed U-boat Tactical Command that she was attacking surface shipping off Cape Farewell, near Greenland. She was never heard from again and was presumed lost with all hands.)

After Vogelsang's attacks in July, navy officials halted traffic in the St. Lawrence and moved five more Bangor minesweepers from the Western Local Escort Force to HMCS *Fort Ramsay*. After a short break, Québec-Sydney convoys were inaugurated with the limited protection of the newly-strengthened Gaspé force.

In 1942, RCN officers estimated that as many as 20 U-boats were operating in the western Atlantic at any one time, with several being ordered to lurk and kill in the waters of the St. Lawrence.

The Strait of Belle Isle is a narrow exit from the Gulf between the tip of Newfoundland and the southeast coast of Labrador. The strait was an important route for ships going to northern Canadian air bases and to U.S. bases in Greenland and Iceland. In August and September 1942, *BdU* (U-boat tactical command) Admiral Dönitz dispatched three of his U-boats to pinch off this narrow bottleneck. The most notorious of the three were U-517 and U-165.

Kapitänleutnant Paul Hartwig commanded the IXC-type submarine *U-517*. Hartwig joined the U-boat force in July 1940. At age 26, on March 21, 1942, he commissioned the boat. He took it from Kiel on August 8, 1942, on its first patrol—to Canadian waters. Its crew (Number 35) admired their commander as much for his competency in handling his boat as for his reputed proficiency at drinking. He took *U-517* across the Atlantic and on August 26 reported being at the mouth of the Strait of Belle Isle. Dönitz insisted upon his U-boat commanders giving complete and timely reporting. These radio broadcasts sometimes aided the Allied anti-submarine effort.

Dönitz also sent *U-165* to the Strait of Belle Isle on September 1. This submarine was commissioned in Bremen on February 3, 1942, and *Korvettenkapitän* (the German rank equivalent to Commander) Eberhard Hoffman took it over. This IXC boat had a crew of 48 to 56 men. Hoffman spent the summer training his crew before sailing for the Gulf of St. Lawrence.

These two boats began a reign of terror in Canadian waters, singly and in tandem. By the time it left Canadian seas in late September, Hartwig's *U-517* had sunk eight merchant ships and one RCN corvette, HMCS *Charlottetown*. Hoffman's *U-165* claimed two merchantmen and the armed yacht HMCS *Raccoon*. The two were responsible for the greatest tonnage of shipping losses during the Battle of the Gulf.

At the campaign's start, Hartwig's submarine worked its way slowly south through the Strait. Hartwig sighted a Sydney–Greenland convoy, SG-6, in the early morning of August 27. U.S. Coast Guard cutters *Mohawk, Mojave* and *Algonquin* escorted this convoy. Closing with the convoy, Hartwig's U-517 fired two torpedoes at 0900 hours. One hit the U.S. Army troop transport ship, USS *Chatham*. *Chatham* was the first United States troopship destroyed during World War II and was carrying 562 passengers. Only 13 of the hundreds on board lost their lives. Some of them floated in the Gulf for a full day, but almost all survived thanks to the courageous rescue efforts of the U.S. Coast Guard cutters and a nearby RCN corvette, HMCS *Trail*. The corvette was escorting another small convoy, LN-6, travelling from Québec to Goose Bay, within sight of SG-6. *Trail* broke from her escort duties to pick oil-soaked sailors and soldiers from the icy waters.

As soon as he fired the torpedo at the troopship, Hartwig turned north to avoid the expected escorts' counterattacks.

One of *Chatham's* survivors was Alabama-born steward Thomas Cooper. After the sinking, he spent a day in an open lifeboat in sub-zero temperatures. In that time he did a lot of thinking about how many men escape when their ships go down in Arctic waters only to fall victim to the temperatures because they were not able to board a lifeboat. When lifeboats were lowered after a torpedoing, lifeboats on the ship's low side capsized immediately because the ship was already listing too far. On the high side, lifeboats fell back onto the deck. When a ship was going down by the bow or stern, lifeboats often were seen hanging from one davit after the falls slacked or snapped on the other davit, in which case the occupants were thrown into the water. Cooper devised a method to launch lifeboats that did not depend on gravity. His invention was slowly put into use on U.S. ships.

During the afternoon of August 27, Hoffman's *U-165* joined Hartwig's *U-517*. That day, near Belle Isle, they found Convoy SG-6 again, and both fired torpedoes. *U-165's* deadly fish hit SS *Laramie*.

At the time, the USCG cutter *Mohawk* was passing through an oil slick believed to have come from *Chatham's* sinking earlier that day. At 2133 hours, its crew heard a torpedo explosion and observed a faint white glow on the port bow of SS *Laramie*. A second explosion and another glow followed. A third explosion sounded one minute later. The *Laramie*, down at the head and listing to port, sent up two white rockets, and *Mohawk* headed in her direction.

USCG cutter *Algonquin* made a depth charge attack on the starboard quarter of the *Laramie*, but to no effect. *Algonquin's* captain decided that the safety of the *Laramie* took precedence over other actions. He reasoned that if the submarine had remained in the vicinity after sinking the *Chatham*, then it might remain in the area again and if the *Laramie* was left unescorted, the submarine might finish her off.

Mohawk made contact with *Laramie* at 2350 hours and learned that she had had an echo bearing 165 degrees true at a distance of 2000 metres. *Mohawk* ran down this bearing, without obtaining a sound contact, and dropped four depth charges from her stern racks in the best-estimated position. Embarrassingly, three of them failed to explode because they were set too deep for the depth of the water.

Although seriously damaged, *Laramie* was not mortally injured and, escorted by *Mohawk*, limped away. USN destroyer USS *Bristol* relieved *Mohawk* on August 29 off Cap Ray in Cabot Straits and escorted

Laramie to Sydney for repairs. The *Mohawk* herself proceeded to Sydney also.

Hartwig's *U-517* had fired a torpedo at about the same time as *U-165*. It too claimed a ship. The U.S. registered tanker SS *Arlyn* took nine sailors down with her. Their day's work done, both submarines left the area and sailed south well into the Gulf. Two days later, they were within sight of Anticosti Island's East Cape. There they struck again.

The setting sun, on the evening of September 2, turned the Gulf waters fiery red and lit up a north-bound convoy. Hartwig's U-boat shadowed it. At 1:30 the next morning, the outbound ships began passing an inbound convoy. With just the decks of his subma-rine awash, Hartwig moved closer. One of the escort-ing corvettes, HMCS *Weyburn*, saw the submarine's wake and then its dim silhouette. The warship's com-mander, A/Lieutenant Commander Tom M.W. Golby, RCNR, of Victoria, ordered rockets to be fired. In their illumination, *Weyburn*'s four-inch gun opened fire. Golby increased speed to ram. The wily Hartwig waited until *Weyburn* was within 1000 metres, then veered away and launched a torpedo past the corvette into the Canadian bulk carrier SS *Donald Stewart*.

With his ship on fire and drifting, the Canadian Steamship Lines captain ordered his entire crew to abandon ship. In due course, one of the *Donald Stew-art's* lifeboats came alongside escort HMCS *Trail*. A surprise reunion took place as one of *Trail's* seamen, Signaller Henry Vondette, helped the survivors aboard.

The first man on board, Gordie Kahl, came from his hometown of Pembroke, Ontario. Kahl and Vondette had been classmates in Pembroke Collegiate Institute less than a year before. Kahl had obtained employment with the Mcnamara Construction Company in the building of Goose Bay Airport. The construction of Goose Bay continued without his help—he and the other survivors were landed at Gaspé. In addition to construction workers, the *Donald Stewart* had been carrying aviation gas and bulk cement destined for the Goose Bay airport runways that USAAF was building. The loss of these vital construction materials set the operation back several months.

As Hartwig's U-boat dived, *Weyburn* closed on its position and dropped depth charges. Hartwig's luck held, and he escaped while a fuming Lieutenant-Commander Golby paced his bridge. *Weyburn*'s depth charge throwers jammed, and only two charges went into the water, hardly enough to threaten Hartwig's U-boat. The two charges roiled the water and caused the loss of ASDIC contact. Unable to re-establish contact, *Weyburn* turned away to assist survivors from the flaming *Donald Stewart*.

Hours later, Hoffman's *U-165* and Hartwig's *U-517* patrolled the Gaspé passage west where the St. Lawrence narrows to 50 kilometres in width. Eastern Air Command crews conducted seven attacks on the two submarines—one by a Douglas Digby (B 18) of No. 10 "the North Atlantic" Squadron and six by Hudsons of No. 113 Squadron.

Flying Officer J.H. Sanderson of No. 10 (BR) Squadron made the RCAF's first attack on a U-boat in the Gulf with his Digby aircraft. Swooping out of a misty sky, he brought his aircraft down to about 45 metres above the waves. Roaring over the diving submarines, Sanderson dropped his depth charges. Unfortunately, some went off prematurely, endangering the integrity of his aircraft, and some seemed not to go off at all. Yet *U-517* had a narrow escape when a depth charge lodged on the U-boat's deck. The charge was discovered the next time the U-boat surfaced. Hartwig, assisted by his engineering officer and two ratings, heaved the charge over the side. It then exploded, presumably at its pre-set depth.

James Harold Sanderson, who grew up in the sleepy Kent county town of Dresden, Ontario, received the Distinguished Flying Cross on January 16, 1945. The recommendation read that he had flown 2017 hours, of which 1190 were on operations (131 sorties):

This officer has had considerable service in anti-submarine operations in the North Atlantic area over a long period. During this time, he has made two attacks on enemy submarines, and after one of these attacks, he brought his aircraft safely back to base despite severe tailplane damage caused by a ricocheting depth charge. By his constant good humour and thoroughness under trying conditions, and his outstanding ability he has been an inspiration to his squadron.

It certainly was a blessed summer for Hartwig and Hoffmann. They worked their way up river and by

September 6 were within 400 kilometres of Québec City. They spotted QS-33, a convoy of eight merchantmen. Escorting the group was the corvette HMCS *Arrowhead,* the Bangor Class minesweeper HMCS *Truro* on her first mission, the armed yacht HMCS *Raccoon* commanded Lieutenant-Commander John Norman Smith, RCNR, and two wooden Fairmile launches, *Q 083* and *Q 085.* While commanding *Arrowhead* during the war, Lieutenant-Commander Edgar George Skinner, RCNR, was awarded the Distinguished Service Cross (DSC).

> *Lieutenant-Commander Skinner has displayed great devotion to duty and given invaluable service in connection with the escort of convoys during exceptionally severe winter months. This Officer, when left as senior officer of the escort, has consistently shown himself capable of carrying responsibility and by his exemplary conduct, initiative and resource, has set an example to others and thus improved the efficiency of those under his command.*

The night of September 6 was dark. U-boat commanders Hartwig and Hoffman had trouble seeing very far. Visibility was not more than one kilometre in haze, with a slight breeze and swell. Fog enveloped Convoy QS-33, as Hartwig's *U-517* jockeyed into position and fired—to no avail. All he did was attract the attention of *Arrowhead.* Hartwig's luck was diminishing, but his nerve certainly held strong. *Arrowhead's* depth charges gave the Germans a severe shaking and knocked out the lighting system. It appeared to the submariner that the corvette's ASDIC had locked on. This was the time

Fairmile *Q 084*

～◦❍◦～

to release his *Pillenwerfer*, a decoy that produced a cloud of bubbles giving the ASDIC a strong return. *Arrowhead* followed the *Pillenwerfer's* false trail, until it suddenly faded and quickly disappeared. Disappointed, Commander E.G. Skinner turned his corvette away to assist survivors from one of the convoy's ships. Hoffman's *U-165* meanwhile had been busy.

While *Arrowhead* was chasing the ghost of Hartwig's *U-517*, the convoy moved off Cap-Chat. The distraction of *U-517* helped Hoffman's *U-165* get into position. Shortly after 2210 hours, she sent the convoy's lead ship, a Greek merchantman, SS *Aeas*, quickly to the bottom, taking two of her crew with her. Twenty-nine sailors were rescued. *U-165* slipped easily away in the darkness. *Arrowhead* launched a star shell to help look for survivors, and lookouts clearly saw *Raccoon* zigzagging behind the convoy. Everyone assumed that she was in a search pattern.

HMCS *Raccoon*, before joining the RCN in June 1940, was the private yacht *Halonia* of millionaire jeweller R.A. Van Clief of New York City. At 1:12 AM, lookouts on several ships saw two large columns of water and heard two loud explosions. They assumed that *Raccoon* was dropping depth charges on a target. In the early morning, *Raccoon*, her 33 ratings and four officers were missing. She was never seen again, and it became clear that the explosions had been torpedoes spelling her doom. The body of Sub-Lieutenant Russ McConnell, a corner of the yacht's wooden bridge structure, some loose signal messages and a life preserver with the word *"Halonia"* still partly visible washed up several days later on Anticosti Island.

At 5:00 PM the next day, the now-smaller convoy was off Cap des Rosiers. Paul Hartwig had it in his sights and fired three torpedoes simultaneously, two from the bow tubes and one from the stern. Each of the homing torpedoes found its target. Two Greek-registered ships, *Mount Pindus* and *Mount Taygetus*, took only 15 minutes to go to the bottom. Two seamen perished in the first and five in the second ship. Hartwig's third torpedo hit the *Oakton*, owned by the Gulf and Lake Navigation Co. of Montréal. The full force of the blast hit the engine room where an oiler and two firemen were killed. The *Oakton*'s cargo of coal, destined for Corner Brook, Newfoundland, went down with her.

Fairmile *Q 083*, under Lieutenant Bill Grant, RCNVR, rescued *Oakton*'s 17 survivors and rescued 61 survivors from the Greek vessels. With the loss of half her merchant ships and one escort, QS-33 was Canada's least successful convoy operation and was a decided low point in the naval war. Escaping unscathed, both submarines remained in the vicinity.

Eastern Air Command sent a detachment of three Hudsons from No. 113 (BR) Squadron to Chatham, NB as a "Special Submarine Hunting Detachment" to protect the convoy routes in the St. Lawrence. They arrived on September 8, and the next day, Pilot Officer R.S. Keetley went out on patrol. Flying at 1200 metres, Keetley swooped down on what he at first thought was a sailboat. It was Hoffman's *U-165* serenely cruising on the surface about 30 kilometres south of Anticosti. On his second pass, Keetley dropped depth charges, but they hit the water eight seconds after the U-boat dived and caused no damage,

A week later, north of Cape Magdalen, Keetley used high-frequency direction-finding (H/F D/F) information to attack Hartwig's *U-517*. Although he caught the boat on the surface, his attack damaged the sub only minimally. Robert Stanley Keetley, from Moose Jaw, Saskatchewan, was mentioned in dispatches in November 1944:

> *This officer has completed many hundreds of operational flying hours over the North Atlantic area. He has*

taken part in attacks on two enemy submarines, both times pressing home his attacks with coolness, courage and skill. As pilot and captain of operational aircraft, his work at all times has been outstanding. His cheerfulness under all conditions, determination and devotion to duty has been an example to all.

Surviving Keetley's attack, Hartwig's *U-517* headed back towards Cap-Gaspé where he found convoy SQ-35. Its escorts, corvette HMCS *Charlottetown* and Bangor minesweeper HMCS *Clayoquot*, had left the convoy in waters thought to be too shallow for submarine operations and were en route to their base at *Fort Ramsay*. The weather was calm. While there was low-lying fog, the ships were clearly visible to curious onlookers on the shore. Without warning, *U-517*'s first strike hit the *Charlottetown* on the starboard quarter at 0800 hours. Seconds later, a second torpedo struck somewhat further forward. Horrified observers on land saw the ship go down stern first in only four minutes.

Charlottetown's captain, Lieutenant J. Willard Bonner, RCNR, of Halifax, had been with the corvette since her commissioning in Québec City. After the torpedoing, he went to the port side to try to free a lifeboat that had hung up because of the ship's extreme list to starboard. Realizing the futility of the task, he gave the order to abandon ship. Over the side went Telegraphist Gerald Martin, Able Bodied Seamen Joe Montgomery, Fred Rush and Ray MacAulay, and Stoker Bill McFadyen. Seaman John "Judy" Garland passed out lifejackets. He gave one to MacAulay, who had just gone on watch as helmsman, then darted below to save the ship's mascot, a dog named Screech. However, Screech had already been thrown overboard and survived the sinking. Garland was never seen again. Weeks later, crewmembers gave Screech to Garland's mother in St. John.

Also on the port side was Seaman Léon-Paul Fortin. He was on deck just above where the torpedo struck. Blown into the air, he somersaulted, and then fell back on the deck, breaking his arm and severely bruising one leg. He threw himself into the water. Fortin estimated that he was in the water for about three hours when a longboat neared. Twenty-nine people were already on it, and they told him to hold the side. Covered with oil and freezing, he said, "I'm at the end of my rope. If I can't get aboard, I'm just going to let go." Two uninjured friends changed places with him. Fortin was hauled on board and laid on the bottom. The group arrived ashore at 10:00 PM. Fortin was delivered to the nuns at the Hôpital de Gaspé. Unable to treat his mangled arm, the naval authorities at *Fort Ramsay* sent him to Halifax via HMCS *Arrowhead* to Sydney and train the rest of the way.

Charlottetown's first lieutenant, G.M. Moore, was the senior officer in the starboard lifeboat. He organized the survivors and collected Carley floats where he put the injured from the overcrowded boat. The captain's body floated against the boat, and they lashed him to the rudder. When they tried to row to shore, both the rudder and the body tore loose and floated away. Nine ratings and the captain were lost.

Seaman Fortin on shore leave

&8c&

Only one man, an engine room artificer, was immediately killed in the explosion, but many others suffered injuries. Six of the nine ratings died when the corvette's own depth charges exploded.

HMCS *Clayoquot* immediately began searching for the submarine and dropped depth charges. She stopped this when her crew realized the exploding charges could kill those in the water. *Clayoquot*'s commanding officer, Lieutenant H.E. Lade, RCNR, set about picking up the sailors, stunned and numbed by the cold water. Later, Henry Ernest Lade, of Brooklyn, Ontario, received a mention in dispatches, partly for his efforts in saving *Charlottetown's* survivors. The *Charlottetown's* yeoman of signals, James Wesley Vincent, RCNVR, from Toronto, was also mentioned in dispatches.

> *Throughout a total of 32 months service at sea during which period he was a survivor of HMCS* Charlottetown, *he has continually received excellent recommendations for good service and devotion to duty....*

The two submarines' reign of terror continued. The RCN and the RCAF harassed them, but, although bloodied, they were not defeated. On September 15, Convoy SQ-36 gave up two ships to Hartwig's *U-517*. The sub caught them off Cap des Rosiers. Within six minutes, it sent the Dutch *Saturnus* and the Norwegian *Inger Elizabeth* to the floor of the river. The loss from both ships was four sailors. Six navy ships, including the Royal Navy destroyer HMS *Salisbury*, counterattacked, but *U-517* sustained only minor damage.

Early next morning Hoffman's U-165 added two more to the score. Off Cap-Chat the Greek freighter SS *Joannis* and the British *Essex Lance* were on the receiving end of her warheads. *Joannis* sank, but all her crew got off the ship. Fairmile *Q 082* recovered SS *Joannis's* survivors and took them to Dalibaire. *Essex Lance* broke in two, but both pieces stayed afloat and were towed to Québec, where they were welded back together.

At the end of September, the two submarines left the Gulf of St. Lawrence. However, five more replaced them. Depth charges from an RAF Wellington aircraft from No. 311 (Czech) Squadron sunk Hoffman's *U-165* on September 27 in the Bay of Biscay, west of its home base, Lorient. All 51 hands were lost.

After reading the report of U-*517*'s Paul Hartwig, BdU Admiral Dönitz commented on the patrol: "Outstanding first patrol of a commander with a new boat." For displaying great nerve and skill Hartwig received the Knight's Cross, the highest class of the Iron Cross. Hartwig's *U-517* was sunk four days after leaving Lorient on her second patrol. A seaplane from the RN carrier *Victorious* caught her off Cape Ortegal and executed a successful attack. Paul Hartwig spent the time from November 1942 to the end of the war in Allied captivity. After the war, Hartwig joined the newly formed *Bundesmarine,* and during the 1970s, he rose to the rank of vice admiral.

On November 8, 1942, the Canadian army intercepted a coded message from a German submarine lurking in Baie des Chaleurs, New Brunswick. According to the message, the submarine was to meet a German spy and take him back to Europe. When the submariners realized that they had been discovered, they left the area, abandoning the spy. The spy, Werner Janowski, hid in an abandoned barn, then took a room in the New Carlisle hotel, managed by Mr. Earl Annett Jr. Annett saw that Janowski was paying his bills with large-sized bills such as were in circulation in Canada in the 1920s. Germany was not aware that the size of Canadian paper money had been reduced. Annett contacted the Québec provincial police, who informed the RCMP. The Mounties arrived too late. Janowski had had time to jump on a train. However, the police stopped the train in Bonaventure. The heavy bag Janowski had with him contained a radio transmitting station. He was arrested, and military authorities questioned him. Possibly he became a double agent in the service of the Allies.

U-boats continued to hunt in the St. Lawrence in 1942. *U-69*, commanded by *Kapitänleutnant* Ulrich Gräf, crept up the river to within 300 kilometres of Québec City. There, off Métis-sur-Mer, on October 9, it sank the Canadian bulk carrier SS *Carolus. Carolus* was in Convoy LH-9 heading for Goose Bay. She sank in only two minutes. Although the escorts searched widely and dropped depth charges, they did not find Gräf's submarine. The explosions awakened many villagers on both shores of the river. Eleven lives were lost in the sinking, including a 16-year-old boy, John Milmine, of Verdun, Québec, a galley boy sailing on his first ship. Robert Dowson, RCNVR, also of Verdun, survived. He was an RCN gunner and had volunteered to serve in Defensively Equipped Merchant Ships.

Two days later, *U-106* nosed through Cabot Strait. It was commanded by *Kapitänleutnant* Hermann Rasch (Knight's Cross), who died at the age of 60 in Hamburg in 1974. His U-boat crossed paths with Convoy BS-31, out of Corner Brook, Newfoundland. Within minutes, Rasch singled out the Newfoundland paper company

Bowood's pulp carrier SS *Waterton* and sent her to the bottom. Her entire crew survived. Her escort, the armed yacht HMCS *Vision* and aircraft from No. 117 Squadron, kept Rasch's *U-106* deep below the surface for eight hours. After three weeks, Rasch left the Gulf.

On October 14, 1942, Gräf's *U-69* was responsible for the worst inshore disaster of the Battle of the Gulf. The U-boat encountered the Newfoundland Railway ferry SS *Caribou* that day and sank it, causing frightful human loss.

Caribou was on its way from North Sydney to Port aux Basques, a 160-kilometre voyage. It was carrying 192 passengers, 45 crew and more than 1200 bags of mail. It also had 50 head of cattle in its holds. She was escorted by the Bangor class minesweeper HMCS *Grandemere*, under command of Lieutenant James Cuthbert, RCN, of Vancouver. The minesweeper had very few instruments to detect the presence of U-boats. The fact the ferry was travelling at night did not make the job of protecting her any easier.

The two ships left the North Sydney harbour and followed their proscribed zigzag course. At 3:00 AM, they were only about 40 kilometres from Port aux Basques. It was then that Gräf in *U-69* floating on the ocean surface sighted them. Gräf mistook the two ships for a destroyer and a freighter. He manoeuvered his boat into attack position and fired a torpedo.

The torpedo tore into the *Caribou*. Its warhead packed with high explosives tore a massive hole in her starboard side. Many passengers and crew were killed outright in the explosion. The lights immediately went out, and the vessel began to sink.

Terrified passengers and crew fought through dark passages to the deck. Two remaining lifeboats were quickly loaded and launched. However, the seacocks in the boats had been opened to allow the drainage of rainwater, so they started to fill with water. Alert crewmen in one boat discovered the source of the leak and quickly closed the seacock. The other lifeboat was so crowded that its occupants could not close the valve before the boat filled and turned over.

Meantime, the ferry began her final slide to the sea bottom. Those still onboard, many still without lifebelts, jumped into the water and attempted to swim to the life rafts, floats and debris that littered the area.

About five minutes after the torpedo struck the *Caribou* was gone. The escorting minesweeper quickly raced to the scene and attempted to ram the U-boat, still on the surface. Gräf ordered his boat to crash-dive, and the U-boat went under the waves. *Grandemere* quickly arrived above the U-boat and dropped a pattern of depth charges, apparently without success. *Grandmere*'s commander Cuthbert saw the survivors in the water, but he could not spare time to help them as he had been instructed to seek out and destroy the attacking submarine in cases like this.

Gräf knew the escort commander would hesitate to drop depth charges near the survivors floating in the water. So *U-69* slipped through the water and came to rest under them. Running silently, the U-boat later slunk away. It eventually made its way to the submarine pens at Lorient, France. (Four months later, Gräf and his *U-69* tried their luck again in the North Atlantic east of Newfoundland. The British destroyer HMS Fame met the U-boat there and sunk it with depth charges, killing all aboard.)

Grandemere searched for the *U-69* for several hours. As dawn was breaking, Cuthbert's *Grandemere* broke from the unsuccessful hunt and rushed to the assistance of the floating survivors. By then only 103 were still alive. After *Grandmere* rescued them, she was ordered to hurry back to North Sydney with the survivors as Port aux Basques had no hospital. Two of the survivors died from exposure before the ship arrived back at North Sydney.

Just hours after the sinking, fishermen from nearby Newfoundland communities set sail to search for survivors. However, at first, they were given incorrect information about the site of the disaster. Perhaps this was done on purpose to keep the small craft out of harm's way while *Grandemere* searched out the U-boat, or perhaps it was because of the chaos of the moment. Either way, by the time the local volunteers were on the correct site, there were only a handful of bodies to be found.

The loss of life in this disaster was 137 lives. Many of the dead were military personnel stationed in Newfoundland. One of the bodies recovered belonged to

Lieutenant Agnes Wightman Wilkie, the only Canadian nurse killed by enemy action in World War II.

After the ferryboat sinking, Admiral Dönitz pulled his submarines out of the St. Lawrence. The five boats that had followed Hartwig and Hoffman had sunk only five ships. A more aware RCN and RCAF had presented much opposition to them. The river's defences had improved enough to become a real deterrent. The U-boats waged war in other seas in 1943 and did not return again to the St. Lawrence until 1944.

On October 10, 1944, the *Schnorkel*-equipped *U-1223*, carrying GNAT homing torpedoes, nosed into the Gulf. The class IXC boat encountered HMCS *Magog* near the Pointe-des-Monts light. *Magog*, a River Class frigate, had her original commanding officer on the bridge, Lieutenant Lewis Dennis Quick, RCNR. Later he was mentioned in dispatches:

> *This officer has served for three and a half years in Escort Vessels engaged in the Battle of the Atlantic, frequently under trying and arduous conditions. By his zeal, industry and wholehearted devotion to duty, he has set a fine example to those serving under him.*

Lewis Dennis Quick was born in Devon, England in 1912. He went to sea at age 14 and received his master's papers at the age of 22. He was master of freighters in the Far East until World War II. He joined the RCN in 1940 and commanded corvettes and frigates. After the war, he made a career in the Canadian Hydrographic Service. He and his wife, Evelyn Fiendel

(Bridgewater), retired in 1971 in Yarmouth, Nova Scotia. Quick died on October 30, 2001, in the DVA Wing of Fishermen's Memorial Hospital, Lunenburg.

Quick's opponent this October night was 23-year-old *Oberleutenant Zur See* (senior lieutenant) Albert Kneip. Kneip took command of *U-1223* in March 1944 and was on his first patrol with her.

Magog and her sister frigate, HMCS *Toronto*, were part of Escort Group 16 (EG-16) and were on their way to join a Sydney–Québec City convoy. On the afternoon of October 14, they were eight kilometres offshore. Visibility was clear under a low overcast. At 1:25 PM, Kneip fired two GNAT torpedoes. The first tore 20 metres off the stern of *Magog*. The second also hit the stern and killed three crewmembers instantly. The frigate's damage control parties went into action. Shoring up the remnants of bulkheads they kept *Magog* afloat. Ships from EG-16 and a Catalina flying boat searched extensively, but Kneip's *U-1223* escaped to safety. *Toronto* took the stricken frigate in tow, and she eventually reached Québec City. The damage was so extensive that *Magog* was declared a total loss.

The last major confrontation in the Battle of the St. Lawrence came in the Cabot Strait (between Nova Scotia and Newfoundland) on the night of November 24–25, 1944. Since the loss of the *Caribou* two years earlier, the Sydney–Port aux Basques ferry *Burgeo* had always been escorted. This day a Canadian corvette, HMCS *Shawinigan* (Lieutenant W.J. Jones, RCNR, Commanding), and the USCG cutter *Sassafras* had the duty. After an uneventful crossing to Port aux Basques, *Shawinigan* left on an anti-submarine patrol. She was scheduled to rendezvous with *Burgeo* the following morning. She did not make the date.

When *Shawinigan* arrived at the meeting place, *U-1228*, under *Oberleutnant zur See* Friedrich-Wilhelm Marienfeld, was nearby, trying to repair a faulty *schnorkel*. In September, a Liberator from No. 224 Squadron had attacked and damaged the sub's *schnorkel*. This damage resulted in carbon dioxide poisoning of its crew. One man died. On the moonlit night of November 24, Marienfeld tested his repairs and found them ineffective. He decided to return to Germany. Then he sighted the *Shawinigan*. *U-1228* had not yet attacked any enemy shipping. Twenty-four-year-old Marienfeld smelled blood and let loose a GNAT torpedo. Four minutes later, HMCS *Shawinigan* disappeared in a plume of water and a shower of sparks. All 91 members of her crew were killed, the RCN's greatest loss in the Battle of the Gulf of St. Lawrence. Soon afterwards, winter ice formed in the Gulf, and the U-boats departed, never to return.

Marienfeld's *U-1228* surrendered at Portsmouth, New Hampshire, USA five months later, on May 17, 1945. She was scuttled on February 5, 1946, off the east coast of the United States. Marienfeld died on August 20, 1973, at age 53.

In September 1992, Governor-General Ramon Hnatyshyn approved the "Gulf of St. Lawrence" battle honour. This honour recognizes 29 corvettes,

29 minesweepers, 13 frigates and four armed yachts that served on patrols or as convoy escorts in the Gulf of St. Lawrence from Québec City to the Cabot Strait and the Strait of Belle Isle. Battle honours are only awarded to named ships. Thus, the battle honours do not go to the brave little Fairmiles, which were numbered craft.

CHAPTER SIXTEEN

Hank Vondette

Captain Henry William (Hank) Vondette
April 14, 1924–July 20, 2006

RENÉ VANDÉ (VANDET) WAS BORN in 1637 in the Poitou area of France. Marie Hariot, born in 1655, was also a native of France. They came to Canada while they were still quite young. They married on April 11, 1671, at Québec City. The name Vandé, or Vandet, gradually evolved into Vondette. They began a dynasty that eventually produced a boy named Henry William. Both Henry's great-grandfather and grandfather married Irish wives, Relehan and Scully respectively, in 1848 and 1879, at Mount Saint Patrick's Church in Renfrew, Ontario. His mother was a Fitzpatrick, and her mother was a Kelly. Their families came to Canada from Ireland around 1840. By the time Henry was born, in 1924, the family had settled in Pembroke, Ontario, 160 kilometres north of Ottawa on the Ottawa River opposite Allumette Island.

Young Henry Vondette was raised as a staunch Irish Catholic. He was baptized, confirmed and in regular attendance at St. Columbkille Roman Catholic Cathedral. He attended a separate school operated by the Roman Catholic Church and was taught by nuns.

They encouraged Henry's musical talent and enrolled him as a member of the boys' choir. After completing grade 10, Henry Vondette, now preferring the nickname "Hank," continued his education at Pembroke Collegiate Institute until he was 17 years old. While he enjoyed school and did very well, in 1941, he heeded his country's call to arms, joined the navy as an ordinary seaman and trained as a visual signaller. The teenager's duties became the transmission of visual signals, communications generally and the use of codes.

After completing new entry training, which involved little more than learning how to march, physical training and how to salute properly, Vondette went to the Signal School at St. Hyacinthe, Québec, to start signal training. St. Hyacinthe, situated 55 kilometres east of Montréal, was the Royal Canadian Navy's communications school during World War II. St. Hyacinthe was a busy, thriving naval establishment, and Vondette's course load was heavy. The skills of semaphore, flashing light, Morse telegraphy and typing were instilled into any young man determined to go to sea as a signaller. Coders spent many hours learning the secret ciphers and techniques required for wartime communications. In charge of visual instruction was Lieutenant J.C. O'Brien, known affectionately by all as "Scruffy" O'Brien. He later became commander of Maritime Command during the rocky integration years of the late 1960s.

Vondette was trained to read a message sent by semaphore flags at the rate of 24 words per minute.

As well, he had to learn Morse code, transmitted by flashing light, at a minimum speed of 14 words per minute. The students learned special naval abbreviated symbols and their meanings. They also learned the different flags of the Naval Code and International Code and their meanings. As well, signalmen had to learn the meanings of naval manoeuvering signals, especially important for visual communications while in convoy.

Their instructors were highly trained and knowledgeable. Many of them were pensioned chief yeomen of signals from the Royal Navy. The RCN did not have sufficient trained personnel to fill both shipboard positions and those in schools. After training to the level of a proficient navy signalman, Vondette went to the manning depot at Halifax. There, he was immediately assigned to HMCS *Trail* and sent to join her in Levis, Québec. HMCS *Trail* was a Flower Class corvette, commissioned in April 1941. Named for Canadian cities, towns and villages, the corvettes' crews formed bonds with the communities their ships were named after. *Trail* was assigned to sea duty, escorting convoys in the St. Lawrence and the Gulf of St. Lawrence.

Trail had a displacement of 950 tons. She was 62 metres long and 10 metres wide. She drew 3.5 metres of water, and her top speed was 16 knots. She was built by the Burrard Dry Dock Company in Vancouver and launched on October 17, 1940. Her weaponry was a four-inch gun forward, a "two-pounder" gun aft (which fired shells weighing a little less than a kilogram), two 20-millimetre Oerlikons, one on each side, depth charges and a hedgehog (capable of throwing anti-sub mortar bombs 80 metres from the ship). In addition to being a signalman, Vondette had an action station position—on the stern as a member of the hedgehog's loading crew.

Trail carried six officers and 79 ratings. Her captain was A/Lieutenant Commander G.S. Hall, RCNR. Hall was *Trail*'s first commanding officer, dominating the bridge from April 30, 1941, to October 8, 1943. One of her deck officers was Lieutenant James B. Lamb, RCNVR, of Toronto. Lamb became a successful author of naval tales after the war. He wrote *The Corvette Navy, On the Triangle Run* and many other well-received books on navy lore.

While the ship was at sea, lookouts on the bridge rotated in their duty, giving them a change of scenery and respite from the weather. On the other hand, signalmen stood their entire four-hour watch on the open bridge with the officer of the watch and often with the captain of the ship. Signalmen prided themselves on the fact they were the first to see anything. They read all signals to the ship and interpreted them to the officer of the watch and the captain. Although the captain and the officer of the watch were responsible for the actions they took, signalmen felt that they shared the responsibility and that they were an important part of the bridge team and were respected as such.

Trail was blessed with a nucleus of experienced seamen. They were endlessly teaching the raw recruits about anchors and cables, boat work, rigging and splicing, and more.

Trail sailed shortly after Vondette reported for duty. During her second year of service, the ship saw action on the night of September 3, 1942. Heavily laden SS *Donald Stewart* was ploughing north towards the Strait of Belle Isle. She was loaded with aviation gas, bulk cement and construction materials destined for the Canadian air base being built at Goose Bay. The USAAF decided the airport there would be a great staging base for its overseas flights. However, it had to improve and extend some runways and build other facilities. The merchantman was carrying needed materiel for this construction.

Just south of the Strait of Belle Isle, a torpedo tore through *Stewart's* hull just ahead of the engine room. The explosion killed three of the engine room crew and set the aviation fuel ablaze. The ship rapidly became a roaring inferno. Hartwig's notorious *U-517* had struck again.

A corvette, HMCS *Weyburn,* saw the submarine, turned and tried to ram it at full speed. On the run in, *Weyburn's* forward gun crew opened fire, but the U-boat dived. Running over the bubbles where they had last seen the boat, *Weyburn* dropped depth charges. The sub's commander, Paul Hartwig, was an officer with plenty of nerve and luck. The German vessel escaped *Weyburn's* attack.

HMCS *Trail* joined in the ensuing action. She dropped many depth charges but had no success. In due course, one of the *Donald Stewart*'s lifeboats came alongside *Trail*. From the lower railings on the stern, Vondette helped pull survivors aboard. The first man on board, Gordie Kahl, came from Hank's hometown of Pembroke, Ontario. The two had been classmates in grade school less than a year before. Kahl had obtained employment with the Mcnamara Construction Company in the building of Goose Bay Airport. Goose Bay continued without his help—he and the other survivors were shortly afterwards landed at Gaspé.

HMCS *TRAIL*

The Canadian government could not completely hide the Battle of the St. Lawrence from Canadians during the war. The government downplayed debate about the battle and censored most media reports of the sometimes deadly action on the country's own seacoast.

Hundreds of men, women and children in tiny French-speaking fishing villages on both shores witnessed Allied ships in flame at night and the sound of Allied ships exploding anytime. They saw *Kreigsmarine* sailors plying our inland waters and indiscriminately killing Canadians who had volunteered to defend our shores. Starting when a German submarine sunk its first ship in the St. Lawrence (the *Nicoya* on May 11–12, 1942), Canadians, especially those living on the Gaspé coast, questioned why the disasters were allowed to continue. The answers they received did little to assuage their cries. Only some of the convoys going to the United Kingdom went through the great St. Lawrence. In relation to the whole Battle of the Atlantic, the seaway was a minor theatre. The government of the day forbade the publication of any reports of action on its waters. It also seemed not to have any plan to defend the waterway.

Vondette later transferred to HMCS *Arrowhead*, which, under its captain, Lieutenant-Commander E.G. Skinner, RCNR, fought three actions in the St. Lawrence during 1942. *Arrowhead*, a Flower Class corvette, was named for a park north of Huntsville, Ontario. She was similar to *Trail* except that *Arrowhead* was two months older. She was launched in August 1940 at the Marine Industries Ltd. yard in Sorel, Québec.

Food aboard most ships was generally good. The sea air and a tot of rum every day at 1130 hours made a man eat, even if he was not hungry. Most Canadian stomachs got used to a breakfast of kippers, herring, red lead (a concoction of tomatoes) and bacon for breakfast. Skinner, however, very much enjoyed smoked kippers for breakfast, and when he had kippers, the whole crew had kippers. Many Canadians never ate kippers again.

In June 1942, Lieutenant-Commander Skinner was awarded the Distinguished Service Cross.

Lieutenant-Commander Skinner has displayed great devotion to duty and given invaluable service in

*connection with the escort of convoys during exception-
ally severe winter months. This officer, when left as
senior officer of the escort, has consistently shown himself capable of carrying responsibility and by his exem-
plary conduct, initiative and resource, has set an
example to others and thus improved the efficiency of
those under his command.*

On July 1, E.G. Skinner was promoted to the rank
of commander.

The first week of September 1942, *Arrowhead* was
the lead escort for the eight-ship convoy QS-33. The
convoy was enveloped in fog when night fell on the
September 6. The ships were sailing past Cap-Chat.

The convoy's sailors knew U-boats were in the
vicinity. A few days earlier, the escort HMCS *Raccoon*,
an armed yacht, had some tense moments near
Matane and Cap-Chat when her bridge lookouts spotted the wakes of two torpedoes perilously close to her
bow. Forewarned, she successfully avoided being hit.

Shortly after 10:00 PM on September 6, the lead
ship of convoy QS-33, SS *Aeas,* exploded in a shower
of cold, grey water and sparks. Hoffman's *U-165* had
attacked. *Arrowhead* turned back to pounce with
depth charges on the bubbles showing where the
U-boat had submerged.

Lead by the pulsing beam of its ASDIC, *Arrowhead*
inched closer and closer to the submarine when
Hartwig released an ingenious decoy. The corvette's
ASDIC picked up the false target, and *Arrowhead*
altered course to follow it. Other escorts joined the

chase of this contact, but suddenly the target faded and disappeared. With the loss of any ASDIC return, the escorts returned to the convoy.

Arrowhead went to assist the survivors of the torpedoed ship. At one point, *Arrowhead's* executive officer, Lieutenant Lester Alton Hickey, of Dartmouth, Nova Scotia, remarked that he saw HMCS *Raccoon* zigzagging behind them in the glow of star shells used to illuminate the scene. Everyone assumed the little yacht was searching for the submarine.

About midnight the rescue of survivors was complete. Officers on the senior ship noted that *Raccoon* was nowhere to be seen. She did not respond to Vondette's visual light signals. However, two heavy explosions were heard from considerable distance behind the convoy. Skinner sent one of the Fairmiles back to investigate, but *Raccoon* was never seen again. The only trace came several days later when the body of one of *Raccoon's* officers and some relics washed up on a beach on Anticosti Island.

A month later, on October 9, 1942, corvettes HMCS *Hepatica*, under Lieutenant Commander T. Gilmour, RCNR, and HMCS *Arrowhead*, under Commander E. G. Skinner, DSC, RCNR, were sailing 24 kilometres southwest of Rimouski. The two cooperated to pick up 19 survivors from the Canadian freighter *Carolus*. Gräf's *U-69* torpedoed and sunk *Carolus* near Bic Island. Five nights later, the same U-boat sank the Newfoundland ferry *Caribou* with the loss of 136 lives. She was the last loss of the 1942 shipping season.

The U-boats returned to Europe. Many of the escorts, including *Arrowhead*, were reassigned to North Atlantic duty out of St. John's.

Arrowhead arrived in St. John's, Newfoundland, and Vondette was transferred to HMCS *Trillium* in early March 1943. The corvette *Trillium*, Vondette's new ship, spent the entire war in one of the escort groups of the Mid-Ocean Escort Force, on the Newfoundland–Londonderry ("Newfie–Derry") run. She participated in three major convoy battles, SC-100 in September 1942, ON-166 in February 1943 and SC-121 in March 1943. Henry Vondette was *Trillium*'s visual signaller during the Convoy SC-121 battle. Twenty-six U-boats attacked this convoy of 59 ships. On average, the submarines outnumbered escort ships about two to one. Thirty ships were torpedoed in convoy, and eight more were torpedoed as stragglers. Twenty-one ships arrived safely.

Convoy SC-121 started from New York on February 23, 1943. Fifteen more merchant ships, including the rescue ship *Melrose Abbey*, joined the convoy from Halifax on February 25. HMC Ships *Trillium* and *Rosthern* shepherded the American tanker *L.V. Stanford* and the British *Empire Bunting* and *Empire Planet* from St. John's to join the convoy on March 1.

The Canadian warships joined the convoy's nine other escorts and took their positions in the Canadian-American A-3 Group. This group consisted of the USN destroyers *Babbitt* and *Greer*, USCG cutters *George M. Bibb*, *Ingham* and *Spencer* (carrying the

Senior Officer) and four corvettes, HM Ships *Campion,
Dianthus, Dauphin* and *Mallow.* The convoy commodore was Henry C. Birnie, RNR, sailing in the Norwegian *Bonneville,* and the vice commodore was Arthur
Cocks, RNR, aboard the British merchantman *Empire
Keats.* Bringing up the rear, on her sixth voyage, was
the rescue ship *Melrose Abbey.*

Continuous westerly gales dogged the convoy until
March 12, two days before it reached Liverpool.
Rough weather scattered the ships, and bad weather
reduced the efficiency of the escort's detecting devices.
At any one time, three H/F D/F sets were inoperative,
four radar units were defective, and three ASDIC
machines were not working. Radio communication
was also often unreliable.

The convoy took a northerly route past the south
coasts of Greenland and Iceland to take advantage of
airborne surveillance and in the mistaken belief that
they would avoid the main concentration of U-boats.

By March 6, the senior officer had significant intelligence that the convoy was headed into a concentration of U-boats. Throughout the day, he sent his fast
corvettes out chasing down H/F D/F contacts. Before
dark, the commodore ordered a sharp course change
in an effort to shake his pursuers. The first attack
came at 2345 hours when the USS *Spencer* sighted two
red flares. Without further information, no action
was taken and the sinking of the first convoy ship
went unnoticed in the gale. The British ship *Egyptian,*
from Lagos and New York to London, was the first

to go. *U-230* sunk this ship. *Egyptian* had a crew of 38 sailors and nine gunners. All the gunners and 35 crewmembers perished. HMCS *Rosthern* picked up the three survivors. *Empire Impala* lagged behind to pick up other survivors and, searching in vain, became a straggler herself. Just before dawn on the seventh, *U-591* sent the *Impala* to the bottom with her general cargo, including mail, and a crew of 48 men, including six gunners.

All day on March 7, the gale kept the submarines below the surface, and convoy SC-121 suffered no successful attacks. Early in the morning, a Flying Fortress on anti-submarine patrol sighted a U-boat on the surface. The aircraft dropped seven depth charges with no results. On March 8, the weather improved, and *U-527* scored two at once. *Fort Lamy* had become a straggler and paid the price. She was carrying general cargo and explosives in her hold and a tank landing craft on deck. From her crew of 43 and eight gunners, only three crew and two gunners made it into a lifeboat. HMS *Vervain* picked them up two weeks later.

Another straggler, the Russian *Vojvoda Putnik*, carrying about 7500 tonnes of wheat for London, was last heard radioing "S.O.S.—Abandoning Ship." *U-591* torpedoed this ship, killing her crew of 38 and six gunners. Two more merchantmen met their doom on March 8. The British ships *Guido*, carrying sugar and cotton from St. Kitts, and *Leadgate*, who joined from Halifax, fell prey to the sea wolves. *U-633* torpedoed the *Guido*. Of her crew of 37 and eight gunners, eight crew and two gunners died. USS *Spencer* recovered the 35 survivors. *Leadgate,* sunk by *U-642,* took all her hands, 26 crew and four gunners, and her 2500 tonnes of flour with her.

During the afternoon, two Liberators from No. 120 Squadron based at RAF Nutt's Corner in Northern Ireland sighted submarines near the convoy. Both dropped depth charges with no obvious effect. One of the Liberators made another sighting and attacked, but her depth charges hung up in the bomb bays.

On March 9, five more ships in convoy SC-121 were sunk. Commodore Birnie and his staff of seven went down with the *Bonneville,* a victim of *U-229.* Again, the U-boats claimed two ships. The landing craft *LCT 2341,* carried on deck, also was lost. Only seven crewmembers survived. *Melrose Abbey* rescued four from a capsized lifeboat and one found in a different boat. USCG *Bibb* saved two from the sea. *U-409* torpedoed the *Malantic,* with a cargo of 5500 tonnes of bombs and 4500 tonnes of ammunition, then sank the *Rosewood* and her load of fuel oil. Twenty-five of her complement of 47 died with the American *Malantic.* *Melrose Abbey* located a lifeboat with 11 men and brought 10, including the captain, aboard. The 11th man was swept away in the rough sea and drowned despite a *Melrose* officer diving into the water to assist him. A further search located a second boat with 10 more survivors. The boat capsized during recovery, and several occupants were trapped and died. The *Rosewood* lost her entire crew of 33 and nine gunners.

Bibb's gunfire scuttled her wreckage later in the day. Two other torpedoes narrowly missed HMCS *Rosthern*.

None of Swedish *Milos'* crew of 30 survived when *U-530* destroyed her. HMCS *Rosthern* got an ASDIC contact at 600 metres and carried out five attacks with 44 depth charges. After the attacks, a large oil slick with a piece of wood floating in its middle covered the target area. HMCS *Trillium* assisted *Rosthern* in the prosecution of these attacks.

The next day the weather deteriorated again. *U-229* was the only successful boat on March 10, claiming two merchantmen from convoy SC-121. The *Nailsea Court* had a complement of 37 crew, nine gunners and two passengers. She was carrying copper bars, nickel ore and asbestos. Thirty-four crewmembers, all the gunners and both passengers were lost. *Melrose Abbey* found a raft with two crewmen on it. They had been in it for eight hours. One was rescued, but the other was trapped in the raft and drowned.

U-229 then turned her attention to *Coulmore*, which she severely damaged to the extent that 25 of the ship's crew of 43 were killed.

On March 10, one of the Sunderland flying boats from No. 201 Squadron at Castle Archdale on Lough Erne, Northern Ireland, flew an anti-submarine sweep ahead of convoy SC-121. The aircraft crew's job was made more difficult, because the attackers and the foul weather had scattered the convoy's ships widely. About noon, the aircrew sighted a submarine, but it submerged too quickly for an attack to be carried out.

The remnants of convoy SC-121 limped into Liverpool on March 14. Thirty ships in convoy and eight stragglers had been torpedoed. The escort groups were too few, too small and too overworked to cope with the growing submarine threat. The convoy system seemed less and less secure as the wolf packs decimated convoy after convoy. Royal Navy officers, however, were quick to point out that the majority of ships lost were stragglers without escorts that were sunk outside the convoy. Still all agreed the number of escorts had to increase.

Trillium's coxswain, William Clifton Pickering, RCNR, of Toronto, earned the British Empire Medal in 1944. The commendation read:

> *This rating has served continuously at sea since October 1940, during which time his ship has been under air attack in the Western Approaches with loss of life, and has repeatedly engaged in anti-U-boat encounters whilst escorting convoys across the North Atlantic. By his faithful and cheerful performance of duty, as a leading seaman and coxswain, and by his outstanding skill and presence of mind as a helmsman in countless emergencies, and during the initial experiments in oiling at sea, this rating has been an inspiration to the whole ship's company.*

After rounding the northern tip of Ireland, the Canadian corvettes *Trillium* and *Rosthern* veered off to Londonderry. The Americans ran the repair facilities there, and they were excellent. As well, Canadians were welcome in Derry, especially in the pubs. Going ashore, sailors usually made their first stop at Cassidy's Bar, just across the street from the dockyard. Having just completed their first North Atlantic run, many young Canadians shared stories of danger and great adventure over booze in Cassidy's. *Trillium* was due for a scheduled refit and sailed to Boston to have the work done.

At the Davie Shipbuilding and Repairing Co. Ltd. in Lauzon, Québec, the River Class frigate HMCS *Sea Cliff* was launched on August 7, 1944. Her first and only commanding officer was an ex-stockbroker from Québec City, Lieutenant-Commander Eric Harrington, RCNVR. Hank Vondette, yeoman of signals, was among her first crew. The yeoman of signals was a signaller responsible for transmitting both visual and radio signals.

The new frigate was scheduled to join Close Escort Group C-3 but first had to complete her workups at the RCN training establishment in Bermuda. *Sea Cliff* began her operational service in December 1944.

Sea Cliff's first convoy escort duty was with the eastbound HX-327. The Canadian escorts with her were HMC Ships *Kokanee,* another River Class frigate, *St. Thomas,* a Castle Class corvette, and the Flower Class corvettes *Trillium, Riviere du Loup* and *Stellarton.* Castle Class corvettes differed from Flower Class corvettes in that they had 15 metres more length and were equipped with the forward-throwing Squid anti-submarine mortar. The Squid was directly connected to the ASDIC, giving a kill rate of up to 50 percent. Vondette's

Sea Cliff was the standard Flower Class frigate, with up to 200 depth charges and the original hedgehog controlled manually by the ASDIC team on the bridge.

Convoy HX-327 began in New York on December 19, 1944 and arrived in Liverpool on January 2, 1945. Escort Group C-3, including *Sea Cliff,* departed St. John's on December 23, with two ships to join the convoy. She accompanied the British ship *Caxton,* carrying newsprint, and the American ship *William S. Baer,* loaded with general cargo. All the ships celebrated a quiet Christmas at sea.

The first few days they experienced typical North Atlantic miserable weather. Then December 27 dawned cold, windy and rainy. About the same time *U-877*, a large type IXC/42 submarine commanded by 27-year-old *Kapitänleutnant* Eberhard Findeisen, left her patrol area west of Ireland to try her luck off North America.

On December 27, the westbound U-boat's radar warning gave an alarm, and she crash-dived. Escort ships' ASDIC reported contact with the sub but then lost it. HMCS *St. Thomas*, however, did not give up that easily. She regained contact and immediately fired one of her Squids. *Sea Cliff* left the convoy to assist in maintaining ASDIC contact. *St. Thomas* positioned herself directly behind the target and fired another Squid. This one was set to explode deep, at 130 metres. It went off above the stern of *U-877*. It damaged the submarine's hull, and water flowed in at the stern. The submarine's pumps stopped functioning, and her propellers were damaged. Out of control, the boat sank to over 350 metres before her ballast was blown and her crew applied full speed to take her back up to 150 metres. She still could not maintain trim, however. All tanks were blown, and she rapidly surfaced, nose up. The hatches opened, and the entire crew bailed out into the cold and choppy water.

St. Thomas and *Sea Cliff,* slowly circling, saw the U-boat surface and, within a few minutes, slide down and sink out of sight. Both corvettes closed on the 56 survivors, floating in rubber life rafts and swimming in yellow lifejackets, struggling to keep their heads up. The two Canadian ships pulled the entire crew onto their decks. On board *Sea Cliff,* taking passage to Londonderry was Lieutenant Peter Chance, RCNVR, of Ottawa. He later recalled seeing the German prisoners huddled in the frigid air on the upper decks. The Canadians provided them with blankets and took them below to the warm mess decks. Chance was the only officer who spoke German, albeit from high school. The sub's first lieutenant, a 21-year-old Austrian, spoke some French and English. The prisoners were a sorry lot but quite grateful for their humanitarian treatment.

In the early darkening December afternoon, *Sea Cliff* and *St. Thomas* rejoined the convoy. There was no vestige of hatred from the German prisoners. They seemed to believe that they and their captors were simply sailors that the fortunes of war at sea had brought together. The sub's entire crew was saved, and their morale remained high. On December 31, they berthed in Gaurock on the Firth of Clyde along-side a jetty with a railroad spur nearby. Before being marched off to a train headed for a prison camp, the submarine's crew formed up in ranks facing the Canadian ships. With typical German gusto, they yelled out three cheers to their rescuers.

Lieutenant-Commander Leslie Perman Denny, RCNR, from Chester, Nova Scotia, commanding *St. Thomas*, received the Distinguished Service Cross "for services in HMCS *St. Thomas* in action against a German boat." On January 12, Escort Group C-3, with the same Canadian warships, departed Southend with a 47-ship convoy travelling west. The escorts halted in St. John's, while the convoy proceeded with different escorts to New York, arriving on January 31.

In April 1945, *St. Thomas* left Londonderry for the last time for a refit in Halifax. *Sea Cliff* continued convoying until May 12, 1945, when she slipped down the River Foyle from Londonderry for the last time. She was paid off in Halifax on November 28.

Hank Vondette ended his wartime service as yeoman of signals on the destroyer HMCS *Restigouche*. She had been one of Canada's first ships to go to war, leaving Halifax on December 10, 1939, to escort convoy TC-1 to England. Convoy TC-1 consisted of five massive ocean liners carrying the 7400 men of the First Canadian Division to war. *Restigouche* performed various local duties in early 1945. After VE-Day the destroyer was employed for three months bringing home military personnel from Newfoundland. *Resti-gouche* was paid off in Halifax on October 5, 1945.

Painted bands on the funnels began to be used to signify the group to which ships belonged. The design on the funnels of Mid-Ocean Escort Group C-3 (and later C-5) was red and white stripes. Thus, the "Barber Pole Brigade" was born. *Restigouche* was one of the original ships in this "brigade."

It's away outward bound the swinging fo'c'sle's heel,
From the smoking sea's white glare upon the strand.
It's the grey miles that are slipping under keel,
As we're rolling outward bound from Newfoundland.
From Halifax to Newfie John to 'Derry's clustered towers,
Through trackless paths where conning towers roll.
If you know another group in which you'd sooner spend
your hours,
Ye've never sailed beneath the Barber Pole.

Henry Vondette's service to his country and to his navy did not stop with the end of hostilities in Europe. He later forged an illustrious career in Canada's peacetime Royal Canadian Navy.

❧◆❧

With the war in Europe over, there was a call for volunteers for the Pacific. Vondette volunteered and was sent to the Signal School at St. Hyacinthe to become familiar with USN Signal Communications and USN Signal Publications. That was where he met Ursula, his wife-to-be. She was training as a radar plotter. Ursula returned to Halifax, where she was employed working in the captain's office at the drafting depot at HMCS *Peregrine*. Vondette's early life had been very much church-oriented and involved in Christian teachings. Until Ursula eventually left Halifax, he accompanied her to Evensong at the Halifax Cathedral.

During the war, many people suggested to Vondette that he should become an officer, but he found his job as a signalman most interesting. After the war, his captain again recommended him as a commissioned by warrant candidate. This time Vondette accepted. While he was awaiting selection, the navy put him on board HMCS *Micmac*, a Tribal Class destroyer. Construction on four Tribal Class destroyers had started at Halifax Shipyards Ltd. in 1942 and 1943, but the first of them, HMCS *Micmac*, was not combat-ready before September 1945.

From *Micmac*, Hank Vondette joined HMCS *Warrior*, which took him via Panama Canal to Victoria. *Warrior* was the first aircraft carrier commissioned in the RCN, although she was loaned from the Royal Navy. She was not equipped with the proper heating she needed for operations in the harsh North Atlantic, as the RN had been using her in the warm Indian Ocean. On her first winter in Canada, she sailed to the west coast to escape North Atlantic's ice and cold. In 1948, she was sent back to the RN in exchange for HMCS *Magnificent*, which was much better suited to the rigors of operation in the Atlantic Ocean.

Magnificent visited Vancouver, and Vondette was invited to Ursula's home in Kerrisdale for Christmas

in 1946. At the Christmas Eve service at St. James'
Anglican Church, Vancouver, they became engaged.
Because he had joined the navy at 17, his education
required enhancement to meet the academic standards for officer training as an upper yardman. He
studied hard, reading many hours each day, and
wrote the required exams during transit of the Panama Canal in early 1947. He qualified academically.
When he left *Warrior* at Portsmouth, England, he was
sent ashore in the commodore's barge after attending
a lunchtime farewell in the wardroom.

Vondette now had to learn how to be an officer
according to the Royal Navy. He completed the upper
yardman's course at the Upper Yardman's College at
HMS *Hawke*, Exbury House, the Baron de Rothschild's
Estate, near Beaulieu Abbey, and was promoted to
sub-lieutenant. Then he attended the Royal Naval
College Greenwich for two semesters to complete the
Junior Officers' War Course.

During the 1948 Christmas vacation, at the end of
the first semester at Royal Naval College, Ursula and
Henry married at the Royal Naval College Chapel.
Before the event, while Ursula was travelling from
Vancouver, Hank Vondette had arranged for the wedding to take place at St. Alphege's Anglican Church,
Greenwich. However, at a holiday reception, the captain's wife asked, "What's wrong with the Royal Naval
College Chapel? It has been good enough for kings
and queens down through the years!" Therefore, the
venue was changed. The reception was in the head
table area of the Painted Hall. A boys' choir from the

chapel sang during the service. The Royal Naval College staff wore their traditional Beefeaters-type dress. Expecting war rationing still to be in effect in England, Ursula had taken the precaution of bringing a small wedding cake made in Vancouver. This became the top layer of a splendid Royal Naval College three-tier wedding cake.

When the couple returned from England in 1949, Vondette was an officer on watch-keeping duties in HMCS *Micmac*. Vondette, as was the custom, joined the ship at 0900 hours on the day of his appointment, wearing his medals and a sword. Vondette had served in *Micmac* during 1946, where the chief boatswain's mate taught him seamanship. It was a happy circumstance for that same person to welcome Vondette back aboard.

The following year, 1950, Vondette became an officer in HMCS *Crescent*, a C-Class destroyer that had been commissioned in September 1945. In early 1949 she was at Nanjing, China—at the time the last mainland holdout of Chiang Kai-shek's Nationalist Chinese. The Communist People's Liberation Army overran Nanjing a month later. From there, Vondette volunteered for service in the Korean War and served in HMCS *Cayuga*. *Cayuga* left Esquimault on July 5, 1950, and carried out three tours of duty in Korean waters.

The infamous American impersonator Ferdinand Waldo Demara Jr. joined the RCN posing as Dr. Joseph Cyr using false credentials. He was quickly inducted and posted to *Cayuga*. His medical training was self-taught, yet while at sea in 1951, his treatment of three wounded Republic of Korea guerrillas won the respect of the captain and the ship's crew. When the real Dr. Joseph Cyr saw the imposter interviewed in the news, he notified the authorities. *Cayuga's* captain, Commander J. Plomer, DSC, immediately relieved the pretender of his duties. In order to avoid embarrassment, the RCN agreed to drop charges provided that Demara left Canada immediately and not return.

When HMCS *Cayuga* returned to Victoria mid-1952, Vondette was sent to England to carry out naval gunnery courses, which included two semesters at the Royal Naval College. He then spent one year at HMS *Excellent*, a gunnery-training establishment at Whale Island, Portsmouth.

Vondette returned to Canada to watch-keeping duties in RCN destroyers. In 1961, in the rank of lieutenant commander, he was appointed in command of a River Class frigate, HMCS *Stettler*. His family left Esquimault in November 1962 when he was posted to Halifax. Vondette was promoted to commander on January 1, 1963, and became commander sea training at Maritime Command Headquarters. In 1965–66, he returned to HMCS *Restigouche* as her commanding officer. Then came three years as commander sea training again, plus involvement in considerable parade and ceremonial occasions, including welcoming the Princess Royal, Princess Margaret and Her Majesty, The Queen, for the 50th anniversary of the RCN, which included the consecration of the Queen's Colour.

Vondette was appointed Executive Officer and Training Commander at HMCS *Cornwallis*, the land-based training establishment for the RCN. He was responsible for courses in communication and bos'n's trades, petty officer and junior officer leadership and recruit training. From *Cornwallis*, he was selected as a student for the U.S. Naval War College at Newport, Rhode Island, for a one-year senior staff course. When he left the war college in 1969, Vondette went to HMCS *Bonaventure*, Canada's last aircraft carrier, as executive officer. When her captain left to a senior staff course, Vice-Admiral J.C. "Scruffy" O'Brien decided that Vondette should stay on as commanding officer of *Bonaventure*.

After *Bonaventure*, Vondette was appointed director, naval reserves. This was the first time he had served ashore where universities were located within reach. He enrolled at Saint Mary's University, for part-time evening and summer courses. By continuing a hectic pace for three years, Vondette achieved straight As and was one of only two students who finished with "summa cum laude" level graduation. In hockey terms, Henry Vondette was allowed a goal—and Ursula earned an assist.

Encouraged to continue with post-graduate work, he applied to Dalhousie University and was accepted. After completing the required number of subject courses, he was required to write a thesis. His chosen

topic "National Defence Policy—An Area of Irrespon-
sibility" was changed to "The Logic and Rhetoric of
Defence Policy Debates from Confederation to the
Present" (an early example of political correctness!).
He eventually completed the thesis during command
time in the operational support ship HMCS *Preserver*
and received his Master of Arts degree in Political Sci-
ence during the 1976 convocation. His academic education, suspended in 1941, was completed more than
35 years later.

Vondette's next posting was to the position of
Queen's Harbourmaster. On December 13, 1973,
Henry Vondette was awarded the Order of Military
Merit at the officer level by the Governor General at
Rideau Hall. This final honour recognized "outstanding meritorious service in duties of responsibilities."
He was simultaneously promoted to captain. When
he returned to Halifax, Admiral D.S. Boyle told him
that he was to be the command personnel and training officer, an office he held for two years. Then, when
he least expected it, he was appointed commanding
officer of HMCS *Preserver* for two years.

It was time to haul anchor and retire from his
beloved navy. His career ran from 1941 through 1978,
37 years from ordinary seaman to signalman to yeoman of signals throughout World War II and during
the Cold War from sub-lieutenant to captain. In
retirement, Henry Vondette was employed as harbourmaster for the Port of Vancouver.

Ursula and Henry always enthusiastically supported their church from St. George, the Martyr, Cadboro Bay, Peter's, Birch Cove, Halifax All Saints' Bedford, Immanuel, Newport, Rhode Island, at Cornwallis and in England. When they arrived in West Vancouver, on retirement, the rector at St. Stephen's invited them to attend. Later they moved on St. Timothy's Anglican Church in North Vancouver. Along the way, they produced a daughter, Nancy, and three sons, Michael, Christopher and Timothy.

On July 20, 2005, Henry William Vondette, BA, MA, OMM, CD, RCN (Captain retired), passed away, leaving Ursula and his family to mourn.

~✲~

CHAPTER SEVENTEEN

WRCNS—So Men May Sail

THE WOMEN'S ROYAL CANADIAN NAVAL SERVICE, its members known as Wrens, officially came into being in July 1942. In 1941, forces senior officers were interested in the idea of women serving in the armed forces. However, the commonly held view was that only a few women were needed as drivers for vehicles. Initially, the RCN was not interested in recruiting women. Many old-school commanders would not tolerate the thought of women in uniform. At best, they thought, women would be a nuisance.

Canadians mostly took a dim view of women in uniform. The new recruits soon realized they would need to convince their families and the wives of servicemen that they were not wanton females with designs on the men and that they were no threat to familial harmony. They had to measure up to the job—they had to be twice as good as the men to get half the respect!

On July 2, 1941, an order-in-council established the Canadian Women's Auxiliary Air Force, which became the RCAF Women's Division. The following month, the Canadian Women's Army Corps was created. By 1942, the Admiralty realized that women in the RCN would free up men for duty at sea. The Admiralty then asked the Royal Navy for the loan of qualified officers of the Women's Royal Naval Service (WRNS). Three WRNS officers, Superintendent Joan Carpenter, Chief Officer Dorothy Isherwood and Second Officer Elizabeth Sturdee, arrived in May 1942.

The task of forming the new branch of the RCN was enormous. The initial complement was set at 150 officers and 2700 ratings. Where would they be trained? Where would the officers and senior ratings come from? How would they be recruited? This was all at the time that the RCN itself was undergoing a major expansion. The main problem that immediately arose as more women were attracted to the WRCNS was accommodation. Wrens would be employed across Canada and in Newfoundland, but appropriate housing was hard to find on short notice.

The navy appointed Adelaide Sinclair, a former Wartime Prices and Trade Board official, as director. Superintendent Joan Carpenter and two other senior WRNS officers accompanied Sinclair on a Canada-wide tour to select the first "suitable" recruits. An initial group of 67 women was recruited to serve as the core of the new service. Beginning on August 29, 1942, the Wrens trained at Kingsmill House in Ottawa, named for Rear-Admiral Sir Charles Kingsmill, RN, the founding director of the Naval Service of Canada. On September 19, the first selection board met at Kingsmill House. Twenty-eight of the 67 appeared before the board, and 22 were passed as officers of His Majesty's Royal Canadian Navy—the first women ever to carry the King's commission in any British navy. Although the WRNS was a far older service, it was an auxiliary to the Royal Navy, not an essential part of the senior service as in Canada.

The WRCNS was established as an integral part of the RCN, not as an auxiliary service. Officers held the King's commission. Non-commissioned ranks were the same for women as for men. A significant difference in officers' uniforms was that, instead of the gold sleeve braid topped by a circular loop worn by men, the Wren officers wore sky blue braid with a diamond-shaped loop. It was not until June 1943 that they shed the unwieldy rank names of the WRNS and began to use the same ranks as RCN officers.

The first Wren class graduated October 1, 1942, and most were immediately dispersed from Kingsmill House. Their task was to help organize a service that eventually saw 6783 Wrens in uniform. Two months later, Wrens were being recruited in the same way men were recruited into the RCN.

All Wren officers after this first group enlisted as ratings and then were commissioned from the ranks. A selection board interviewed them, and applicants, if successful, underwent rigid officer training at Hardy House in Ottawa. They studied responsibility and leadership, morale and social problems, officers' duties, pay accounting, public relations, growth of British sea power, the art of instruction and naval regulations.

Basic training for Wren ratings was done at HMCS *Conestoga*, at Galt, Ontario. This ship was under the command of First Officer (later Lieutenant Commander) Isabel J. Macneill. Although it was not a seagoing vessel, it was the first RCN ship to be commanded by a woman. Commander Macneill, in June 1944, became an Officer of the Order of the British Empire for her service and responsibility for the basic training of almost every member of the WRCNS. Training of the Wren ratings started in October 1942. At any one time there were likely to be 600 women in residence. The three weeks of basic training was devoted to converting civilians into Wrens, all on the double! Physical training, drill and naval customs made up a major portion of the training. They learned how to salute and who to salute. When Wrens left *Conestoga*, they were sternly lectured on behaviour. They were told clearly that the reputation and future of women's service rested with them.

Initially, women were paid two-thirds that of a man. This was later raised to four-fifths. Probationary Wrens' pay was 90 cents a day during basic training, increasing to 95 cents a day on completion of basic training, with extra daily allowances given according to the Wren's ability in a particular branch. Ratings received a free issue of winter and summer uniforms and a grant of $15.00 to kit themselves up with personal underclothing and toilet necessities. A quarterly upkeep allowance of $3.00 was also allotted.

There was much discrimination, both from within the ranks of the military and from the wider community.

Women in the Navy were not always taken seriously, as this contemporary newspaper article makes clear:

We don't know how to spell that two-note whistle, with the emphasis on the last note that is, we believe, the equivalent for "Not bad!" or "Woo-Woo!" but that's the one we almost gave a few moments ago. We just saw the trimmest little craft we've seen since coming to Navytown.

Talk about lines! Why, she was sweeping along there with her sails trimmed and with her soft colors showing up against that blue background—just the loveliest sight a sailor would want to set his eyes on. Is she a schooner or a sloop? You got it all wrong, chum. Heck no, she was a Wren!

(From the March 1943 issue of *The Crow's Nest*, the RCN newspaper.)

Women officers, in February 1943, trained at Hardy House. The course was initially two weeks but eventually became five weeks. There neither ratings nor officers trained in a particular trade or for specialized employment. Advanced training, for both officers and ratings, for the most part took place at HMCS *Cornwallis* and St. Hyacinthe.

Situated on the southern shore of the Annapolis Basin, HMCS *Cornwallis* was located at Clementsport, NS. The name honours Edward Cornwallis, the founder of Halifax and governor of NS from 1749 to 1752. St. Hyacinthe, 55 kilometres east of Montréal, was the location of the Royal Canadian Navy's Communications School. While attending the best-equipped signals school in the British Empire, Canadian Wrens lived in wooden huts condemned by the army after World War I.

Initially, however, specialized training took place in Galt (now part of Cambridge), Toronto, Ottawa and Halifax.

After basic training in Galt, 40 Wrens selected to be wireless telegraphists went to a resort hotel called the Guild of All Arts in Scarborough, Ontario. Many more were to follow them. For three months, instructors, such as Leading Telegraphist Irene Carter, introduced the Wrens to the mysteries of Morse code. The students were surprised to find that they would be taught German naval procedure, the location and call signs of German navy coastal stations, and the makeup and probable meaning of various types of messages. They were also taught to distinguish between the incessant, low-interest traffic from German shore stations and the infrequent vitally important broadcasts from U-boats. They were also trained in the use of direction-finding sets.

Meantime, an intercept station, No. 1, was built 30 kilometres outside Ottawa. When the Wrens arrived, they found Gloucester had four buildings. Building No. 1 was the barracks with accommodation, sickbay, mess and galley. Building No. 2 was the Operations Building with its light, airy Operations Room. There the operators worked 24/7 at a continuous table that ran around three walls. The fourth wall had a table for the watch supervisor who walked

Wren operating direction-finding equipment at HMCS *Coverdale* station near Moncton, New Brunswick, August 1945

around collecting messages to be transmitted to Naval Headquarters in Ottawa. Building No. 3 was a garage housing panel trucks, called liberty boats in navy parlance, which were used to ferry personnel and supplies to and from Ottawa. A mile away, across five fields, stood a small shack that was Building No. 4. Its single room held three direction-finding (D/F) sets. Some Wrens were trained as D/F operators. Each change of watch meant Wrens had to cross the fields and go through fences of barbed wire, lugging sand-wiches, water, coal, pads of paper and flashlights. The trip was quite formidable during winter months.

In spite of stiff discrimination, the Wrens perse-vered and took advantage of the new opportunities that opened up to them. In May 1943, courses started in *Cornwallis* for: writers and supply assistants, cooks, wardroom assistants, sick berth attendants, laun-dresses, M/T drivers and photographers. At first, there were 22 different job categories open to women in the WRCNS. Wrens were sorted for the different jobs, based on their background and experience. The Naval Service drew up specific guidelines to measure a job candidate's ability and aptitude. Here are some exam-ples of how Wrens were evaluated for certain jobs:

- Steward: Previous employment in general domes-tic service preferred. Women who are used to housework and like it can be trained.

- Plotter: Secondary school education. Neat at fig-ures. Should have a quick, clear brain and some mathematical ability. Must be steady and not eas-ily flustered.

- Sick berth attendant: Of good education, preferably two years or more of high school. Should not be timid when exposed to sickness or disease or sight of blood.

- Coder: Secondary school experience. Must be able to type. Bright, intelligent girls are required for this work.

Eventually, 39 occupational branches of the WRCNS were created, although most Wrens served as messengers, cooks, messwomen, writers and wardroom attendants. By 1943, others were employed as clerks, stenographers, writers, cooks, drivers, sick berth attendants, supply assistants and photographers. Later, Wrens were employed in a wider variety of trades such as radar operators, wireless and switchboard operators, cypher clerks and teletype operators. They took on the responsibilities of assistants in the operational training centre at RCN Headquarters in Halifax, HMCS *Stadacona*, and the one at HMCS *Avalon* in St. John's. They operated a spotting table for gunnery training. They managed the complex duties to run the night escort teacher apparatus developed by Commander J.D. "Chummy" Prentice. They manned special wireless and LORAN shore stations in isolated locations on the coast. They kept operational plots of the war at sea. They operated base signal towers. By November 1943, there were 80 Wren officers and 1000 ordinary Wrens at *Stadacona*, some training and some working.

Just one year after the WRCNS was established, Wrens were earning high praise for their efforts. Vice Admiral Percy W. Nelles, Chief of Naval Staff, noted their contribution to naval morale and efficiency. He addressed the 400 Wrens celebrating their first anniversary on parade in Ottawa.

I wish to thank the patriotic women who have entered their country's service and have added so capably to the combat strength of the navy by helping to man the shore establishments in this country. In one short year, you have proved yourselves of immeasurable value to the naval service by taking over many tasks with skill, diligence and cheerfulness. As Chief of Naval Staff, I am proud of your record and the contribution you are making to the final victory.

Some Wrens performed duties that were traditionally those of women: office work, household chores, food preparation. Others were singers and dancers for the "Meet the Navy" show.

The RCN soon realized that women could be skilled communication and intelligence operators. Although they worked in cooperation with sailors, Wrens were not authorized to serve onboard seagoing ships. Some Wrens worked in merchant navy coordination, information processing and signals. They were posted to the East Coast starting in March 1943. They served at Halifax and St. John's naval bases and at radio detection and plotting stations, such as the newly built Coverdale base south of Moncton, New Brunswick. As soon as the Coverdale base was ready, the senior operators at Gloucester were reassigned there. A new batch from St. Hyacinthe replaced them at Gloucester.

HMCS *Coverdale* was established as a special wireless station (H/F D/F) in 1941. The name "Coverdale" came from a nearby village. The wireless station was built in a tremendous bog. The location was selected for H/F D/F operations because it provided a good electronics grounding.

Construction was completed in January–February 1944. Operations began when Wrens started arriving in numbers. The initial personnel consisted of three male officers, four WRCNS officers, three male ratings and 140 Wrens. The major activity was obtaining directional finding (D/F) bearings on German U-boats and assisting with search and rescue operations for aircraft in distress.

When a D/F bearing was obtained at a Canadian station, it was plotted on a large wall map. Coloured pieces of string were drawn across the map according to the bearing obtained. Then operators heard from stations in the UK, Bermuda, Labrador or Africa that had received the same signal. The intersection of strings indicated the source of the signal. Within minutes, aircraft flying on patrol were dispatched to investigate. At the intercept point, determined within a 40-kilometre accuracy margin, the aircraft dropped sonobuoys to detect, track and ultimately target the source of the signal.

The following are vignettes of women who served in the Wrens. They are courtesy of The Dominion Institute, Veterans Affairs Remembrance program and the veterans themselves. The Memory Project Digital Archive is an initiative of the Dominion Institute. The Archive contains the memories of more than 300 servicemen and women from across Canada who served the country in many capacities. Without the Dominion Institute's generosity and commitment to the preservation of history, the Archive would not be possible.

Noreen Helena MacDonald—WRCNS No. 1

As her service number, WRCNS No. 1, reveals, Noreen Harper was the first enlistee in the Women's Royal Canadian Naval Service.

Born and educated in Ottawa, Noreen Harper was working in Naval Headquarters when news of the formation of a Canadian women's naval service was announced. When Women's Royal Naval Service officers arrived to put the plan in motion, one of the first to knock on their door was Noreen. Her father strongly opposed her career choice, but with her mother's blessing, Noreen proceeded.

The recruiters liked what they saw, enlisted her and sent her to Hardy House in Ottawa as a member of the first class training for selection as an officer.

After graduation, Noreen enthusiastically joined the WRCNS recruiting team. Within the year, she was promoted to petty officer, chief petty officer and sub-lieutenant, becoming one of the first officers in the WRCNS. She served in various postings to schools in Toronto and Ottawa before her appointment, in May 1945, as a lieutenant to HMCS *Stadacona*, in Halifax, as East Coast personnel officer for both male and female seamen in the supply trade.

That same year, Lieutenant William MacDonald, of Bedford, Nova Scotia, was posted to HMCS *Micmac* as that ship's supply officer. *Micmac* was the first Tribal Class destroyer built in Canada. She was launched on September 18, 1943 at the Halifax Shipyards Ltd. and was commissioned on September 18, 1945, after the war in Europe was over. She was the only Canadian Tribal not to see any action.

Noreen and Bill worked closely together during the preparation for the ship's commissioning. The two young lieutenants married on January 22, 1945. The ceremony took place aboard HMCS *Micmac* and was the first naval wedding performed in a Canadian warship.

With the end of the war, Noreen was employed demobilizing the disbanded WRCNS. She aided in the release of many of the same Wrens she had enrolled. The MacDonalds left the navy but stayed in Halifax. Their union produced three sons, John, William and Michael.

In the late 1980s, in retirement, the MacDonalds moved to New Glasgow, Nova Scotia.

Jenny Pike—WRCNS Photographer

Jenny (Whitehead) Pike was one of a groundbreaking wave of female recruits to the Forces during World War II. She was among the first group of young women to train as photographers and photo technicians. She helped process the first pictures of the D-Day invasion to liberate northwest Europe.

Jenny Whitehead was born in Winnipeg in 1922, the youngest of four children. As young as age 11, Jenny used to help in her brother's photo lab and was sure she was destined to become a photographer. This experience stood the young shutterbug in good stead when she began work in the photography department of Eaton's Portage Avenue department store.

In 1943, with World War II underway, Jenny's father helped her write a letter to the Secretary of the Naval Board offering her services as a photographer. His support was unusual in an era when many parents disapproved of their daughters joining the Forces. There were no vacancies in the photography trade at the time, but Jenny was encouraged to join the Naval Service as a Probationary Wren.

The Women's Royal Canadian Naval Service (WRCNS) seemed to her like a good life and, in February 1943, at age 21, Jenny enlisted. She trained at HMCS *Conestoga* in Galt, Ontario. As Jenny later said, it was her first time in a "Home for Wayward Girls," which was what the buildings at *Conestoga* were used for before the Wrens took up residence.

In August, Jenny was posted to Ottawa for photography training, one of only seven women in the first photography class. She went on to Halifax in October 1943, and in February 1944, sailed in the third draft of WRCNS women to London, England. She had been in London just four months when the D-Day invasion began.

Jenny's proudest memory of the war was her recollection of developing photographs from the D-Day landings. They were the first pictures released of the Allied onslaught and were picked up by the newspaper wire services. Jenny, then 22, was the only woman working in the darkroom at the time.

She returned home from England in April 1945. In 1949, Jenny married Chief Petty Officer Second

Class Donovan Pike, a boy she had grown up with and met again in Winnipeg when they were both discharged from the Navy. Donovan loved navy life and with Jenny's encouragement, he re-enlisted. The couple moved to HMCS *Esquimalt* in Victoria, a city they both loved. They had two children, a son, Jim, and daughter, Susan. Donovan Pike died in 1977.

In 1969, Jenny became a darkroom technician for the Victoria City Police. She retired in 1983. Despite problems with her sight, Jenny continued to be an avid photographer and camera club enthusiast, always looking for the perfect shot.

She also maintained her interest in service organizations. She joined the Royal Canadian Legion in Winnipeg in 1946 and later transferred to Ex-Service Women's Branch 182 in Victoria, of which she was president from 1982 to 1983. She was also active in the Ex-WRCNS Association of Victoria.

"Jenny was so proud to have served her country," recalls Barbara Fosdick, current president of Ex-Service Women's Branch 182, Victoria." I think that my favourite memory of her is from the recent Remembrance Day Parade, when all of the women were told they must march at the back of the parade. Jenny in her wrath was mighty to see."

"With fists clenched, she yelled, 'We are women veterans, we will NOT march at the back, we're going to join the men where we belong.' And we did."

Jean Adams—Sick Berth Attendant

The following is a transcript of an interview given in Toronto by Jean Adams in 1997. It has been collected and preserved by The Memory Project Digital Archive. Jean was a Wren who served during World War II. This is her story in her own words.

My name is Jean Adams and I'm an ex-Wren. I was a member of the Women's Royal Canadian Naval Service in the Second World War. My service number was W5440. We had over 6000 Wrens registered by the end of the war.

My basic training, like every other Wren in the Navy, was at HMCS Conestoga *in Galt, Ontario. When that was finished, I was drafted to HMCS* Protector *in Sidney, Nova Scotia to get my medical training as a sick berth attendant. When I finished that, on New Year's Day 1945, I was drafted to HMCS* Stadacona *in Halifax and served as a sick berth attendant at the Royal Canadian Naval Hospital in Stadacona navy dockyard in Halifax. While there, I was asked to join special services as a dancer and singer. We put on shows and entertained troops up and down the Atlantic seaboard.*

In September 1945, after VE-Day and VJ-Day, I was sent to HMCS Niobe *in Scotland to join the Royal Canadian Navy show for a filming of "Meet the Navy."* (Niobe *was a shore establishment situated in the misty hills above Greenock, Scotland. Its primary mission was the manning of Canadian ships in the European theatre. It was housed mainly in a collection of brick and stone buildings which pre-War had been a poorhouse and insane asylum, a fact which gave rise to many bad jokes about the inhabitants having only changed uniforms.)*

The Navy Show was a musical performed by sailors and Wrens relocated from various navy duties or recruited especially for service in the show. Most were talented amateurs, but some were professional, like dancers Alan Lund and Blanche Harris and the producer, music director and choreographer. The Radio City Rockettes–style chorus line was composed of Wrens who may have studied tap or ballet but had had little opportunity to use their skills or to perform professionally. The "Meet the Navy" show performed for the first time in Toronto's Victoria Theatre on September 2, 1943. Ticket prices ranged from $2.50 to $0.75. The troupe travelled by special train back and forth across the Dominion. In early October 1944, they sailed on the troopship Ile de France *for performances in front of Canadian servicemen in the U.K. In June 1945, they flew to Paris, then Brussels, Amsterdam and Oldenburg, Germany, where the curtain fell on September 12, 1945.*

Elstree Studios in England made a film in late 1945. It benefited the Royal Canadian Navy Benevolent Fund by more than $200,000.

I actually joined the show to make the movie. The entire show had been on a very long, long tour two or three years and then sent overseas. It played Britain and as countries were freed, they not only played for the military but also for civilians. The movie tried to re-enact those tours. I have to give credit to the people who built the sets because they tried to build the sets as close as possible to the original theatres that the Navy show played in. Therefore, many of the numbers were done as if they were on that stage. It was a lot of fun. We all learned a lot about making movies.

The participants certainly earn their dough. We had a captain of the Navy show, Captain Connelly, who insisted that the Navy show be Navy. We had to get up in the morning, fully dressed in rig of the day, outside for divisions, raised the flag, then dash to breakfast or whatever, off to makeup, which took hours, and then onto the set. So we were there a long, full day. Moreover, I think that is what taught everybody who had any illusions about going into movies to have second thoughts. A travelling show and a show that is at a movie studio making a movie are certainly two different things, I must admit.

I returned to Canada in February of 1946. Instead of getting my discharge as I thought I would, sick berth attendants were considered compulsory. So I was kept in the Navy and sent to HMCS Carleton at Dow's Lake in Ottawa where we were busy doing medicals on young 17-year-old men who wanted to join the Navy. (In 1944, the barrack blocks were occupied by the Women's Royal Canadian Naval Service.) I was finally discharged in Toronto on April 24, 1946.

Margaret Los—H/F D/F Operator

Margaret Haliburton (nee Los) was a Wren H/F D/F operator. She operated high-frequency direction-finding apparatus. Margaret was born in Prince Albert, Saskatchewan, in 1922. She was still young when the family moved to Petrolia, Ontario, where her father established a butter-and-cheese factory. Both parents were in their 40s when Margaret and her sister were born. Her father died while she was a young girl, and the family then moved to Toronto. There Margaret's mother went to teacher's college and, as a skilled seamstress and tailor, began teaching dressmaking and tailoring. Margaret received her senior matriculation with honours from Central Technical School in Toronto. In 1939, further studies in engineering at the University of Toronto was not an option for young ladies, so she took a job with the plant department of Bell Telephone.

Margaret's mother encouraged her to join the service. Her mother did not want to get rid of her but instead was an adventurous woman. Her mother was born in 1879 and did not get married and have children until later in life. She had travelled all across Canada, primarily on horseback and simply did not understand her daughter's reluctance. "If I'd had a chance," she told Margaret, "I would have joined up the very first day!" The two women exchanged looks and Margaret replied "Weelll!" and the next day enlisted in the WRCNS. She was interested that the army and air force were recruiting women, but she selected the navy because, she would facetiously say,

"The uniform was nicer." On her application, she found no categories that matched her education or work experience so she marked the boxes for dancer, stock keeper and wireless operator.

In the early summer of 1943, Margaret did her basic training at *Conestoga,* as did all the Wrens. The day she arrived there was a production crew on site making a publicity film. There she was, in her civilian clothes, baggage in hand, watching all the beautiful girls in marvellous uniforms doing precision marching while being filmed. She thought it all was just wonderful and was quite rueful that she was not included.

The next day she reported to the supply section to get her kit, her uniform and be fitted out. There were a few steps down into a terrace in front of the kitting office. When she exited, she saw photographers filming the girls and was not watching where she was going. Her hands were piled high with boxes and folded clothes over which she could barely see. She tripped on the stairs and fell flat on her face. The crew ran over, to help, she thought—but no, they kept the camera running on all the equipment scattered on the ground. After determining that she was all right, they asked if she would do it again because they did not get it on film. It took her about two seconds to agree. She later said that her entire movie career consists of a tiny figure in the background making a fool of herself.

Being 21, she was a bit older than most of the other girls. Her maturity resulted in her basic training only lasting a few days. She was drafted to No. 1 Radio Station at St. Hyacinthe with the first Wren contingent taking an intense course in wireless radio. She went to a camp that was still being built. "A most desolate and uninviting place," she later recalled. The 25 Wrens reported in and found that the captain had not been warned of their arrival. No one knew if he was laughing or crying when he put his head down and lamented, "Here I am with a camp being built. I have hundreds of sailors living in very poor conditions in tents with improper toilet facilities. What am I going to do with 25 girls?" With the base under construction, the Wrens were billeted in a convent school until the end of September. They then moved into new but inadequate accommodations unsuitable for girls. They had double bunks, plastic screens for windows and washrooms designed for males. However, Margaret recalls her months there as "some of the most enjoyable times I have ever experienced."

Qualified as an H/F D/F operator, Margaret climbed on the train to the radio station at Coverdale. She recalled it was quite a beautiful spot if you ignored odours from the nearby pig farm. One bonus was the nearby British Commonwealth Air Training Scheme Manning Depot. She stayed until after VE Day at Coverdale, intercepting enemy messages and getting directional bearings on submarines. She volunteered for duty in the Pacific and went back to St. Hyacinthe for Japanese code training. She said she would have been happy to stay in the service, but when the war ended, the WRCNS was disbanded.

Margaret married in August 1946 when her air force fiancé, Gordon Haliburton, returned from England. He was an air force communicator, and he stayed in the service after the war. When Canada took control of the Alaska Highway from the U.S., the RCAF assumed responsibility for communications in the area. Gordon and Margaret moved to Watson Lake in the Yukon where Gordon was manager of the telephone and telegraph station. Their son was born prematurely in Whitehorse in December 1948. At two months of age, he contracted meningitis. Margaret flew to Edmonton with him where he was hospitalized for six months.

The family stayed on with the highway after the Canadian National Railway took over communications in the area. When Margaret got pregnant again, the couple decided not to risk the experience they had with their first child. Gordon left CN for a job with Bell Telephone in Hamilton, Ontario. A daughter was born in 1952. The family lived in several northern Ontario towns and finally in Toronto. Gordon and Margaret separated in the early 1960s. He moved to Calgary, where he later died. Margaret spent the last eleven years of her working life with the Government of Ontario in Toronto.

In retirement, Margaret has been active in veterans' organizations, especially the Ex-Wren Association. At 85 years, she still marches in Remembrance Day parades.

Marie Duchesnay—Coder

Mary (Marie) Duchesnay was born in Québec City in 1920. In 1939, she passed the civil servant's examination for bilingual shorthand and typing, but with no jobs readily available, she stayed home to help her mother. She was called by the naval control office of National Defence in Québec City and started to work there. Marie thought she would be a stenographer, but they immediately taught her to code and decode messages. After a few months, all civilian female National Defence employees were invited to join the Wrens if they wanted to have a chance to continue this work. The offer pleased Marie since she found the work unusual and interesting.

She joined up because she felt war was a terrible thing and because her brother, not yet 17, had enlisted in 1939 and was already in service. Her father had served in the Canadian Army—the Princess Patricia's Canadian Light Infantry—in 1914. Members of her family had a history of becoming involved when it thought people were in danger.

Marie joined the WRCNS in June 1943 and went by train to Galt. After a month's training, she was sent to St. Hyacinthe to the first school in coding and decoding in the Commonwealth. There were 23 girls in that first draft, and they all passed.

She did coding work for the duration of the war and afterwards. In the navy, she learned to improve her English writing and speaking and made wonderful friends. For Marie Duchesnay, it was a great experience.

C.P.O. Irene Carter, B.E.M.—Telegraphist

This news clip appeared in the *Winnipeg Star* newspaper on March 28, 1945:

> *A Winnipeg girl who had virtually a ringside seat at the sinking of the mighty battleship HMS* Hood, *heard the first word to be received in Canada of Hitler's death and intercepted messages from the German surface raider* Prince Eugen *and dozens of U-boats, has been awarded the British Empire Medal. Now she is back at her peacetime job as a Canadian National Telegraph operator.*

The "girl" in the article is Irene Carter, who served during the war as a Wren chief petty officer in radio intelligence, Foreign International Branch, Ottawa Intelligence Centre. Commodore E.R. Brock presented Carter with the British Empire Medal at an investiture at HMCS *Chippewa* (Winnipeg).

During the war, Carter was in charge of a station at Moncton, New Brunswick where she had 200 Wren operators working under her. This station was part of a chain of more than 100, which maintained listening posts for wireless signals from enemy craft. By working closely with coastal radar units, the stations were quickly able to establish a "fix" on the location of the enemy craft.

"On many occasions, we listened to naval engagements on the North Atlantic and even as far as the Baltic Sea," said Carter. "After D-Day, we could tell the progress of Allied troops in France from the German High Command messages which we intercepted. We heard the frantic messages for help of a wireless operator on a German submarine as the craft, which was one of those taking part in the naval engagement in which HMS *Hood* was sunk, also went to the bottom."

Carter continued, "He was frantically giving signals and he must have been an old commercial operator, possibly on a German merchant ship before the war because he broke out with S.O.S. instead of the usual German naval distress signal of K.R., just before the signals were cut off."

Word of Hitler's death was dramatically broadcast to U-boats and German warships before being announced to the rest of the world. Carter received the word even before the Ottawa authorities. On many occasions, the sending of an aircraft or warship to the place where signals were heard at the station resulted in further radio traffic from the enemy craft to the effect that it was being attacked. Carter says that her station also listened to reports from life rafts with Canadian and British seamen aboard. These reports gave their location and speed of drift.

After tracing the signals of U-boats for so long, Carter states that her greatest thrill of the war came when she heard the general orders given to German submarines and surface craft to surrender after the Nazi defeat.

Headquarters commended Carter's work:

> CARTER, Irene Francis, Chief Petty Officer Telegra-phist (W-187)—British Empire Medal (BEM)—WRCNS—Awarded as per Canada Gazette of 16 June 1945 and London Gazette of 14 June 1945.

Home: St. Boniface, Manitoba.

This Wren rating has made an outstanding contribution to the training and supervising of telegraphists in the Women's Royal Canadian Naval Service at a Naval W/T Station staffed principally by W.R.C.N.S. personnel. By her qualities of leadership and loyalty, she has secured the confidence and respect of all those working with her.

Elsa Lessard—Wireless Telegraphist Special Operator

Elsa Lessard was in her senior matriculation year (Grade 13) of Lisgar Collegiate Institute in 1940. Born on July 2, 1922, she had lived in Ottawa all her life and had grown up during the Depression. Anyone who lived through those years learned and remembered the value of a dollar. In 1940, she was offered, and quickly accepted, a job with a finance department in the federal government. The pay was good for the time—$55.80 per month. The federal civil service needed thousands of young women. She gave that up for a monthly salary of $27.00 in February 1943, when she joined the navy.

Her work in the government gave her a decided affinity for military folk. She was in the section responsible for sending cheques to dependants of servicemen. She often had to deal with the personal circumstances of the families so soon learned the hardship imposed on those left behind when men went to war.

She had a soft spot for the navy because her older brother, Francis Arthur (Frank), had joined the RCN in 1928. He was serving at sea as a chief petty officer telegrapher aboard a destroyer. It was simply a matter of fact that Elsa and her brother Thomas Oscar (Ossie) Lessard would be eager recruits for the navy with the hopes of becoming telegraphists. Later in the war, Frank was posted to instructor duties at the communications school in St. Hyacinthe and Ossie transferred to become a visual signaller, serving aboard the corvette HMCS *Moose Jaw.*

In February 1943, Elsa completed the requirements to join the service and signed on to the WRCNS. She had to wait until April to go to her "training ship" for basic training. Travelling by train through Ontario in the springtime was interesting for an adventurous young lady. She arrived in the city of Galt and was taken by a navy vehicle to HMCS *Conestoga.* Elsa was excited to begin her navy service. After receiving a host of medical shots to vaccinate her against every known ailment, she attended a series of 24 lectures intended to familiarize her with all things naval. She learned to march in step and wheel left and right, co-ordinated with the rest of her class on parade. This did have a practical application as the young women were often sent to neighbouring towns to march in Victory Loan parades. After two weeks, she was declared a bona fide Wren, a member of the Women's Royal Canadian Naval Service. Entitled to wear the uniform with pride!

Each Wren indelibly learned the dress of the day. Each day, appropriate uniform was spelled out in detail from underwear to galoshes. For example, one day's uniform was black lisle stockings, white shirt with separate collars, black tie (neatly knotted), navy blue serge skirt, matching double-breasted jacket with two rows of black buttons engraved with an anchor, polished black oxfords, round rig hat, black leather purse slung across the chest, black leather gloves and Burberry. After dressing, they emerged en masse from barrack blocks to march to the mess hall for breakfast, identically clad in proper uniform.

Elsa was not selected to train as a telegraphist. Instead, she was ordered, with 13 other women, to report to HMCS *Jellicoe,* a former luxury hotel and spa, the Preston Springs, in Preston, Ontario, just down the road from *Conestoga.* Elsa, who had worked two years as a government clerk, was to be instructed to be a captain's writer. The RCN Chief teaching the women told them that the most important requirement to be a captain's writer was a firm and extensive knowledge of navy regulations. Since it was impossible to learn all this in two weeks, their most important key to success was in knowing where to find the pertinent regulation. First in the pile of books requiring at least their nodding acquaintance was *KR&AI* (*King's Regulations and Admiralty Instructions*). This three-volume book replaced their bibles as the most valuable publication in their personal libraries.

As a captain's writer, Elsa's first posting was to HMCS *Cornwallis,* a newly built base on the shore of the Bay of Fundy near Digby, Nova Scotia. The streets were unpaved and in the rain turned into a morass of slippery red clay gumbo. During or after a rainfall, marching was impossible. Just getting to work required Wrens to be quite nimble-footed. Elsa's first job was in the new entry administration office. The room held an information counter with three desks lined up behind it. One of her jobs was to hand out assigned barrack and bunk numbers to sailors newly arrived for their basic training.

Space was reserved in front of the counter for the "quarter deck." It was there that sailors with special requests, for example, for compassionate leave, or facing minor disciplinary charges appeared before the duty officer. Young sailors also had to appear there to request permission to stop shaving and grow beards. Once permission to grow facial hair was granted, the sailor had to appear before the officer again in six weeks for permission to keep the beard. The navy did not allow scruffy-looking facial hair on anyone in navy uniform. Elsa later recalled one matelot's response when asked why he wanted to keep his beard. Standing stiffly at attention, wearing a gorgeous, flaming-red beard, he replied, "I've grown attached to it, sir."

A Royal Navy submarine, HMS *Seawolf,* was at *Cornwallis* for use as a target vessel for ASDIC training. The English submariners, always anxious for the companionship of females, invited Wrens to dinner on board. On one of these occasions, the commander invited Elsa and a friend to sail on a diving exercise. To get permission, the two Wrens appeared before the duty officer. They were firmly and flatly denied. There was a *KR&AI* regulation expressly forbidding Wrens on seagoing ships.

Elsa's brother Ossie arrived in *Cornwallis* for basic training as a new entry seaman. Elsa always knew, as she neared the Fleet Mail Office, if a parcel from her mother was there for her, because when there was one there, Ossie would be waiting for her. Someone in the mailroom would tip him off, and he would claim his share of their mother's goodies. Elsa does not recall if he shared his boxes with her.

The Red Triangle club in Digby frequently held dances. It was impossible for a girl to be a wallflower since the men outnumbered them by a considerable margin. Being of quite small stature, Elsa was always in demand as a partner for the jive contests. Any good male dancer could throw her around quite easily. The evening always ended with coffee and cake from the *Cornwallis* mess.

In September 1943, Elsa's long-awaited draft for the six-month telegraphists' course in St. Hyacinthe came through. She was off to Montréal and the communication school. The Wrens lived in an old, previously condemned army barracks. It was a long shed with a row of double-decker bunks along each side wall and pot-bellied coal stoves down the center aisle. The stoves had to be continuously stoked, which meant a rotating roster of Wrens for night duty. The Wren on fire duty crept around with a flashlight tending each stove as quietly as possible. Often the most difficult part was waking the replacement Wren without disturbing the whole barracks.

In Elsa's class were 25 Wrens spending untold hours copying Morse code. Day in and day out they copied letters, numbers, special Q and Z codes and plain-language text in many languages. After a time every noise seemed to be sending Morse code messages—rattling water pipes, radio static and music. They attended lectures in electronic theory. Elsa later benefited from these classes. After the war, she graduated from the Radio College of Canada as an electronic technician and spent 30 years working in the field as a purchasing agent for electronic companies.

Elsa's first posting was to the Wren-operated station at Gloucester. Then, in February 1944, as a trained Wireless Telegraphist Special Operator, Elsa went by train to HMCS *Coverdale* near Moncton. The living quarters were a marked improvement. There were large dormitory rooms with four double-decker bunks, built-in lockers, a floor mat and a four-drawer dresser, luxury living compared to St. Hyacinthe. The Wrens worked eight-hour shifts around the clock so there were always Wrens trying to sleep. Those awake confined their activities to the forecastle, a nearby community room.

Elsa's duty was in the Operations Room where about two dozen Wrens sat with headphones at radio receivers on a continuous table along the outside walls. Some distance away was the H/F D/F shack.

When the Wrens listening in the Ops Room alerted the H/F D/F Wrens that a submarine was transmitting, the H/F D/F Wrens took the broadcast's bearings and passed them to Whitehall (RN) or Ottawa (RCN). The map plotters took over, determined a "fix" and transmitted that information to the air squadrons. Occasionally the Wrens at *Coverdale* were told that their traffic resulted in a U-boat being put out of action. By 1944, this was occurring quite frequently. Elsa spent the remainder of her war at *Coverdale*. In retirement, Elsa has become an active member of the Wren Association.

It was not all plain sailing for the Wrens. They were paid two thirds of what servicemen earned, in keeping with the misguided (and soon to be disproved) notion that it took three women to do the work of two man. They were also paid less than what civilians were making. A chief petty officer in the WRCNS made in three years the same amount of money earned by a male civilian worker in one year.

Between 1942 and 1945, 7122 women served with the RCN. The first Wrens to go to Great Britain sailed aboard a troopship on September 4, 1943. Nearly 1000 of them served overseas. Many served in Londonderry, Northern Ireland and HMCS *Niobe* in Scotland. Fourteen women were assigned to RCN Headquarters in London, England. More than 500 Wrens served in Newfoundland; and 50 went to New York and Washington.

The Wrens' determination was instrumental in the Allies' victory at sea. Women helped win the war in many ways. They proved their worth in the armed forces and won a victory for emancipation and recognition. They proved beyond doubt that they had the skills, stamina and intelligence to master almost any job a man could do.

In May 1945, the war ended. Troops began coming home. The war effort was winding down. There was a discussion on the desirability of retaining a number of Wrens in the navy. It would have been advantageous to keep a disciplined group, both to carry on the excellent record that had been established and to maintain the nucleus of a women's service ready for expansion in any future war. The director of the WRCNS argued that it would be too costly to maintain a group of Wrens in peacetime. By August 31, 1945, the Women's Royal Canadian Naval Service had ceased to be.

But six years later, there were Wrens in uniform once again. With the establishment of a regular women's component in the air force, permission was given for the establishment of women's components in the army and navy as well. Approximately 60 officers and 650 Wrens joined the RCN(R). On January 26, 1955, Cabinet approved the creation of a nucleus of regular-force Wrens for the Royal Canadian Navy. A month later, the Minister of National Defence announced that approval had been given for the establishment of a women's component in the regular force of the Royal Canadian Navy. The women were referred to as

Wrens, but, with the unification of the armed services in the late 1960s, the names of the women's groups in the services were dropped.

The fact that women today serve in all aspects of naval operations is mainly due to the hard work and adventurous spirit of the Wrens, who celebrated their organization's 60th anniversary in 2002. Elsa Lessard was one of these ladies, marching tall, head held high, enjoying the accolade "World War II Veteran."

CHAPTER EIGHTEEN

Eastern Air Command

IN MARCH 1938, HITLER ANNEXED PART of Czechoslovakia, producing the crisis that shook the world from its lethargy. Canada began to look realistically at her armed forces. On March 1, 1938, Western Air Command of the RCAF came into being, and on September 15, 1938, Eastern Air Command (EAC) was formed. Eastern Air Command's area of responsibility stretched from eastern Québec out over the Atlantic Ocean beyond Newfoundland (at that time a British colony). EAC had its headquarters in Halifax and directed air operations on the Atlantic coast of Canada throughout the war. Western and Eastern Air Commands became the two operational commands for the defence of Canada.

Disbanded on February 28, 1947, EAC was succeeded by 10 Group, which became Maritime Group and then Maritime Air Command on June 1, 1953. Unlike EAC, which had a geographical basis, Maritime Air Command became a functional command controlling all maritime air operations of the RCAF.

The RCAF and the Royal Canadian Navy maintained separate commands on the east coast during the Battle of the Atlantic. Unlike the co-operation between the RAF and the Royal Navy, the Royal Canadian Air Force and the Royal Canadian Navy maintained their independence, as seen on the east coast during much of the Battle of the Atlantic. Before the war, the British government placed the RAF's Coastal Command under the direction of the Royal Navy. Royal naval and air commanders responsible for a particular maritime area shared a common operations room where they worked from the same intelligence plots. The RCN and RCAF stubbornly refused to follow this lead. Both were insecure new services, and each jealously guarded its independence. Not until early 1943 did the RCAF accept naval direction. It took sharp criticism from British and American experts to finally persuade the RCN and the RCAF to establish a combined operations room at Halifax.

RCN operations were split between the flag officer, Newfoundland, in St. John's and the commanding officer, Atlantic Coast, in Halifax. Beyond the Canadian 19-kilometre territorial limit, naval operations were under the control of the USN admiral based in Argentia, Newfoundland.

Air operations on Canada's east coast were the sole prerogative of Eastern Air Command. EAC was a regional command tasked with many roles. Only part of its mandate was to help the RCN protect convoys and attack U-boats.

After Canada's declaration of war, Eastern Air Command, under Air Vice Marshall N.R. Anderson, scrambled to develop bases and to provide qualified personnel to meet its increasing commitments. The best modern aircraft, from U.S. manufacturers, began to arrive in the latter part of 1941.

The RCAF and the RCN were not prepared in January 1942 when Germany responded to the United States' entry into the war by dispatching the first of several waves of U-boats to North American waters. There, the U-boats slaughtered independently routed shipping.

The United States removed warships from the North Atlantic to protect its coastal waters and to reinforce the Pacific. Although USN forces in the North Atlantic were greatly reduced, the USN kept their grip on the North Atlantic held by the American admiral in Argentia.

Meanwhile, RAF Coastal Command aircraft were successful in pushing enemy U-boats out of British inshore waters by concentrating air patrols in areas where naval intelligence suggested U-boats were located. RAF aircraft flew at high altitudes, giving the greatest effectiveness for radar and visual observation. Using these and other innovations, in early 1942, Coastal Command aircraft began to impose heavy losses on U-boats. It soon proved impossible for submarines to locate and destroy shipping by making fast surface runs.

Canada's Eastern Air Command aircraft, on the other hand, were flying low-altitude close cover over convoys. A motivated Canadian air officer, Norville Everett Small, independently began using the British

Squadron Leader Norville Everett Small, AFC, DFC

methods in July 1942 with dramatic results that included the destruction of a U-boat off Yarmouth. However, the whole of the EAC did not adopt the improved tactics until October.

In May 1942, Small, promoted to squadron leader, had been given command of No. 113 Squadron. On July 31, 1942, he was flying his Lockheed Hudson on patrol southeast of Yarmouth when his wireless operator received information of a suspected submarine's position gained from H/F D/F bearing triangulation. Approaching the area off Cape Sable, someone on his crew spotted a German VIIC submarine, *U-754*, on the surface. The vessel's captain, *Kapitänleutnant* (Lieutenant Commander) Hans Oestermann, ordered a crash dive. His crew rushed to close the conning tower hatch. When Small released his depth charges, *U-754* was still visible. Small neatly bracketed the boat just forward of its tower. On Small's third orbit over the place where the U-boat was last seen, the U-boat's conning tower broke the surface. This was followed by a large explosion. A quantity of oil on the water marked the final resting place of *U-754*, barely 11 months old, and the grave of her 43 crewmembers. Squadron Leader Small had claimed Eastern Air Command's first kill.

Small's success was as much by design as it was by accident. He had implemented RAF Coastal Command's innovations. He had painted the bottom of his aircraft white, making it difficult for it to be seen against the sky. He had been flying at 900 metres, instead of the standard 150 metres. This gave his crew a better chance to spot a U-boat. As squadron commander, he ensured that his whole squadron adhered to the innovations. It took many months for other squadron commanders to follow his lead.

A few hours after Small's attack, armed with fresh D/F information, Pilot Officer G.T. Sayre, of No. 113 Squadron, attacked *U-132* but did little damage. D/F information led to Small attacking other U-boats in the following week: *U-458* on August 2 and *U-89* three days later. Although Small did not sink either boat, he was proving that the new tactics worked in surprising submarines on the surface.

By October, Eastern Air Command had adopted Small's new tactics and delivered a nasty surprise to the Kreigsmarine soon after. Within the space of a few hours, EAC aircraft sank two submarines on the ocean route east of Newfoundland.

In the last days of October 1942, U-boats massed to intercept Convoy SC-107 plunging eastward from October 24. U-boat headquarters positioned a wolf pack of 13 boats against the convoy. U-boat headquarters also stationed two more boats south of Newfoundland.

On October 30, 1942, Lockheed Hudson "Y" from No. 145 (BR) Squadron flying out of Torbay discovered and sunk *U-658* 460 kilometres northeast of Torbay. She went down with all hands, a crew of 48 men.

That evening, a Digby 747 from No. 10 Squadron in Dartmouth, with Flight Lieutenant D.F. Raymes and crew, was returning from a patrol over another convoy in the area. Raymes found *U-520* 180 kilometres east of St. John's and sank her with four 250-pound depth charges. The U-boat's entire crew of 53 sailors died. This was the squadron's seventh attack and Eastern Air Command's third kill.

In early 1942, as the RCN and RCAF reduced shipping losses off Nova Scotia and Newfoundland, the

Gulf of St. Lawrence was vulnerable to U-boats. The huge commitments on the ocean shipping routes left very few aircraft and almost no warships to defend this inland sea. U-boats crept in, and on the night of May 11, they torpedoed the freighters SS *Nicoya* and SS *Leto* off the Gaspé Peninsula. The war was suddenly close to home and in sight of shore.

A few days earlier, Eastern Air Command responded to a report of a U-boat off Newfoundland's south coast with the establishment of anti-submarine patrols over the gulf. They began operations on May 11. When news of the sinking of *Nicoya* that same day reached it, EAC deployed No. 130 Squadron, RCAF, flying Curtiss Kittyhawk fighters, to the air gunner-training base at Gaspé Peninsula's Mont-Joli. Later, No. 117 (Bomber and Reconnaisance) Squadron, flying Canso and Catalina aircraft, was established at North Sydney, NS, with a large detachment based at Mont-Joli. No. 113 (BR) Squadron, flying Hudson aircraft, moved to Yarmouth, Nova Scotia, and by 1944 its pilots were making many anti-submarine attacks in the Gulf. By the end of the war, 14 RCAF squadrons had provided air cover over the St. Lawrence.

Ernst Vogelsang penetrated the Gulf on July 6, 1942. His U-boat, *U-132*, took aim at a slow-moving convoy. In quick succession, she torpedoed three merchantmen. The escort, HMCS *Drummondville*, hastened to the scene but did not make contact with the enemy so directed her attention to rescuing survivors. Meanwhile, No. 130 (Panther) Squadron at Mont-Joli scrambled four of their Kittyhawk fighters to join in the search. After having no success, they turned for home. But only three landed. The aircraft of the flight leader, Squadon Leader J.A.J. Chevrier, disappeared and was never found.

Based on Small's encounters, No. 113 Squadron sent, on September 8, a three-aircraft detachment of Hudsons to the air base at Chatham, New Brunswick. This "Special Submarine Hunting Detachment" was to protect convoys in the Gulf. It produced immediate results. On September 9, Pilot Officer R.S. Keetley was on a patrol based upon D/F reports of U-boat transmissions in the area. Thirty kilometres south of Anticosti Island, from 1200 metres, he sighted and dove on a contact that he first thought was a sailboat. The "sailboat" was *U-165* under the command of *Fregatten Kapitän* (Captain Junior Grade) Eberhard Hoffmann, serenely cruising on the surface.

Because he had incorrectly identified the vessel, Keetley was unprepared to attack on his first pass. All he accomplished was to alert the submarine of his presence. On his second pass, he dropped depth charges, but that was eight seconds after the sub had dived. Although he did not damage the target, Keetley proved again the efficacy of flying at higher altitude. Six days earlier, a No. 10 Squadron pilot flying at 270 metres spotted a U-boat but was unable to get into an attack position until 20 seconds after the boat had submerged. Keetley's attack on *U-165* had an effect on the boat's operations. After his contact, air and sea patrols kept it submerged as the U-boat crew tried to avoid detection. Hoffmann reported to U-boat headquarters that it was "difficult to contact convoys east of Gaspé and south of Anticosti."

While escorting the Québec-to-Sydney convoy QS-37 on September 24, Flight Sergeant A.S. White sighted *U-517*, with *Kapitänleutnant* Paul Hartwig in command, southeast of Sept-Îles, Québec. P/O Keetley had seen this same boat a week earlier north of Cape Magdalen. The U-boat dove too quickly for White to make an attack, so he dropped sea markers and flew off to warn the convoy. The U-boat rose to the surface. White returned to attack, and the U-boat submerged. Only five seconds after the sub went under, White released his depth charges. However, three of his four depth charges hung up in his aircraft's bomb bay, so Hartwig escaped undamaged.

But the presence of the enemy submarine was noted, and a major search effort was launched. Shortly before midnight, Flying Officer M.J. Belanger from the Chatham detachment found Hartwig's U-boat sihouetted in the moonlight. Taken completely by surprise, Hartwig held on as depth charges dropped close astern and violently rocked his boat. But again, the submarine suffered no significant damage. The next morning, Flight Sergeant M.S. Wallace, flying top cover over QS-37 in his Hudson, found Hartwig's *U-517* twice. Both times, he forced the U-boat to dive. Later that afternoon, Belanger, flying just below clouds, again sighted the German submarine and dove to attack. Hartwig crash-dived his boat and got under the waves soon enough to avoid any damage.

Kapitänleutnant Paul Hartwig and his crew certainly appeared to lead charmed lives.

No. 113 Squadron and its detachment based at Chatham had an impressive record of seven sightings and three attacks on the same boat within 24 hours. Five days later, Belanger again found Hartwig's boat riding completely on the surface off the Gaspé coast. Belanger's Hudson was at 1500 metres. He dove to attack and placed five depth charges close to the sub. The pilot claimed a successful attack, but once again *U-517* survived.

Small, who had brought these anti-submarine tactics to Canada, made another attack on a U-boat in 1942. On November 24, while flying from Yarmouth, he spotted a U-boat 10 kilometres ahead of him. In the fading afternoon light, the vessel was barely discernable and was able to submerge while the aircraft was still about three kilometres away. Small dropped depth charges 50 metres ahead of the swirl but got no confirmation of any damage to the boat. After this, Small was posted to Eastern Air Command Headquarters Operations Room. On December 11, EAC discontinued operations from Chatham, but No. 113 Squadron continued anti-submarine sweeps from Yarmouth.

No. 113 Squadron's tally for the year was 22 sightings resulting in 13 attacks, 12 occurring in the six months between June and November. This record was better than that of all other EAC squadrons combined.

Only one attack proved fatal, that of Small on Oester-mann's *U-754*.

However, the other attacks kept the submarines below the surface and forced them to run at slow underwater speeds, preventing them from interdicting convoys. The anti-submarine aircraft were doing their job. The psychological stress on the U-boat crews was summed up later by former U-boat captain Hartwig, noted by historian Michael Hadley.

> *...the stress that RCAF surveillance, "scare charges" and attacks caused his watch officers. Planes would unexpectedly swoop down on them, buzz them, drop out of a cloud, skim low over the water out of the sun and drop bombs. Even when the attacks were inaccurate, the bombs made "one hell of a ruckus." All his officers had been badly shaken by such attacks and consequently preferred to stand their watches submerged.*

No. 113 Squadron's successful attacks in the summer of 1942 were more often than not the result of D/F information. Consequently, the chief of the air staff, Air Marshall L.S. Breadner, ordered that D/F plots be sent immediately from Ottawa to EAC headquarters in Halifax and to the No. 1 Group in St. John's. This, he reasoned, would provide pilots with accurate and current information with which to plan their anti-submarine patrols. To ensure that Operations Room personnel in EAC headquarters more clearly appreciated how to handle D/F information, he posted Small to the Ops Room as a controller. However, the RCAF simply did not have enough officers to properly man the Operations Room and the flying squadrons, so officers without operational experience often staffed controller positions.

The exploits of No. 113 Squadron's aviators did not go unrecognized. For his success, Small was awarded the Distinguished Flying Cross. For his repeated attacks on *U-517*, Belanger was also awarded a DFC.

S/L N.E. Small, AFC, DFC

According to Richard Goette, in his 2003 study on leadership successes and failures, Norville Everett "Molly" Small had the intellect and work ethic that made him a great squadron commander. By the time he reached No. 113 Squadron, Molly Small was an "old man" by air force standards at the age of 34. He was born on December 7, 1908, in Allandale, Ontario but grew up in Hamilton. His secondary education was in Hamilton Technical School, where he studied motor mechanics. On May 23, 1928, he joined the RCAF at Camp Borden as a mechanic but was soon selected for pilot training. He received his wings in Vancouver as a sergeant pilot on June 2, 1931.

Small's first flying duties took him to the west coast, where he gained experience on seaplanes and flying boats, logging some 2000 hours. He flew an additional 1000 hours on twin-engine aircraft. His superiors were most impressed with his work ethic and his dedication to the service. However, greener fields beckoned, and in 1937, he resigned to fly commercial aircraft with Canadian Airways. Canadian Airways reluctantly released him in 1939, when he got a better position with Imperial Airways. He was described as a "pilot with outstanding ability and sound judgement."

In September 1939, with the outbreak of war, Small re-enlisted as a pilot officer and was assigned to instructor duties on the new Douglas Digby aircraft acquired from the United States. In the spring of 1941, he was seconded to the RAF's Ferry Command, flying from Bermuda to Great Britain. He was primarily ferrying the Catalina aircraft and made five ferry flights, one of them in record time. He added 125 flying hours to his log. The RCAF formed No. 116 Squadron at Dartmouth, Nova Scotia, and in July 1941 it began taking delivery of the new long-range Catalina. Because of his experience, Small was transferred to the new squadron.

By March 1942, Small had been promoted to flight lieutenant and was given command of No. 10 (BR) Squadron detachment in Yarmouth, Nova Scotia. On April 28, 1942, while flying a Canso, a Canadian amphibian version of the Catalina, on patrol south of Yarmouth, he sighted a U-boat on the surface. He was at 150 metres and dove to attack. When he tried to release his depth bombs only the first and fourth dropped. Release mechanisms in anti-submarine aircraft were more often than not defective. The attack was not lethal, but Small believed he had "definitely made their back teeth rattle."

On May 19, 1942, the Yarmouth No. 10 Squadron detachment, having received additional aircraft, was

Squadron Leader Small (centre) and crewmembers

re-formed as No. 162 (BR) Squadron with newly promoted Squadron Leader Small as its commander.

He was only there a month organizing the new
squadron and then went to command No. 113 (BR)
Squadron, also at Yarmouth. Small was decorated on
June 11, 1942, with the Air Force Cross. The recommendation read:

> *Flight Lieutenant Small is an outstanding pilot who*
> *has been utilized as an advanced instructor and ferry*
> *pilot most of the time since the start of the war. He is*
> *extremely keen in all phases of his work. He was picked*

to captain the Catalina *which did a reconnaissance flight around the Labrador Coast, Hudson Strait and Hudson Bay this fall. During the spring and summer of 1941, he made five ferry flights from Bermuda to the United Kingdom, one of them in record time, and has completed 125 hours of flying on this type of work. He has flown a total of 1224 hours. This officer's devotion to duty deserves recognition, and I strongly recommend him for the above award.*

Small had the distinction of sinking Eastern Air Command's first enemy submarine on July 31, 1942. He was flying a Hudson aircraft southeast of Yarmouth when he surprised *U-754* on the surface. After an accurate dropping of depth charges, an explosion and floating debris on the surface confirmed EAC's first kill.

Small had early recognized the efficacy of using H/F D/F information. After a long study of the Command's operations, he concluded "it may be advantageous to concentrate on an area known to contain a submarine rather than to make regular wide sweeps of fixed areas." He kept an aircraft on 24-hour readiness, able to react at a moment's notice to D/F information. Thus he had aircraft airborne 12 to 15 minutes after receiving news of a "hot" fix.

Bypassing both Ottawa and Halifax, he arranged a direct line of communication between the director of bombing and reconnaisance operations at Air Force Headquarters and his squadron in Yarmouth. Thus he was able to receive timely information that allowed him (and his crew) to destroy *U-754*.

It was at that time that Small instituted Coastal Command's innovative tactics that aided EAC's success against U-boats. Small's final attack on a German submarine was on November 24, 1942. Shortly thereafter Small was posted to Eastern Air Command Headquarters Operations Room as a controller to coordinate D/F information from the receiving station with the squadron's aircraft prosecuting targets.

For his achievements with No. 113 Squadron, in January 1943, Small received the Distinguished Flying Cross with this commendation:

> *This officer has displayed outstanding airmanship, courage and devotion to duty on operational flying in the face of the enemy over the sea off the coast of Nova Scotia. During the last few months he has carried out five attacks on enemy submarines carrying armament considerably superior to that of the aircraft. Three of these attacks were successful; two of the successful attacks were made within a recent period of six days on fully surfaced submarines with their decks manned.*

> *In the course of 335 hours operational flying during the last four months, this officer has on several occasions distinguished himself by his initiative and by the completion of difficult tasks under adverse weather conditions; in particular he has been of prime assistance in effecting more than one sea rescue of survivors of sunken or damaged vessels.*

The award was made posthumously. On January 7, Small died when his Canso crashed shortly after take-off for a test flight from Gander, Newfoundland. Not surprisingly, he was involved in trials attempting to extend the range of aircraft so they could provide air cover to convoys out in the Atlantic. He had decided to reduce equipment weight in order to carry more fuel. He eliminated 575 kilograms by removing guns and ammunition and changing from larger depth charges to smaller ones. He hoped this would increase the range of the aircraft from 800 kilometres to 1100 kilometres. Small took off in his reconfigured Canso at 0630 hours. At his expected time of return, 1830 hours, he was discovered to be missing. A search, begun at first light on January 8, found the wreckage six kilometres away from the base. Only the plane's two gunners survived the crash. "Equipment failure" was determined as the cause of the accident.

Small left an impressive legacy to aid the Allied victory in the Battle of the Atlantic. Historian W.A.B. Douglas points out, "it was largely due to the efforts of Small that Gander-based Cansos were able to make a series of promising attacks at maximum range" during early 1943. It seems appropriate that Small died while testing modifications to an aircraft made by him to extend and improve its anti-submarine capability.

F/L M. J. Belanger, DFC

Maurice John Belanger was born in Ottawa on June 25, 1919. His family moved to Vancouver. It was there that he was educated. While attending university, he earned tuition money by working as a steward for one season with the White Pass and Yukon Company Railway and one year as a Hudson Bay Company clerk. Extra-curricular activities included the Vancouver Sea Cadets from 1935 to 1938.

Belanger joined the RCAF in Vancouver on June 15, 1940. He began flight training at No. 1 Initial Training School at the old Toronto Hunt Club. This was basically a ground school. He didn't start flying until July when he went to No. 8 Elementary Flying Training School at Moncton, New Brunswick. From there he went to No. 1 Service Flying Training School at Camp Borden where he graduated and won his wings and a promotion to sergeant pilot.

Sergeant Belanger attended No. 1 Air Navigation School in Rivers, Manitoba then went to No. 3 SFTS in Calgary and then to No. 11 SFTS in Yorkton, Saskatchewan. At Yorkton, he taught navigation to other fledgling pilots. He was commissioned as a pilot officer on March 1, 1942 and on May 8 left Yorkton to return to the Air Navigation School in Rivers for a month. By this time he had accumulated 1000 flying hours, being trained and training others, and was pestering his senior officers for an operational posting. On June 27, 1942 he reported to No. 113 (BR) Squadron in Yarmouth. He and Small gave navigation training to squadron crews.

Over a period of five days, September 25 to 29, 1942, Belanger made three attacks on submarines in the Gulf of St. Lawrence, including one at night without flares. For these exploits he was awarded the Distinguished Flying Cross with the following commendation:

> *This officer has completed a total of 1200 hours flying. His devotion to duty has set an example and has been a source of inspiration to the members of his squadron. In addition to demonstrating his ability as squadron navigator and pilot he has carried out three attacks against U-Boats, inflicting damage on one, probably sinking a second and possibly sinking a third. Two of these attacks took place within a period of 18 hours, during which time he was on continuous duty. During one attack, which was carried out at night, he displayed tenacity of purpose, courage and skill when taking advantage of occasional moonlight he pressed home a good attack at extremely low level.*

From May to November 1943, Belanger left the squadron, going to a desk job on staff of RCAF Station Sydney, Nova Scotia. He was posted overseas and arrived in the United Kingdom on January 31, 1944. After training on four-engine bombers, Belanger, now a flight lieutenant, was posted to No. 425 "Alouette" Squadron at Tholthorpe. The squadron had recently been re-equipped with the Handley Page Halifax Mk III bombers. Over the following year, the squadron flew on every night it was required against the Third Reich. It dropped more than 10,000 tonnes of bombs during its operational career.

Belanger flew 20 bombing missions over Germany and received a Bar to his DFC before being repatriated to Canada on February 15, 1945. He was released from the RCAF on April 23, 1945.

ᨠᦂᦂᨡ

By late 1942, Eastern Air Command (EAC) was doing its best to help the beleaguered convoys and was pushing its aircraft to the limits. Canadian flyers achieved outstanding results on several occasions. They damaged and destroyed U-boats 800 kilometres out in the Atlantic. They did not, however, have the latest "very long range" (VLR) aircraft needed to reach the dreaded "Black Pit" where the U-boats attacked in relative freedom.

Then, in the spring of 1943, EAC finally was allocated American four-engine VLR B-24 Liberator bombers. With these planes, EAC intersected with RAF patrols from Iceland and closed the lethal air gap over convoy routes. The nose guns on these aircraft offered greatly improved forward firepower on the final run in on a submarine. The ammunition belts were well laced with tracer bullets to convince submarines, well protected by armour, that they were in grave danger.

The appropriateness of the term "very long range" for this bomber became apparent after 12 hours of flight with the plane still out of sight of land. The absence of the Sunderland's galley or the Canso's bunks contributed to crew discomfort. "Very long range" was a term no doubt coined by the first returning weary crew. It is perhaps significant that all the major improvements later made to the Liberator detracted from its speed. To those who flew the "Lib" she was an absolutely reliable aircraft—mild-mannered, if somewhat ponderous; stable to the point of being unmaneuverable; dry in wet weather; quiet on the flight deck and unbearably noisy aft; with a long, gymnastic trek from its nose to its tail turret while in flight.

On July 3, 1943, a No. 10 Squadron Liberator, based in Gander, Newfoundland attacked *U-420*, under *Oberleutnant* Hans-Jürgen Reese. The plane launched a FIDO homing torpedo, which hit the boat, killing two submariners and wounding another. The boat was severely damaged and limped back into Lorient two weeks later. (*U-420* was repaired and set out again to wreak havoc a couple months later. Its crew made a radio transmission for the last time on October 20, 1943, while enroute to its operational area of Newfoundland. It has been missing in the North Atlantic since then.)

In September 1943, No. 10 Squadron, flying its B-24 Liberators, made transatlantic flights from both sides of the ocean to support the embattled convoy ONS-18/ON-202. An aircraft of No. 10 Squadron, based at Reykjavik, Iceland, drew first blood in the convoy's protection. At 0430 hours on September 19, 1943, Flight Lieutenant J.F. Fisher sighted a submarine on the surface 260 kilometres west of the convoy and moving toward it. *U-341*'s commander, *Oberleutnant zur See* Dietrich Epp, elected to stay on the surface and use his boat's heavy AA armament to defend himself from Fisher's attack. That proved to be a mistake as

Fisher's well-placed depth charges blew the U-boat's bows out of the water. *U-341* was no more, and all of the 50 hands on the submarine were lost. The battle was joined.

Three days later, on September 22, another Liberator, piloted by Warrant Officer J. Billings, attacked *U-270* in the face of the U-boat's intense anti-aircraft fire. The Liberator's attack damaged the submarine such that its captain, *Kapitänleutnant* Paul-Friedrich Otto, had his boat retreat on the surface for its homeport in St. Nazaire.

Another Liberator, this one piloted by Flight Lieutenant J.R. Martin, engaged a second U-boat, *U-377*, the same day. Martin attacked with depth charges, machine-gun fire and torpedoes, wounding the commander *Oberleutnant zur Seer* Gerhard Kluth. The boat returned to Brest, France, under the command of its executive officer.

Admiral Karl Dönitz hoped to revive pack tactics in the mid-Atlantic with the attack on this convoy, but the appearance of the very-long-range air coverage convinced him that the effort had failed.

On October 26, Flight Lieutenant R.M. Aldwinkle attacked *U-91* in his Liberator, dropping depth charges and torpedoes. The sub, under command of *Kapitänleutnant* Heinz Hungershausen, was not damaged.

Eastern Air Command and the three RCAF squadrons in RAF Coastal Command at this time (No. 404 Buffalo, No. 407 Demon and No. 413 Tusker) obtained outstanding results against U-boats. They destroyed or shared in the destruction of six submarines prior to September 1943 and destroyed 11 more the following year. The three RCAF anti-submarine bomber squadrons had been organized in the RAF's Coastal Command to carry out patrols from Great Britain. Many RCAF personnel also served in British anti-submarine squadrons. Thus the RCAF, like the RCN, had a major presence across the entire Atlantic. Technological developments helped the Allied cause as well, with new weapon, radar and code-breaking developments, such as Ultra, contributing to turning the tide against the U-boats.

❧❖❧

The RCN and the RCAF assumed an increased share of convoy defence in the North Atlantic, releasing British warships and aircraft to prepare for the invasion of France. During the last months before D-Day, the RCN took responsibility for all convoy escorts in the North Atlantic. As well, Canada's large and capable anti-submarine fleet and air squadrons played a prominent part in protecting the D-Day invasion fleet as it crossed the English Channel. Canadian air and naval units were among the most successful in finding and destroying U-boats during and after the landings.

In the English Channel during the weeks following the D-Day landings, a destroyer group sank three U-boats that were attempting to interdict supply of the armies.

Eastern Air Command's No. 162 Squadron and its No. 117 Squadron had been loaned to Coastal Command. Off Norway, in June 1944, No. 162 aircraft sank four German submarines and shared in the destruction of a fifth. No. 162 Osprey Squadron was formed as a bomber-reconnaissance squadron at Yarmouth, Nova Scotia on May 19, 1942, with Consolidated Canso A aircraft, the truly amphibious version of the Catalina. The squadron spent an uneventful 18 months on East Coast anti-submarine duty. In January 1944, it was loaned to RAF Coastal Command and stationed in Iceland to cover the mid-ocean portion of the North Atlantic shipping route. During June and July, the squadron operated from Wick, Scotland, and scored a series of brilliant successes by sinking at least four German submarines that were attempting to break through the North Transit Area to attack the Allied D-Day invasion fleet. In one of these engagements, Flight Lieutenant D.E. Hornell won the Victoria Cross.

On June 3, 1944, a Canso "A," of No. 162 Squadron with Flight Lieutenant R.E. MacBride and crew, sank *U-477* in the face of the U-boat's intense anti-aircraft (AA) fire. On June 11, a Canso aircraft "B," with Flying Officer L. Sherman and crew, sank *U-980*. Two days later, Wing Commander C.G.W. Chapman and crew sank *U-715*. As a result of AA fire from the U-boat, the Canso had to ditch. The crew spent nine hours in the water, and one crewman drowned.

On June 24, a Canso aircraft "P," with Flight Lieutenant D.E. Hornell and crew, sank *U-1225* north of the Shetland Islands. Damage from the U-boat's AA

A Canso crew serving on maritime patrols along the Atlantic seaboard

fire forced the Canso to ditch. The crew spent 21 hours in the water floating in and beside a dinghy. Two members died before the crew was rescued. Thirty-four-year-old Flight Lieutenant David Ernest Hornell, of Mimico and Toronto, died shortly after rescue and was posthumously awarded the Victoria Cross for inspiring leadership, valour and devotion to duty.

An air force honours and awards website has Hornell's recommendation:

Flight Lieutenant Hornell was captain and first pilot of a twin-engined amphibious aircraft engaged on an anti-submarine patrol in northern waters. The patrol had lasted for some hours when a fully surfaced U-boat was sighted, travelling at high speed on the port beam. Flight Lieutenant Hornell at once turned to attack.

The U-boat altered course. The aircraft had been seen and there could be no surprise. The U-boat opened up with anti-aircraft fire, which became increasingly fierce and accurate.

At a range of 1200 yards, the front guns of the aircraft replied; then its starboard gun jammed, leaving only one gun effective. Hits were obtained on and around the conning tower of the U-boat, but the aircraft was itself hit, two large holes appearing in the starboard wing.

Ignoring the enemy's fire, Flight Lieutenant Hornell carefully manoeuvred for the attack. Oil was pouring from his starboard engine, which was, by this time, on fire, as was the starboard wing, and the petrol tanks were endangered. Meanwhile, the aircraft was hit again and again by the U-boat's guns. Holed in many places, it was vibrating violently and very difficult to control.

Nevertheless, the captain decided to press home his attack, knowing that with every moment the chances of escape for him and his gallant crew would grow more slender. He brought his aircraft down very low and released his depth charges in a perfect straddle. The bows of the U-boat were lifted out of the water; it sank and the crew were seen in the sea.

Flight Lieutenant Hornell contrived, by superhuman efforts at the controls, to gain a little height. The fire in the starboard wing had grown more intense and the vibration had increased. Then the burning engine fell off. The plight of the aircraft and crew was now desperate. With the utmost coolness, the captain took his aircraft into wind and, despite the manifold dangers, brought it safely down on the heavy swell. Badly damaged and blazing furiously, the aircraft settled rapidly.

After the ordeal by fire came ordeal by water. There was only one serviceable dinghy and this could not hold all the crew. So they took turns in the water, holding onto the sides. Once, the dinghy capsized in the rough seas and was righted only with great difficulty. Two of the crew succumbed from exposure.

An airborne lifeboat was dropped to them but fell some 500 yards down wind. The men struggled vainly to reach it and Flight Lieutenant Hornell, who throughout had encouraged them by his cheerfulness and inspiring leadership, proposed to swim to it, though he was nearly exhausted. He was with difficulty restrained. The survivors were finally rescued after they had been in the water for 21 hours. By this time Flight Lieutenant Hornell was blinded and completely exhausted. He died shortly after being picked up.

Flight Lieutenant Hornell had completed 60 operational missions, involving 600 hours flying. He well knew the danger and difficulties attending attacks on submarines. By pressing home a skilful and successful attack against fierce opposition, with his aircraft in a precarious condition, and by fortitude and encouraging his comrades in the subsequent ordeal, this officer displayed valour and devotion to duty of the highest order.

The officers and crew of No. 162 Squadron still had some fight left in them. On June 30, Flight Lieutenant R.E. MacBride and crew, in action for a second time, damaged *U-478*. The U-boat was subsequently sunk by a Liberator of No. 86 (RAF) Squadron. Finally, on August 4, a Canso, with Flying Officer W.O. Marshall and crew, damaged *U-300*.

Also decorated for their actions during these trying days were Lawrence Sherman, Robert Ernest MacBride and Cecil George William Chapman.

Headquarters awarded Sherman a Distinguished Flying Cross:

Recently this officer captained an aircraft which attacked a U-boat. In spite of heavy fire from the submarine's guns, Flying Officer Sherman pressed home his attack with great determination. His depth charges were released with such accuracy that within a few minutes of the explosions, the U-boat sank. In this well executed operation, Flying Officer Sherman displayed courage and coolness of a high order.

Flight Lieutenant Robert Ernest MacBride of Woodstock, New Brunswick, was mentioned in dispatches and awarded a Distinguished Flying Cross.

Flight Lieutenant MacBride has a fine record of operational flying. He is a most skilful pilot, fully qualified to fly both land and sea aircraft and has operated from some of the most difficult bases, never allowing adverse weather to deter him from completing his mission. On one occasion while on an anti-submarine patrol this officer sighted a U-boat. Despite intense and heavy anti-aircraft fire he pressed home an excellent attack and the U-boat was probably destroyed.

Wing Commander Cecil George William Chapman of Fredericton, New Brunswick, was awarded the Distinguished Service Order:

This officer has completed a large number of sorties and has displayed a high degree of skill, courage and devotion to duty, qualities which were well in evidence on a recent occasion when he successfully attacked a U-boat. In the fight his aircraft was struck by anti-aircraft fire and extensively damaged. Height was rapidly lost but Wing Commander Chapman skilfully brought the aircraft down on the sea. The crew got safely aboard the dinghy and, some four hours later, were rescued. During the time spent in the dinghy, Wing Commander Chapman set a fine example which greatly inspired his comrades in a trying period. He has invariably displayed high qualities of leadership and tenacity.

By the autumn of 1943, H/F D/F stations were reading much of the U-boat radio traffic and, with only a few hours' delay, transmitting the information to Eastern Air Command. With this information, EAC's anti-submarine aircraft surprised and paralyzed two intruders with four near-miss attacks. Those boats had dared to make long runs on the surface. Those that followed seldom surfaced except at night. From the spring of 1944, all boats that came into Canadian waters were equipped with *schnorkel* and remained submerged for the whole of their six-week missions in the coastal area. They showed only the tip of their breathing tubes, which could not be located by radar in rough seas.

These actions were the focus of great individual efforts by Canadian aviators. Their aircraft closed the mid-Atlantic gap in air coverage for the convoys travelling between North America and Britain. Canadian aviators were the decisive element in the ultimate defeat of Dönitz's wolf packs, which had lost their ability to roam the surface of the ocean in search of "sitting duck" targets.

In May 1940, during the Battle of France, the British, in a process dubbed "Ultra," learned how to read and de-code German intelligence. Ultra intelligence was carefully guarded and sanitized before being passed on. The word "Ultra" was never mentioned. Ultra gave Eastern Air Command the general course and destination of a boat but was unable to determine a U-boat's actual location. However, anti-submarine aircraft were able to harass the boats by constantly flying over water where they were thought to be lurking.

Harassment, however, was not effective with bold submariners. Three of them, *Kapitänleutnant* Klaus

Hornbostel on *U-806*, *Oberleutnant zur See* Hans-Erwin Reith on *U-190* and *Kapitän zur See* Kurt Dobratz, Knights Cross, on *U-1232* penetrated close in to the mouth of Halifax harbour in late 1944 and early 1945. They destroyed five merchant vessels and severely damaged a sixth and sank two Bangor minesweepers between December 24, 1944, and April 16, 1945. They escaped massive air and sea searches. Other boats that operated in Canadian waters during the last year of the war also escaped unscathed.

At the end of January 1944, Eastern Air Command reached a peak strength of 21,233 personnel, including 1735 members of the RCAF's Women's Division. Of this total, only a little more than 1200 were aircrew. The rest managed the bases, communications, navigation systems and other services needed to operate multi-engined aircraft over vast expanses of the northwest Atlantic. In addition to EAC's 21,000 personnel, nearly 2000 RCAF aircrew were serving in Canadian and British squadrons of the Royal Air Force Coastal Command. Seven hundred and fifty-two members of the RCAF died in maritime operations because of enemy action and flying accidents in the unforgiving environment.

The naval and air forces of Britain and Canada struggled to maintain the upper hand in the North Atlantic until the last U-boats surrendered in May 1945. Eastern Air Command's contribution cannot be measured in the number of U-boats they sunk, nor does the number of sightings and attacks express it. A better indication is found in the thousands upon thousands of hours flown by its vigilant aircrew, through weather that was often appalling, while they carefully searched the grey expanse of water. Although often unseen, their presence forced the enemy to surface for only short periods or to remain submerged altogether. They drove U-boats away from convoys and permitted merchant ships to continue on their way unmolested. It was weary and unglamorous work, but critical to the successful prosecution of the war. Its importance cannot be over-emphasized. The battle lines of Western Europe were fed by the long Atlantic sealanes.

As the Allies advanced through northwest Europe capturing U-boat base after U-boat base, EAC reduced its number of men and aircraft. After Germany's surrender, EAC airmen were gradually demobilized. By September 15, 1945, Eastern Air Command and Western Air Command no longer had men on active duty.

CHAPTER NINETEEN

Home is the Sailor,
Home From the Sea

IN OCTOBER 1944, ALLIED FORCES encountered only one German sub in the entire North Atlantic. A VII/41 boat, *U-1006*, was detected—and sunk—on October 16 southeast of the Faeroes. Six of the submariners were lost, but 46, including her commander, *Oberleutnant zur See* Horst Vogt, survived.

Escort Group 6, including His Majesty's Canadian Ships *Arran*, *Loch Achanalt*, *New Waterford* and *Outremont* were on patrol in the North Atlantic when *Arran* and *Achanalt* picked up radar contacts from a surfaced submarine that was moving away at maximum speed. HMCS *Arran* was a River Class frigate commanded by A/Lieutenant Commander Charles Patrick Balfry, RCNR, of St. Jean d'Iberville, Québec. HMCS *Loch Achanalt* was an anti-submarine frigate under command of Lieutenant Richard Wallace Hart, RCNVR, of Belleville, Ontario. The two ships opened fire with their forward guns. The submarine's return fire wounded several of *Arran's* crew. *Arran* closed and fired two shallow-set depth charges, which sank *U-1006* in two minutes. *New Waterford* and *Outremont* provided support with star shells and gunfire and helped rescue survivors.

Arran's commanding officer, A/Lieutenant Commander Charles Patrick Balfry, RCNR, was later awarded the Distinguished Service Cross for "outstanding skill, courage and zeal in anti-U-boat operations while serving in His Majesty's Canadian Ships *Arran* and *St. John.*"

The last campaign of the Atlantic war began in autumn 1944. Few of the enemy were left except *schnorkel*-equipped U-boats, which proved to be the bane of existence for the anti-submarine forces. Radar and human eyes could not detect the *schnorkel*, at least until late 1944. At that time, Canadians developed an efficient radar that could detect "planks with nails in them." Unfortunately, the RCN never got its hands on any of these sets before May 1945.

The war ended before the Kreigsmarine put into operation their newest type of U-boat, the XXI. These new boats were too fast, both on the surface and submerged, for anti-submarine weaponry to deal with. They could change position at depth before weapons could reach them. None of the escort vessels could catch them in a surface sprint.

Even without the new boats, the final campaign was rough enough. The final frenzy of U-boat attacks began on Christmas Eve when *U-806* torpedoed the Bangor minesweeper HMCS *Clayoquot* in the approaches to Halifax harbour. The submarine, under the command of 28-year-old *Kapitänleutnant* Klaus

Hornbostel, claimed her only confirmed warship when she sank the minesweeper with a GNAT torpedo. Lieutenant P.W. Finlay, RCNVR, of Montreal, was sailing *Clayoquot* five kilometres off Sambro light at 1437 hours. She was escorting convoy XB-134 when her stern erupted in flame and torn steel. The ship sank in 10 minutes, taking eight of her crew, including her captain, to the bottom. Sub hunters gathered, but Hornbostel's U-boat lay on the channel bottom until they departed.

On January 4, 1945, *Kapitän zur See* Kurt Dobratz sailed *U-1232* on her first patrol. She was off Egg Island when he made his first attack, on a Halifax-to-Sydney convoy, and sank two ships. Ten days later, Dobratz was in the final approaches to Halifax when he spotted a convoy strung out in the channel. He sank two merchant ships and destroyed a third before the convoy's escort, HMCS *Ettrick,* a River Class frigate under command of A/Lieutenant-Commander Edward M. More, RCNR, MiD, of Halifax, began high-speed sweeps and dropped depth charges. On duty at *Ettrick's* ASDIC set was 19-year-old John Stables of St. John. The shallow water presented poor conditions. The signals bounced randomly off the hard, boulder-strewn bottom, but Stables detected and warned the bridge of an approaching torpedo. As the frigate took evasive action, she ran over the conning tower of the U-boat, bending its periscope and tearing away some of its combing. The poor ASDIC conditions covered the U-boat's escape.

The last Canadian warship lost to enemy action in World War II was torpedoed in the approaches to Halifax in the morning of April 16, 1945. The sinking came only three weeks before Germany's surrender. HMCS *Esquimalt* sank with heavy loss of life within sight of the coast. Forty-four Canadian sailors were lost. Her commander, Lieutenant Robert Cunningham MacMillan, DSC & Bar, RCNVR, a native of Charlottetown, PEI, and others were rescued after six hours clinging to rafts in the frigid water.

Their nemesis, *U-190*, piloted by 25-year-old *Oberleutnant* Hans-Erwin Reith, was on its sixth patrol. Skulking off Chebucto Head, near dawn on April 16, the U-boat went up to periscope depth. Reith easily saw the Canadian minesweeper at about 900 metres in the early morning twilight. The water was calm with a long swell as *Esquimalt* passed within five kilometres of the Halifax East Light Vessel. Her ASDIC had given no contact before *U-190* fired a stern torpedo tube. At 0630 hours, the torpedo opened a gaping hole in *Esquimalt*'s starboard stern quarter, and she began to list. Her commander, Robert MacMillan, ran from his cabin to the bridge and gave the order to abandon ship. Everyone got off the ship, but 44 of the crew did not last in the Atlantic water. Six men made it to the light ship. HMCS *Sarnia* picked up 21 and took them into Halifax.

U-190 remained submerged in the shallow coastal waters until April 29, and then she headed for home. The war ended before she got there. On May 11, 1945, the *Kreigsmarine* signalled all submarines to surface and surrender.

Reith's *U-190* surrendered on May 12, 1945 at Bay Bulls, Newfoundland. The navy transported the submariners to Halifax for interrogation. The boat was taken to St. John's in June and then to Halifax, where it was commissioned into the RCN. She served the navy for two years then naval aircraft sunk it on October 21, 1947. Her periscope was removed and remains operational in the Crow's Nest Officers' Club of St. John's.

~✶~

Afterword

Britain's Prime Minister Sir Winston Churchill said the only thing that really worried him during the war was Hitler's U-boat campaign during the Battle of the Atlantic. If Germany had starved the United Kingdom into capitulation, Hitler would have gained control of almost all of Europe and beyond. Without Canadian seamen, the Battle of the Atlantic might well have been lost. Unprepared ordinary sailors went to sea in the most unglamorous, dangerous and uncomfortable conditions imaginable. Many never saw nor heard the torpedo that snuffed out their lives. Canadian boys from schools, shops, factories and prairie farms went out time and again into the freezing night without adequate protection or equipment to battle Nazi submarines.

Unfortunately, an embarrassing incident in victory marred the triumph and glory of the wartime RCN. The city leaders of Halifax closed all the bars and liquor stores to celebrate VE Day. The servicemen reacted to six years of overcharging, overcrowding and priggish disregard for sailors by rioting, which was incited by civilians at every street corner. Together, civilians and sailors virtually destroyed downtown Halifax. The RCN's most distinguished flag officer and its only operational commander, Admiral Murray, resigned and fled to England. He never returned.

From a pre-war force of 1800 all ranks, the RCN blossomed into a modern navy of nearly 100,000 sailors plus 6000 women. It took responsibility for the vital security of north Atlantic trade routes and more. The RCN escorted about half of the 25,000 ship crossings during the war. They sunk, or shared in the sinking, of 31 U-boats and 42 enemy warships. They lost 24 of their own ships and almost 2000 Canadian lives.

During the Battle of the Atlantic, losses mounted, and survival seemed bleak. Without the stubborn endurance of the RCN, the battle at sea could easily have become defeat. The Canadian navy followed Churchill's edict to "succeed in doing what is necessary."

Canadian navy's expansion was remarkable. Becoming a large, modern naval service, it built new bases in Canada and Newfoundland and accumulated more than 400 various types of ships. It stood, in 1945, as the third largest navy in the world. After the war, the majority of the bases and ships were sold or scrapped. On February 1, 1968, Defence Minister Paul Hellyer effectively extinguished the Royal Canadian Navy for his personal political ambitions. His unified Canadian Armed Forces included only remnants of a once-proud navy.

"For These Thy Children of the Sea"

Notes on Sources

Beattie, Andrew P. *The Wandering Scot, The Memoirs of Andrew P. Beattie, A Gift to his Family.* Scarborough: [unpublished], 1994.

Benedict, Michael (Ed.). *Canada at War.* Toronto: Viking Penguin, 1997.

Bishop, Arthur. *Courage At Sea, Volume III, Canada's Military Heritage.* Toronto: McGraw-Hill Ryerson, 1995.

Bishop, Arthur, *Unsung Courage.* Toronto: Harper Collins, 2001.

Broadfoot, Barry. *Six War Years 1939–1945.* Toronto: Doubleday Canada, 1974.

Buchheim, Lothar-Günther. *U-Boat.* Glasgow: William Collins Sons & Co., 1974.

Burrow, Len and Emile Beaudoin. *Unlucky Lady—The Life and Death of HMCS Athabaska.* Toronto: McClelland and Stewart, 1987.

Christie, C.S. (Stu). *My Life.* Ottawa: [self-published], 2000.

Gardam, John. *Fifty Years After.* Burnstown, Ontario: The General Store Publishing House, 1990.

Geisler, Patricia. *Valour Remembered: Canada and the Second World War.* Ottawa: Veterans Affairs Canada, 1998.

German, Tony. *The Sea Is At Our Gates: The History of the Canadian Navy.* Toronto: McClelland & Stewart, 1990.

Granatstein, J.L. and Desmond Morton. *A Nation Forged in Fire.* Toronto: Lester & Orpen Dennys, 1989.

Gray, Larry. *Fathers, Brothers and Sons.* Victoria, BC: Trafford, 2004.

Greer, Rosamond "Fiddy." *The Girls of the King's Navy.* Victoria, BC: SONO NIS Press, 1983.

Griffin, Anthony. *A Naval Officer's War.* [Ottawa?]: Starshell, Newsletter of the Naval Officers' Association of Canada, 1999/2000.

Johnson, Mac. *Corvettes Canada.* Toronto: McGraw-Hill Ryerson, 1994.

Lamb, James B. *On The Triangle Run.* Toronto: Macmillan of Canada, 1986.

Lawrence, Hal. *Tales of the North Atlantic.* Toronto: McClelland & Stewart, 1985.

Lessard, Elsa. *A Wren Reminisces. Salty Dips, Vol 6.* Ottawa: Ottawa Branch, Naval Officers Association of Canada, 1999.

Macpherson, Ken & Marc Milner. *Corvettes of the Royal Canadian Navy, 1939–1945.* St. Catherines: Vanwell Publishing, 1993.

McKee, Fraser & Robert Darlington. *The Canadian Naval Chronicle 1939–1945.* St. Catherines: Vanwell Publishing, 1998.

Middlebrook, Martin. *Convoy*. New York: William Morrow and Company, 1976.

Milner, Marc. *Canada's Navy: The First Century*. Toronto: University of Toronto Press, 1999.

Milner, Marc. *The U-Boat Hunters*. Toronto: University of Toronto Press, 1994.

Milner, Marc. *North Atlantic Run*. Toronto: University of Toronto Press, 1985.

Pedersen, Dorothy. *Convoys of World War II*. Canmore, Alberta: Altitude Publishing Canada, 2005.

Sarty, Roger. *Canada and Submarine Warfare, 1909–1950, The Maritime Defence of Canada*, Toronto: Canadian Institute of Strategic Studies, 1996.

Schull, Joseph. *The Far Distant Ships*. Ottawa: King's Printer, 1950.

Shortridge, Audrey Sim. *On the Double, Matilda*. Victoria, BC: Lookout Publishing, 2006.

Taylor, Scott R. (Ed.). *Canada at War and Peace, II*. Ottawa: Esprit de Corps Books, 2000.

Whitby, Michael J. *The "Other" Navy at War: the RCN's Tribal Class Destroyers 1939–1944* [unpublished master's thesis]. Ottawa: Carleton University, 1988.

http://frankcurry.ncf.ca/sailors.html

http://jproc.ca/rrp/coverdale.html

http://uboat.net/boats

http://webhome.idirect.com/~kettles/uncle/powtest.htm

http://www.airforce.ca

http://www.airmuseum.ca/mag/exag0209.html

http://www.cbrnp.com/contact.htm

http://www.cda-acd.forces.gc.ca

http://www.civilization.ca/academ/articles/sart1_5e.html

http://www.jproc.ca/cta/athab.html

http://www.mnq-nmq.org/english/vivez/impacts/fortin.htm

http://www.navalandmilitarymuseum.org

http://www.rafcommands.com/index.html

http://www.readyayeready.com

http://www.rcnvr.com

http://www.thememoryproject.com/digital-archive

http://www.vac-acc.gc.ca

http://www.vondette.com/index.php

http://www.warsailors.com/convoys/index.html#links

http://www.warsailors.com/convoys/index.html#norway

Index

Larry Gray

Larry Francis Gray is a retired member of the Canadian Armed Forces. He served as a radio officer, air navigator and information officer before becoming the managing editor for the newspaper of the Canadian Army in Europe. He has also been a United Nations military observer and served as part of the Commonwealth Election Team in Zimbabwe in 1980. After he retired from the RCAF, he served with the Royal Canadian Legion, the Veterans Review and Appeal Board and the Office of the National Defence and Canadian Forces Ombudsman.

Gray has received the Minister of Veterans Affairs Commendation, the Queen's Jubilee Medal, the United Nations Peacekeeping Medal, the Canada Celebration 88 Medal for Voluntarism, the United Nations Service Medal and the Canadian Forces Decoration. He has published several articles on World War I in *Esprit de Corps* magazine, has written two books on the war dead of Carleton Place. This is Larry's second book for Folklore Publishing; the first was *Canada's World War II Aces*.